THE CENTER FOR CHINESE STUDIES

at the University of California, Berkeley, supported by the Ford Foundation, the Institute of International Studies (University of California, Berkeley), and the State of California, is the unifying organization for social science and interdisciplinary research on contemporary China.

RECENT PUBLICATIONS

Van Ness, Peter. *Revolution and Chinese Foreign Policy: Peking's Support for Wars of National Liberation* (1970)

Larkin, Bruce D. *China and Africa, 1949–1970: The Foreign Policy of the People's Republic of China* (1971)

Schneider, Laurence A. *Ku Chieh-kang and China's New History: Nationalism and the Quest for Alternative Traditions* (1971)

Moseley, George. *The Consolidation of the South China Frontier* (1972)

Rice, Edward E. *Mao's Way* (1972)

Wakeman, Frederic, Jr. *History and Will: Philosophical Perspectives of Mao Tse-tung's Thought* (1973)

THE POLITICS OF CHINESE COMMUNISM

This volume is sponsored by the
CENTER FOR CHINESE STUDIES
University of California, Berkeley

THE POLITICS
OF CHINESE
COMMUNISM

Kiangsi under the Soviets

Ilpyong J. Kim

UNIVERSITY OF CALIFORNIA PRESS
BERKELEY, LOS ANGELES, LONDON

University of California Press
Berkeley and Los Angeles, California

University of California Press, Ltd.
London, England

ISBN: 0-520-02438-9
Library of Congress Catalog Card Number: 73-76101

Printed in the United States of America

To A. DOAK BARNETT

CONTENTS

ACKNOWLEDGMENT

Almost a decade ago, when I became interested in the study of the Chinese Communist movement in general and the Kiangsi soviet government in particular, I was greatly encouraged by Professor A. Doak Barnett, who saw the need for research on this subject and gave me wise counsel and invaluable criticism. Without his persistent encouragement and sustained inspiration this study would never have been possible. It is with profound gratitude and sincere appreciation that I dedicate this modest book to him who taught me not to be biased on such a sensitive subject as Chinese Communism.

I am also grateful to Professors John N. Hazard, C. Martin Wilbur, O. Edmund Clubb of Columbia University, and the late Dr. John M. H. Lindbeck for their comments and suggestions at various stages of the writing. They should not be held responsible, however, for any misinterpretations or errors in the factual presentation of this work. For these I am solely responsible. The Contemporary China Studies Committee at the East Asian Institute of Columbia University gave me financial support at an earlier stage of my research, and a generous grant under the Fulbright-Hays Act facilitated my field research in Hong Kong and Taiwan in late 1964 and early 1965. This book is basically a revised version of my dissertation for Columbia University under the title "Communist Politics in China: A Study of Organizational Concepts, Techniques, and Behavior Developed in the Period of the Kiangsi Soviet."

Dean Hugh Clark of the University of Connecticut Research Foundation not only purchased the Ch'en Ch'eng microfilm from the Hoover Institution for my personal use but also gave generous support to facilitate the editing and typing of the manuscript, and I want to express my appreciation to him. Jane Blanshard did an excellent job of editing and improving the style at various stages of rewriting, and my colleague Gary Clifford in the political-science department read the first three chapters and made many good suggestions for the improvement of my writing style. Their contributions materially aided this work.

Last but not least, I am affectionately grateful to my wife, Hyunyong, who was always patient and willing in bearing the tasks of the household while I was occupied by this work. Irene and Katherene missed their share of their father's time on weekends and holidays when he was hitting his typewriter hard. I would also like to thank the anonymous reader who reviewed the earlier version of my manuscript and offered invaluable comments aimed at improving its structure, and Richard Adloff, who edited the manuscript for the University of California Press and who made a significant contribution to this book.

I.J.K.

INTRODUCTION

The political system established by the Chinese Communist Party (CCP) after its assertion of sovereignty over the mainland in 1949 had its origins, in many respects, in the Chinese Soviet Republic of 1931–1934, the so-called "Kiangsi soviet period." It was in these early years that the Chinese Communists began to develop the organizational theory and practices that later formed the basis of their Chinese People's Republic. In the village of Juichin, which lies deep in the hills of southern Kiangsi province about 400 miles southwest of Shanghai, the Chinese Communist leaders first set up a territorially based regime when they proclaimed the establishment of the Chinese Soviet Republic on November 7, 1931. It was in this period, and in this area, that many of their distinctive organizational forms and behavioral patterns emerged.

The Kiangsi soviet period is considered one of the most important in the development of the Chinese Communist movement, because for the first time since their revolutionary struggle for power had begun a decade earlier, the Chinese Communist leaders were able to establish their own government and rule an extensive geographic area and a large population. It was a unique period because the Chinese Communist leaders were able, under these circumstances, to develop new organizational techniques for conducting Party and government affairs and to work out methods of mass mobilization that had a great impact on the subsequent development of the Chinese Communist movement and, ultimately, the political system that the Communists established in the country as a whole.

The purpose of this study is to explore the development of the Chinese Communist movement during the Kiangsi soviet period in terms of its organizational concepts and behavioral patterns, and the growth of the organizational techniques of "mass line" politics. The study therefore focuses on such issues as how the CCP leaders came to perceive organizational problems within the Chinese Communist movement, especially following the failure of the 1927 revolution; what kind of organizational methods the CCP leadership developed in dealing with the problems that arose in carrying out the revolution; and

1

finally what kind of organizational techniques the CCP leaders had to formulate and implement in order to maintain the balance of power among the three pillars of power (the Party, the government, and the Red Army), administer the expanding territorial base, and manage the complex organizations.

In short, this study is a response to two questions: What were the underlying concepts of organization that governed the principles and procedures of the Kiangsi political system? Who formulated what kind of policies and how were they implemented at the rice-roots level of government?

After the 1927 debacle, the Chinese Communist leaders perceived that in order to seize political power they must execute an "agrarian revolution," continue "armed struggles," and build up "soviet base areas." It is important to understand and analyze these three components of the revolutionary movement in the late 1920s and early 1930s if one is to comprehend fully the revolutionary change that was sweeping through the Chinese hinterland at that time. To evaluate the whole political system that had sustained the revolutionary growth during the Communists' rise to power it is necessary to analyze in depth each of these three components of the Chinese revolution. The following study is primarily concerned with the way in which the Chinese Communist leaders came to grips with the problems of building institutions in rural China by focusing on the growth and development of "soviets" as a technique of mass participation and mobilization. It is not concerned with the CCP's military strategy or with interpreting the agrarian revolution, but it will consider the questions of how the soviets were developed and how the policy-making elites, including Mao himself, formulated their own mass-mobilization policies, and implemented them in the course of the revolution.

After the breakdown of CCP-KMT cooperation in 1927, Mao and his associates gradually came to realize that the KMT organization could never be an effective instrument with which to handle the problems of the Chinese revolution. Therefore, he gradually perceived the necessity for an effective organization through which his concepts of mass mobilization could be implemented. What was now required of the Chinese revolution, as he viewed it, was to establish an organization that would be able to perform the functions of mass mobilization and simultaneously execute the program of land distribution to meet the needs and aspirations of the peasant masses. Mao proposed the idea of a soviet-type institution because, as he analyzed correctly, the China of 1927 was not the Russia of 1905. By 1927, social and economic conditions in China had long since developed beyond those of Russia in 1917.

Therefore, Mao's rise to the undisputed position of power at the Tsun-yi Conference may have had its origin in the organizational theory and techniques that he was able to develop and demonstrate in the Kiangsi soviet base. As the organizer and leader of the peasant masses as well as the Chairman of the Chinese Soviet Republic, Mao had acquired profound knowledge about the exercise of political power, and he also possessed intuitive notions of the functions and processes of political organization. Mao's subsequent rise to power at the Tsun-yi Conference was therefore due, in many respects, to his intuitive understanding of how an organization operates and also to his mastery of organizational techniques. He learned not only how to mobilize the broadest possible segments of the peasant masses and to involve them in the organizational processes, but also how to manipulate and influence the key leaders of certain political institutions so as to win their support for his views and policy positions. Thus Mao's basis of power, in many respects, lay in his ability to manipulate and influence the leadership and organization of the central soviet government, and this same ability enabled him to regain power, if he had ever lost it, at the Tsun-yi Conference.

The approach I have chosen for this study stresses the development of organizational patterns and administrative procedures. The emphasis is on political and governmental structures and their functions in the Chinese Soviet Republic, from the central soviet government in Juichin to the local governments of the *hsiang* and villages in rural areas of China.

I

TOWARD MAO'S THEORIES OF ADMINISTRATION AND ORGANIZATION

The degree of success achieved by the soviet type of government during the Kiangsi period can be explained in part by the backwardness and deteriorating economic conditions in rural China at that time, and by the weakening control of the landlord and gentry class over the rural population. Also important, however, were the highly developed organizational techniques based on Mao's concept of "mass line," which were successfully applied to the realities of Chinese society to build new institutions and win the support of the rural masses. The election process, council meetings, debates, and discussions of policy issues, all of which took place within the institutional framework of the soviet organizations at each level, were organizational techniques that helped the peasant masses express their views and perhaps also find release for their psychological frustrations.

To make some generalizations about the organizational principles underlying the structures and functions of the Chinese soviet government in the Kiangsi base, this chapter will focus on the processes by which the Chinese Communist leaders attempted to establish their political institutions among the rural population, will discuss systematically the political functions of Mao's concept of "mass line," and will explore the possibility of outlining Mao's theories of administration and organization,

Establishing the New Political System

In creating new political institutions in the backward and rural sectors, the Chinese Communist leaders consistently expounded the view that China had two political systems: one representing the ruling class of the landlords, monopolistic capitalists, and compradores, which took the form of the KMT government, and the other representing the workers, peasants, and all toiling masses, which was clearly manifested in the soviet form of government. The organizational goal of the soviet system of government, therefore, was to "liberate China from imperial-

4

ist rule and rescue the workers, peasants, and all toiling masses from oppression and poverty."[1] After reaching such a goal the Chinese soviet government would serve as a leader and organizer of the world revolution.

Inasmuch as the comprador capitalist class, represented by Chiang Kai-shek, Feng Yu-hsiang, and others, was considered the vanguard of the imperialists, their agent — the KMT — had to be overthrown first. Therefore, "The liberation of China (from imperialist rule) and the liberation of toiling masses of workers and peasants (from oppression and exploitation) are inseparable," the program declared. Hence the liberation of China must follow liberation of the toiling masses. The program of the Chinese Soviet Republic, proclaimed in November 1931, was to establish the new political system by overthrowing the KMT government when and if the soviet government was able to free the working masses and win their support and loyalty.[2]

The program assigned organizational tasks to the new system of government: to eliminate all privileges held by the imperialists; to provide land and arms to the workers and peasants, and abolish the warlord system; and to establish councils of workers', peasants', soldiers', and poor-people's deputies (soviets) which would exercise political power by eliminating the traditional system of government. In the process of building a new political system, the old bureaucratic ways of handling governmental affairs were to be replaced by the soviet system of government, which would be the most popular form of government and would enable the masses of people to participate directly in the administration of their own local affairs. It would abolish all existing political institutions, as well as all exploitative economic structures, and replace them with new political institutions known as "soviets." The primary task consisted of consolidating all revolutionary forces around the new political institutions in order to liberate China from the feudalistic and oppressive rule of the KMT government.

It is interesting to note here that the soviet as a new political form and as an alternative to the existing KMT government emerged as a

[1] "Declaration of the Conference of the Delegates from the Soviet Areas" in Shanghai, May 1930, may be found in Hatano Ken'ichi, *Shiryō shūsei Chūgoku Kyōsantō shi* (*Source Materials of the History of the Chinese Communist Party*) (Tokyo: Ji Ji Press, 1961), I, 388–394. Also in Wang Chien-min, *Chung-kuo Kung-ch'an tang shih-kao* (*Draft History of the Chinese Communist Party*) (Taipei, 1964), II, 277–280. Hatano's work hereafter cited as Hatano, *Chūkyō-shi*. Wang's work hereafter cited as Wang, *Chung-kung shih-kao*.

[2] See "Chung-hua su-wei-ai kung-ho-kuo cheng-kang" ("The Political Program of the Chinese Soviet Republic") in Tso-liang Hsiao, *Power Relations Within the Chinese Communist Movement, 1930–1934* (Seattle: University of Washington Press, 1967), II, The Chinese Documents, 432–435. Hereafter cited as Hsiao, *Power Relations*.

dynamic political theory only after the breakdown of CCP-KMT collaboration in 1927. In the search for a new institutional form and a new leadership style the Chinese Communist leaders were thinking in terms of developing a new political institution that would combine the new form and style of leadership and also arouse the revolutionary consciousness of the majority of the Chinese population — the most important factor in the contest for power. Therefore, the key concept was "mass participation." This concept, developed by Mao during his revolutionary experiences in rural China from 1925 to 1930, was formalized later as Mao's principles and procedures of operating the soviet system of government in the Kiangsi base. The organizers of the soviet government, armed with Mao's and his colleagues' concept of "mass line" and his organizational techniques, aimed to create an environment in which the peasant masses could feel for the first time that they were masters of their own destinies. This atmosphere was, of course, to be created by eliminating the minority ruling class and by forming the soviets to provide the peasants and working masses with the opportunity of taking part, both in principle and in practice, in the formulation and execution of policy.

According to a booklet, *Su-wei-ai cheng-ch'üan* (*Soviet Political Power*), a publication to educate and indoctrinate Red Army personnel and the peasants, "The soviet system of government has two important political functions: one is to carry out the bourgeois-democratic revolution in which the workers and peasants take joint leadership, and the other is to achieve the ultimate goal of proletarian dictatorship." [3] Unlike Lenin's concept of "soviet," which stressed only the leadership of the industrial proletariat, Mao's concept consistently emphasized the equality of the peasantry with the industrial workers in the development and operation of the new political system. During the Kiangsi period, the soviet system had the dual function of carrying out the bourgeois-democratic revolution and establishing the basis for the proletarian dictatorship at a later stage of revolution. In outlining the basic principles of the soviet government, *Tou-cheng* (*Struggle*), an official journal of the CCP central bureau of the soviet area (CBSA) under the editorship of Chang Wen-t'ien (Lo Fu), declared in its first issue on February 4, 1933:

Actually the soviet is a system of government which will enable the masses of people to participate directly in the policy-making

[3] Kung-nung hung-chün hsüeh-hsiao, ed., *Su-wei-ai cheng-ch'üan* (*Soviet Political Power*), Juichin, Kiangsi (January 1932), p. 2. Several versions of this booklet may be found in *Ch'en Ch'eng collection* (Shih Sou archival material in microfilm reproduction by the Hoover Institution on War, Revolution, and Peace in 21 reels). This collection hereafter cited as *SSCM* (*Shih Sou Collection in Microfilm*). See Reel 10.

process. The basic principle of soviet government is, therefore, to provide the workers, peasants, soldiers, and all toiling masses opportunities to participate in political processes and to express their own will. The principle of the people's government can only be realized through the means of the "soviet" (a representative council of the workers, peasants and soldiers). This is the soviet system of government.[4]

Confronted with massive military power immediately after the 1927 debacle, the Chinese Communist leaders had no choice but to reorient their political program from an urban-based revolution to revolution in the rural hinterland. However, the process of shifting their strategy from the proletarian revolution of the urban centers to revolutionary change in the rural areas was by no means an easy task because, among other reasons, the CCP's veteran leaders were strongly influenced by an orthodox interpretation and mechanical application of Marxist theory and were also swayed by Comintern policies during the years between 1927 and 1930.

The Comintern-directed policy of urban insurrections — as manifested in the failures of the Canton commune, the Nanch'ang uprising, and the Ch'angsha insurrection — brought about a series of setbacks to the Chinese Communist movement in the late 1920s. While the Comintern leaders and the CCP leaders, who faithfully followed the Comintern's instructions, were preoccupied with the problems of urban insurrections, Mao Tse-tung and his associates continued to organize the peasant movement and establish soviet bases in rural China. The majority of Mao's faithful followers were well entrenched in the local organizations of the peasant movement, and also served as the leadership elite of rural China.

Furthermore, Mao's intuitive understanding of the need for an organization to bring about successful revolutionary change, coupled with his ability to understand and adapt Lenin's concept of soviets to the realities of rural China, enabled him to develop a broad ideological appeal that would gain the CCP the support of the peasant masses without alienating any significant portion of those masses. Mao's genius lay in his understanding of an organization that would close the vast gap between the urban-oriented revolutionary ideology and the revolutionary realities, his perception of the actualities of China's rural society, and his development of the concept of "mass line" as an organizational technique.

It was easy to speak of the organizational goals of mass mobilization, but difficult to attain such goals. One may read through all the resolu-

4 See the editorial in *Tou-cheng*, No. 1 (February 4, 1933); reproduced in *SSCM*, Reel 18.

tions, directives, and documents put out by the CCP's central organ in
the late 1920s and sense the CCP leaders' awareness of the urgent need
to win the support of the masses. But such CCP leaders as Ch'en Tu-
hsiu, Ch'ü Ch'iu-pai and Li Li-san were so preoccupied with orthodox
interpretation and mechanical implementation of Comintern instructions that they could pay little attention to organizational techniques
that might win them mass support. Not only did they fail to perceive
the problems of Party organization and to understand the realities of
Chinese society, but they also neglected to build an organization that
would realize their organizational goals of mass support.

The central leadership of the CCP was chiefly concerned with analyzing essentially trivial issues. What was the current stage of the
Chinese revolution in terms of Marxian orthodoxy? How were the
Comintern's instructions applicable to the present stage of the Chinese
revolution? When and under what circumstances should the Comintern directives be implemented? In the course of debating such strategies, the CCP leaders inevitably split into several factional groups.
The information provided by some of the former Communist leaders
who participated in these debates and were later expelled from the
CCP sheds much light on the policy-making process and on the organizational behavior of the CCP leaders at the time of the crisis.

Faced with the growing problems of Party organization and the factional activities of various rival groups within the CCP, both the Comintern and the CCP leaders continued to search for an institution that
would solve their organizational problems and at the same time close
the wide gap between revolutionary ideology and the realities of
Chinese society. The group alignments in the central organ of the CCP
also constantly shifted in accordance with the vicissitudes of the Comintern's strategy for the Chinese revolution. A detailed analysis of the
organizational behavior of the Party's central leaders in terms of their
attitudes and opinions on various policy issues connected with the
problems of the revolution leads one to a better understanding of the
development of Chinese Communist policy. However, information on
this subject is scanty at best and does not provide a whole picture of
the debates, nor does it disclose who was making the key decisions at
the center of the Party and government organizations.

However, information provided by former Communist leaders gives
some insight into the organizational behavior and policy-making
processes of Chinese Communist politics. A study of the organizational
concepts and techniques of the Kiangsi soviet government will, it is
hoped, help to explain the governmental process of the soviet system
and lay the groundwork for certain hypotheses about the organizational
basis of Communist political development during the Kiangsi period.

The Ch'en Ch'eng Collection on microfilm suggests that even though, in some ways, the Party, soviet, and Red Army organizations were not so closely interrelated as one might expect, they were successful in attaining some of their major organizational goals — i.e., creating a revolutionary base, establishing a new political order, and mobilizing the peasant masses into the political processes of the local soviet government. For example, Ch'in Pang-hsien (Po Ku), the general secretary of the Party, summed up the achievements of the Kiangsi period at the Fifth Plenum of the CCP in January 1934 as (1) the establishment of the central soviet government by grouping and consolidating the scattered soviet areas and (2) the strengthening and expanding of the Red Army to guard the soviet base against external attack.

The Fifth Plenum of the CCP, convened in January 1934, just before the convocation of the Second Soviet Congress in Juichin, Kiangsi, has been interpreted by some scholars as the turning point in Mao's regaining of power, which he was assumed to have lost in 1932 when the CCP Central Committee moved from Shanghai to Juichin. Other scholars conjectured that it may even have marked his total removal from power and the seizure by the returned-student leaders of control over the policy-making machinery of the Kiangsi soviet base. However, if one analyzes carefully the political report delivered by Ch'in Pang-hsien (Po Ku) on "The Present Situation and the Party's Tasks" and the report by Chang Wen-t'ien (Lo Fu) on "The Tasks of Sovietization in China" at the Fifth Plenum, and systematically compares them with the political report delivered by Mao Tse-tung on "The Work of the Central Executive Council and the People's Commissariat of the Chinese Soviet Republic for the Past Two Years" and with a speech delivered by Wu Liang-p'ing on "The Resolution of the Soviet Construction" at the Second Soviet Congress, one finds that the returned-student group was neither monolithic nor cohesive, and that their policy perspectives on such issues as antiimperialism and economic construction were as divergent and diffuse as those of the policy-makers in any complex organization of the contemporary world. Faced with the persistent attacks on the Kiangsi base by the KMT forces, the government bureaucracy led by Mao Tse-tung, on the one hand, and the Party groups led by Ch'in Pang-hsien, on the other, had to search for a compromise solution to the problems of power and policy. The compromise emerging from the conflicts of "left" and "right" policy lines was established by Mao when he asserted in his report on agrarian policy that "The goal of the Chinese Soviet Government and the Red Army is to carry out the land revolution . . . the class line of the land struggles is to suppress the rich peasants and eliminate the landlords by establishing a solid alliance between the farm workers and the poor and middle peasants. Therefore, the Chinese soviet government will correct the erroneous tendencies of attacking the middle peasants (mainly the well-to-do middle peasants) and eliminating the rich peasants, but at the same time it will rectify the error of compromising with the landlords and the rich peasants." Therefore, Mao stressed that "The land revolution is not only to help the peasants acquire the land but also to make them increase its productivity." [5] He thus assumed a middle-of-the-road position by attacking both the "left"-oriented policy of elimination of the middle peasants and the "right"-oriented policy of alliance with the rich peasants and landlords.

The process of compromise had already begun in the fall of 1933 when Mao and Chang Wen-t'ien began to agree on the issue of "economic construction" based on Mao's concept of "mass line." At the same time, some of the returned students, led by Ch'in Pang-hsien, pushed hard for the adoption of a policy based on his concept of "offensive line." This was actually an argument for all-out war on the issue of "antiimperialism" when the Chinese Soviet Republic declared war on Japan in April 1932 and when the KMT's military campaigns threatened the central soviet area. Mao's policy, based on the concept of "mass line," pressed for broader mass support, including the support of well-to-do middle peasants and nonexploitative rich peasants, by deemphasizing the Comintern line of severe "class struggle." Mao's policy line also won the support of such Party leaders as Wu Liang-p'ing, Lin Po-ch'u, and Wang Chia-hsiang. However, the issue of "antiimperialism" based on the Comintern line of "class struggle" and advocated by the Party leader Ch'in Pang-hsien was by no means dead when the final policy decision emerged. Ch'in Pang-hsien continued to urge total mobilization of both economic and human resources and these views were incorporated into the Party's policies of economic development and Red Army expansion. Therefore, the reopening of the Land Investigation Movement in March 1934 was closely connected with total mobilization for the war, which included the enlargement of the Red Army and the collection of fines and contributions from the landlords and rich peasants.

The policy decisions of the Chinese Communist leaders at the Fifth Plenum of the CCP, later issued as policy pronouncements at the Second Soviet Congress (January 22–February 1, 1934), were concrete evidence of the compromise between the two conflicting policy perspec-

[5] See Mao's report in *Chung-hua su-wei-ai kung-ho-kuo ti-erh-tz'u ch'uan kuo tai-piao ta-hui wen-hsien* (*Documents of the Second Soviet Congress of the Chinese Soviet Republic*), published by the People's Commissariats of the Chinese Soviet Republic, March, 1934. *SSCM*, Reel 16. Hereafter cited as *Documents of the Second Soviet Congress.*

tives: Mao's concept of "mass line" and Po Ku's concept of "class line." In the course of establishing and implementing the compromised policy line, certain Party leaders in the camp of Po Ku seem to have gone to the other extreme and used coercion to achieve total mobilization. This prompted Chang Wen-t'ien to denounce his fellow student leaders and their "leftist trend" and call for a turn to the "right" in order to broaden mass support.[6] This was also clear evidence that Chang Wen-t'ien was supporting Mao's concept of "mass line," enunciated during the Land Investigation Movement in June 1933. Even Ch'en Shao-yü (Wang Ming), one of the returned student leaders, criticized "some of his comrades" who took up the "leftist" policy line. In an article in the Comintern journal *Communist International* in 1934, Wang Ming charged that

> These comrades thought that the bourgeois-democratic revolution in the Chinese soviet areas had already been transformed into the socialist revolution. Therefore, they considered the rich peasants to be the most dangerous enemies in the process of achieving socialism, and finally concluded that the main task of the Chinese soviet areas was to struggle against the rich peasant class. The incorrect and leftist program of the government was created as a result of the erroneous theory that the bourgeois-democratic revolution had already been achieved.

Mao's concept of "mass line," on the other hand, reflected two important policies: mobilization of the soviet government and its committees at all levels, and mobilization of all mass organizations in the Kiangsi base. Earlier, in June 1933, Mao had called for the mobilization of all government agencies in his speeches on the Land Investigation Movement.[7] He also proposed the mobilization of labor unions, poor-peasant corps, women's associations, the Red Guard, the Youth Vanguard, and other revolutionary organizations, and called for mass meetings jointly sponsored by the *hsiang* and village soviet governments. As he had said in the booklet "How to Conduct the Work of the *Ch'ü* and *Hsiang* Soviet Government," coauthored with Chang Wen-t'ien in 1933, Mao always envisaged the *hsiang* soviet government

[6] Chang Wen-t'ien, "Shih chien-chüeh ti chen-ya fan-ko-ming, hai shih tsai fan-ko-ming ch'ien-mien ti k'uang-luan" ("Should We Stand Firm in Suppressing the Counter-revolutionaries or Become Angry and Confused in the Face of Them?" *HSCH*, No. 208 (June 28, 1934).

[7] Mao Tse-tung, "Ch'a-t'ien yün-tung ti ti-i pu — tsu-chi shang ti ta-kuei-mu tung-yüan" ("The First Step of the Land Investigation Movement — A Large Scale Mobilization of the Organization"), *HSCH*, No. 87 (June 20, 1933). See also Mao's other speeches in *Ch'a-t'ien yün-tung chih-nan* (*Directives for the Land Investigation Movement*), published by the Central Soviet Government in June 1933 in Juichin, Kiangsi. Collected in *SSCM*, Reel 17.

as the basic unit for mass mobilization. In connection with the mobilization of mass organizations, however, Mao instructed the *hsien-* and
ch'ü-level soviet governments to convene frequent meetings to which
the key leaders of all mass organizations in the region should be invited
to draw up plans and review the work of the local soviet government.

To formulate and implement Mao's "mass line" policies, the central
soviet government called two important conferences in 1933 — one
attended by key leaders of the *ch'ü*-level soviet governments in eight
hsien of the central soviet [8] and the other by key delegates from the
poor-peasant corps of the same eight *hsien*. The first conference took
place at Yeh-p'ing Juichin *hsien*, from June 17 to June 21, 1933. More
than four hundred key leaders of the soviet governments took part,
including chairmen of the soviet governments and heads of land departments, workers' and peasants' inspection departments, and security
bureaus. It was at this conference that Mao delivered a series of important speeches during which he conceptualized and formalized his concept of "mass line" and developed its organizational techniques of
institution-building. These speeches were by far the most systematic
and elaborate statements he ever made delineating the organizational
techniques of a mass political movement.[9]

Political Functions of Mao's "Mass Line"

The central concepts of the Kiangsi political system were the mobilization of the entire population to preserve the revolutionary base and
the development of organizational techniques that would release the
latent power of the masses for the revolutionary cause. Mao's concept
of "mass line," which took shape in the Kiangsi soviet base, also developed there the organizational principles and operational procedures
of the soviet system of government. Liu Shao-ch'i could say confidently
that "in the democratic revolutionary period, the Chinese Communist
Party . . . went deep into the villages and for more than twenty-two
years led the armed revolutionary struggle, which used the villages to
encircle the cities. What the Party adopted was the mass-line policy of

---

[8] The eight *hsien* were Juichin, Hui-ch'ang, Yü-tu, Sheng-li, Po-sheng, Shih-
ch'eng, Ning-hua, and Ch'ang-t'ing.

[9] "Chung-yang cheng-fu t'ung-kao — chao chi pa-hsien ch'ü i-shang su-wei-ai
fu-tse jen-yüan hui-i chi pa-hsien p'in-nung-t'uan tai-piao ta-hui" ("Circular of
the Central Government — Calling a Conference of Responsible Soviet Personnel
of Eight Counties On or Above the District Level and a Conference of Delegates of
the Poor-Peasant Corps of Eight Counties"), *HSCH*, No. 85 (June 14, 1933), p. 3.
See also "Pa-hsien-ch'ü i-shang su-wei-ai fu-tse jen-yüan ch'a-t'ien yün-tung ta-hui
so t'ung-ku chüeh-lün" ("Conclusions Reached by the Conference of Responsible
Soviet Personnel of Eight Counties on or above the District Level on the Land Investigation Movement"). *HSCH*, No. 89 (June 29, 1933), 5–7.

firm reliance on the peasants' political consciousness; it used their organized strength, mobilizing them to save themselves." The organizational achievements of mass mobilization during the Kiangsi period depended largely on local organizations and their cadres, who were trained and charged with the responsibility of maintaining a close relationship with the peasant masses. They not only appealed to the peasants psychologically but also created an organizational outlet to channel their energies into revolutionary change. The peasant masses of rural China, however, like those in any developing society, were passive and unresponsive; therefore, the success of any organization in mobilizing their strength greatly depended upon the organizational skill of the leadership cadres at the local level.

"Mass line," as the technique of leadership and organization in contemporary China, has been explored by a number of scholars.[10] Great similarities exist between the organizational techniques of "mass line" as experimented and developed in the Kiangsi base and those that have been implemented by the Chinese Communist leaders since their seizure of power in 1949. One might conclude that Mao's concept of "mass line" developed in the Kiangsi base in the 1930s was further refined in the base areas of Yenan in the 1940s and finally institutionalized as the organizational principles and operational procedures of the Chinese political system in the 1950s. The essential feature was unequivocally expressed in such campaign slogans of the Kiangsi soviet government as "From the masses and back to the masses." The cadres working in the Party and government organizations, as leaders and organizers of the masses, were charged with the responsibility of maintaining constant contact with the latter, listening to their views and desires, and articulating their wishes through the organizations of the local soviet government. After certain policy decisions were reached at the local level their acceptability had to be tested by projecting them back to the masses to ascertain whether they would enthusiastically support the new policies. The success or failure of such policy decisions, therefore, had to be measured in terms of whether they won the approval of the masses, by which was meant enthusiastic, occasionally blind, support.

[10] A. Doak Barnett, "Mass Political Organizations in Communist China," *Annals of The American Academy of Political and Social Science* (September 1951); also his *Communist China: The Early Years, 1949–55*, pp. 29–44; A. Arthur Steiner, "Current 'Mass Line' Tactics in Communist China," *American Political Science Review* (June 1951), pp. 422–436; John W. Lewis, *Leadership in Communist China*, ch. 3; also his *Major Doctrines of Communist China* (New York, Norton, 1964), ch. 6; James R. Townsend, *Political Participation in Communist China*, chs. 5 and 6: Chalmers A. Johnson, "Chinese Communist Leadership and Mass Response: The Yenan Period and the Socialist Education Campaign Period," in Ping-ti Ho and Tang Tsou, eds., *China in Crisis: China's Heritage and the Communist Political System* (Chicago, University of Chicago Press, 1968), pp. 397–437.

Conceptually, the mass-line approach to the execution of policy sought to maintain a close and correct relationship between the leadership and the masses of the people. Therefore, a close and correct relationship between the leaders of the Party and government and the masses should be built, according to Mao's concept of "mass line," on two-way communication. In such a process, the leadership cadres of the mass organizations were to serve as the link between the Party and government organizations and the people. During the Kiangsi period, therefore, Mao devoted his major writings to the role of social groups in the revolution and the relationship between the basic-level government and the mass organizations.[11]

Mao's concern for the development of organizational techniques to mobilize the masses stems from his active involvement in the peasant movement in the mid-1920s. During the period of the First United Front policy, Mao actively engaged in training the leaders of the peasant organizations at the Peasant Movement Organizations' Training Institute. The trained cadres later became the organizational foundation on which Mao built up his peasant associations in the various provinces. Although the peasant associations in the United Front period were officially an integral part of the KMT's agrarian programs, the CCP leaders, notably T'an P'ing-shan, P'eng P'ai, and Mao Tse-tung, took the most active role not only in directing such organizations as the central training institute but also in building the peasant associations as instruments of mass mobilization in rural China. The rapid growth of the peasant associations in Hunan during the period of CCP-KMT cooperation may be attributed to the leadership skill and ability of Mao's trained cadres. According to Mao, the peasant associations were established between January and September 1926, with a formal membership of 300,000 to 400,000, and the peasant population under the direct influence of the peasant associations numbered more than one million in that province alone. The peasant associations grew even more rapidly, Mao noted, when violent revolutionary activities occurred in rural China. The membership of the peasant associations increased to more than two million between October 1926 and January 1927, and the peasant population under their influence was reported to have exceeded ten million.[12]

[11] All of Mao's writings scattered in *Hung-se Chung-hua*, the government publication, and *Tou-cheng*, the Party paper, and elsewhere in the massive collection of the Kiangsi documents available in Ch'en Ch'eng microfilms have now been conveniently collected in two volumes. See *Mao Tse-tung chi (Collected Writings of Mao Tse-tung)*, supervised by Takeuchi Minoru (Tokyo, Hokubosha, 1970, 1971), vol. 3 (September 1931–August 1933) and vol. 4 (September 1933–October 1935). Hereafter cited as *Mao Tse-tung chi.*

[12] Mao Tse-tung, *Selected Works of Mao Tse-tung* (Peking, 1964–1965), I, 24. This collection hereafter cited as Mao, *SW.*

The ability to build such large peasant associations and to recruit so much of the peasant population in such a short time required not only an understanding of the peasants' minds but also an organizational talent that could make an appeal to the masses and arouse their revolutionary consciousness. Mao's actions during this phase of the peasant movement, however, were destructive and violent, in contrast to his later establishing of the poor-peasant corps and farm-labor unions during the Kiangsi soviet period. After the breakdown of CCP-KMT collaboration in 1927 Mao concentrated on the organizational question of how the peasant associations could be transformed into entirely new institutions by instilling in them a new identity with the Communist movement. The question of how to differentiate the peasant-association membership into two categories — those who would continue to support the KMT and its policy and those who would support the CCP and its revolutionary effort — now became the fundamental issue of organization within the Chinese Communist movement. As the peasant associations were suppressed and destroyed by the KMT, the CCP had to build a new form of peasant organization. Mao therefore had already begun to transform the peasant associations into "soviets" by sorting out friends from enemies even before the CCP's Sixth Congress adopted its ambiguous and inconsistent resolution on the peasant movement. Mao's strategy envisaged that the enemies (the landlords, rich peasants, and all kinds of reactionaries) were to be eliminated from the newly established soviets, and the friends (poor peasants, middle peasants, and farm laborers) were to be recruited into the newly transformed soviets. Using this organizational strategy, Mao put into effect his "left"-oriented agrarian policy in the region of the Chingkang mountains.

Inasmuch as Mao continued to pursue policies based on his own perception of the revolutionary realities in China rather than on an orthodox interpretation of the Comintern policy line, he frequently clashed with the central leadership of the CCP in the late 1920s. He and his associates had already enunciated his program, based on the Resolution adopted by the Enlarged Politburo Meeting of November 1927, of taking over the leadership of the peasant associations and transforming them into soviet-type organizations. However, many differences in both the form and the operational methods of the peasant associations persisted under Mao's control, partly because of the ambiguity and inconsistency of the policy line established at the Sixth Party Congress and partly because of the absence of a revolutionary government and any solid revolutionary base on which to establish the mass organizations. Even the poor-peasant corps and farm-labor unions were not immediately organized when the Chinese soviet government was established

in November 1931, though the resolution adopted by the political
secretariat of the ECCI on July 23, 1930, vaguely mentioned the need
for them. The poor-peasant corps and the farm-labor unions emerged
as dynamic political forces at the local level only after the Land Investigation Movement was launched in June 1933 under the leadership
of Mao. It should be noted here that the two important documents of
the Land Investigation Movement, "How to Differentiate the Classes"
(June 1933) and "Decisions Concerning Some Problems Arising from
the Agrarian Struggle" (October 1933), were later selected by the CCP
Central Committee as the reference work (though somewhat revised)
when the CCP reopened the land revolution in the liberated areas of
Yenan in December 1947.[13] If the Land Investigation Movement was
directed solely by the returned-student leadership, as some scholars
assume, why should Mao select his own documents almost a decade
and a half later as the key reference work for the reopening of the
agrarian revolution in Yenan? This was another indication that by
October 1933 Mao had not lost his power and continued to develop
his theory of organization, perhaps with the support of a group of the
returned students. His original power position within the Central
Soviet government, therefore, was constant. It is difficult, consequently,
to interpret the Comintern resolutions literally and conclude auto-
matically that Mao's activities in the Kiangsi soviet were nothing but a
response to Comintern instructions. The growth and development of
mass organizations in the Kiangsi base must be understood and analyzed in the broader context of revolutionary realities, as well as the
practical experience of Mao in attempting to build the institutions
according to his own concept of "mass line."

The main function of the poor-peasant corps and the farm-labor
unions was to serve as auxiliaries to the basic-level soviet governments,
acting as bridges between the soviet government and the masses. According to the organic law and regulations adopted in early 1931 under
the direct influence of Mao, the poor-peasant corps were to establish
and maintain horizontal communication at the village and *hsiang*
levels of government, whereas the farm-labor unions were to maintain
vertical communication between the higher and lower echelons on the
provincial and county levels. The poor-peasant corps, representing the
broad mass of the rural population in the villages and *hsiang* and concentrating their organizational work at these two basic levels, were

[13] Mao Tse-tung, "Tsen-yang fen-hsi chieh-chi" ("How to Differentiate the
Classes"), in *HSCH*, No. 89 (June 29, 1933), p. 8; "Kuan-yü t'u-ti tou-cheng chung
i-hsieh wen-t'i ti chüeh-ting" ("Decisions Concerning Some Problems Arising from
the Agrarian Struggle"), adopted by the People's Commissariat of the central soviet
government, October 1933, in *Ch'a-t'ien chih-nan*, collected in *SSCM*, Reel 17.

more important in mobilizing the masses to participate in executing agrarian policies than were the farm-labor unions, which functioned as a kind of transmission belt for directives from the central government to the intermediate levels.

Another indication that Mao considered the poor-peasant corps much more important than the farm-labor unions was that in two important reports on the creation of model soviet governments in Ch'ang-kang *hsiang* and Ts'ai-hsi *hsiang* he mentioned only the functions of the poor-peasant corps. One was to establish an alliance between the poor and middle peasants, and the other was to maintain a close and functional relationship between the poor-peasant corps and the *hsiang*-level soviet government under whose direct jurisdiction and supervision the former were organized.[14] Even the uniformity in the organizational pattern of the poor-peasant corps did not emerge until the central soviet government under the able leadership of Mao adopted the "General Principles of Organization and Function of the Poor Peasant Corps" in July 1933.[15] The organizational structure and function of the poor-peasant corps varied from region to region until the Land Investigation Movement was launched under Mao's personal direction.

Under these new principles the basic functions of the poor-peasant corps remained the same, but several important changes were made in their structure and operating methods. All changes were, of course, aimed at establishing spontaneous organizations that would not only win the support of the broadest possible masses but also make the operational procedures as flexible as possible. Therefore, the new principles specifically stressed that the poor-peasant corps were by no means organizations of only one group, but that they were to become organizations of all poor masses, including farm laborers and seasonal workers. Even in recruitment the new regulations opened the door widely to all the rural poor, regardless of age and sex, so that almost everyone in the villages could join the poor-peasant corps. They were to become true mass organizations, and recruitment was

[14] Mao Tse-tung, "Hsing-kuo ch'ang-kang hsiang ti su-wei-ai kung-tso" ("The Soviet Work in Ch'ang-kang Hsiang of Hsing-kuo Hsien"), printed by the central government of the Chinese Soviet Republic on December 15, 1933, and published in *Tou-cheng*, No. 42 (January 12, 1934), pp. 10–16; No. 43 (January 19, 1934), pp. 15–20; and No. 44 (January 26, 1934), p. 16, SSCM, Reel 18. See also Mao Tse-tung, "Shang-hang ts'ai-hsi hsiang ti su-wei-ai kung-tso" ("The Soviet Work in Ts'ai-hsi *Hsiang* of Shang-hang *Hsien*"), *Tou-cheng*, No. 45 (February 2, 1934), pp. 15–16; No. 46 (February 9, 1934), pp. 15–16; No. 48 (February 23, 1934), pp. 18–20, SSCM, Reel 18.

[15] The Central Government of the Chinese Soviet Republic, "P'in-nung-t'uan tsu-chih yü kung-tso ta-kang" ("General Principles of Organization and Functions of the Poor-Peasant Corps"), July 15, 1933, SSCM, Reel 11. Also available in *Ch'a-t'ien yün-tung chih-nan*, pp. 35–40, SSCM, Reel 17.

not to be conducted under any duress or pressure. Mass participation was to be achieved through the educational means of propaganda and political agitation, but not by coercion. The voluntary will of the peasant masses had become an important aspect of Mao's concept of "mass line" politics.

The organizational principles of mass organization based on Mao's concept of "mass line" were crystallized into the operational procedures of the poor-peasant corps when the central soviet government under Mao's leadership adopted the new organic law and established two important principles of organization: the open-door policy and the voluntary basis for recruitment. Poor-peasant corps were established only at the *hsiang* level, in which Mao had the most profound interest, and they were organized in small teams (*hsiao-tzu*). Small teams were not necessarily organized on a village basis; sometimes they were formed by combining a number of small villages, and sometimes several small teams were established in a single large village. Although the chiefs of small teams usually played an important role in the policy-making process of the poor-peasant corps' executive committee, the most important policy decisions were not made by the executive committee but in mass meetings called by the poor-peasant corps. To avoid formalism or mechanical procedure, the leaders of the poor-peasant corps did not schedule meetings regularly but called them according to the demands and needs of the peasant masses. The open-door policy was not always implemented as envisaged by Mao's plan — in some places the poor peasants were denied their right to join and in other places they were not even permitted to attend the mass meetings. These were specific problems of implementing the organizational policy at the rice-roots level.

Even the Red Army, which bore the heavy responsibility of carrying out mass mobilization in the newly occupied areas, was often criticized by Mao for not practicing the principle of voluntary recruitment. He pointed out that without the initiative and approval of the masses themselves, the Red Army frequently exercised a kind of monopolistic authoritarianism. Such practices, however, were reportedly eliminated and rectified when the principles of mass organization based on Mao's concept of "mass line" were established in July 1933. That concept was fully incorporated into the organizational principles of the poor-peasant corps, and the importance of "mass line" in all political campaigns and movements was further stressed in the Land Investigation Movement.

The techniques developed in the Kiangsi base were further systematized as the organizational matrix of Chinese Communist rule in

the early years of the Chinese People's Republic. As A. Doak Barnett
has observed:

> In many respects, mass organizations — including those for peas-
> ants, labor, youth, and women — are the most unique element in
> the structure of Chinese Communist power. They are the princi-
> pal agencies through which the weight of the Communist appa-
> ratus makes itself felt upon the average individual and the means
> through which the Communist Party has its widest impact. . . .
> but in countless ways they are tied to the Party, the army, and the
> government, and they form an essential part of the organizational
> matrix of the Chinese Communist rule.[16]

There are, however, two important differences in the function of
"mass line" between the Kiangsi soviet period and the People's Republic period. In the period of the bourgeois-democratic revolution, including the Yenan phase, Mao insisted that the functions of "mass
line" were to become the organizational techniques of mass mobilization and mass participation in the process of policy execution, but after
1949 he seems to have stressed "mass line" as the mechanism for political and social control. Another difference was that in the Kiangsi
period the concept of "mass line," like the concept of "participatory
democracy" in the contemporary world, was the instrument of radical
change in established policy, but as John Lewis observed, its function
in the post-1949 period has been a continuous process of uniting ideology, policy, and practice.[17] Ideology and policy were formulated by
the Party's central leadership under the principle of "democratic centralism," and the political participation of the masses was needed only
to implement and not necessarily to formulate policies.[18] The reason
for that difference in the functions of "mass line" in these two periods
was perhaps that the policy-making process and the structure of the
central leadership in the Kiangsi period were much more diffuse and
differentiated than under the People's Republic. It was therefore possible for a segment of the policy-making elite — Mao and his supporters — to press hard for the adoption of their policy line by mobilizing
the support of the masses. Once having seized power, the leadership
became more interested in social and political control than in winning
the support and loyalty of the masses. Therefore, the essence of mass-
line politics in the Kiangsi period seems to have been a feeling on the

[16] A. Doak Barnett, *Communist China: The Early Years, 1949–1955*, pp. 29–30.
[17] John W. Lewis, *Leadership in Communist China*, p. 10.
[18] A. Doak Barnett, *Cadres, Bureaucracy, and Political Power in Communist China*, p. 142.

part of the masses that they were more involved in revolutionary social change than in any actual participation in the formulation of policy.

Mao's Theories of Administration and Organization

The development of Mao's thought on the principles and procedures of organization and administration may be conveniently divided into two broad stages: that of bourgeois-democratic revolution, in which Mao was primarily occupied with the development of an organization that would not only provide an alternative political system contrasting with KMT rule but also win the support and loyalty of the masses and transform their latent energies into a dynamic revolutionary force; and that of socialist construction, in which Mao was more concerned with the problems of institutionalizing the organizational procedures of government, which he had developed in the first stage of revolution, and creating new ways to exercise control over the society. Some of the important elements of Mao's thinking on the principles of governing a revolutionary society and managing its administrative organization not only persisted in both stages but are also a recurrent, predominant aspect of Mao's theory of organization.

The formal organizations created by Mao on the basis of his concept of "mass line" in the stage of bourgeois-democratic revolution were the most salient features of the revolutionary society in China. One finds in the base areas of the Kiangsi soviet such organized groups as trade unions, army battalions, cooperatives, banks, hospitals, schools, factories, and professional societies — all of which resembled, at least in their formal structure, those of contemporary China. Did these organizations operate in the same ways as do their counterparts in the People's Republic? Did these groups behave in ways resembling their counterparts in the Western countries? If they did, there might be a good possibility of applying the theory of organization, which is primarily intercultural, "still deeply rooted in and engaged with the American experience,"[19] to the analysis of the organizational behavior of a non-Western society such as that of contemporary China.[20] However, our primary concern here is to identify comparable characteristics of organizations that existed in both stages of the Chinese revolution and ascertain whether the Western theory of organization has any relevance to the analysis of Chinese administrative behavior.

[19] Dwight Waldo, "Theory of Organization: Status and Problems," paper for the American Political Science Association meeting, September 1963, p. 12.

[20] Fred Riggs, "Organization Theory and International Development," paper for the Carnegie Seminar on Political and Administrative Development of Indiana University, 1969.

In making some generalizations about the bureaucratic procedures of contemporary China, Michel Oksenberg concluded that the organizational behavior of the People's Republic of China is as complex as that of any bureaucratic organization in the West.[21]

When we analyze the peasant associations, the soviets, the poor-peasant corps, and the farm-labor unions of the Kiangsi period in terms of the Western theory of organization, they can be classified as "formal organizations" because they satisfied such criteria as "an *unequivocal collective identity*, an *exact roster of members*, a *program of activity*, and *procedures for promoting and replacing members.*"[22] To distinguish the organizations established in the Kiangsi base from those of the previous Kiangsi social system, one must use precise criteria. These include an organization name (to establish collective identity); identifiable membership at any given moment (exact roster); definite goals, including means to attain them and a calendar (program of activity); and means of moving members from one position to another (procedures for promoting and replacing members). All of these criteria were the central focus of Mao's thinking on organization when he wrote *Nung-ts'un tiao-ch'a (Rural Survey)*[23] and "How to Differentiate the Classes," and when he delivered his speeches to the conferences of the Land Investigation Movement. Mao's primary concern with methods of class analysis, the essential theme of his writing on organizational principles and procedures, may be considered, in modern sociological terms, as including the assignment of roles to such social groups as the poor, middle, and rich peasants as well as farm laborers and the proletariat, and the definition of the structures of the revolution by establishing the relationship of each group to it. Therefore, Mao's analysis of class structure in rural China was the heart of his theory of organization. In order to establish collective identity among the peasant masses and assign a specific role to each social group, he was always concerned with the scientific analysis of classes in rural China. In all of his work on *Rural Survey*, from his earliest article "Analysis of the Classes in Chinese Society" (1926) to his speech "How to Differentiate the Classes" (1933), Mao was particularly concerned with identifying the majority group of the

[21] Michel C. Oksenberg, "Policy Making under Mao Tse-tung, 1949–1968," *Comparative Politics*, III, No. 3 (April 1971), 323–360.

[22] See Theodore Caplow, *Principles of Organization* (New York, Harcourt, Brace & World, 1964), p. 1 (italics in original). See also Peter M. Blau and W. Richard Scott, *Formal Organizations: A Comparative Approach* (San Francisco, Chandler Publishing Co., 1962), ch. 1.

[23] Mao Tse-tung, *Nung-ts'un tiao-ch'a (Rural Survey)* (Yenan, Chieh-fang-she, 1941).

peasant masses and differentiating them in terms of friends and enemies, prorevolutionaries and antirevolutionaries. After identifying the majority groups of friends or prorevolutionaries such as the poor, middle, and nonexploitative rich peasants as well as the farm laborers, Mao promptly established an exact roster by recruiting them into such organizations as the poor-peasant corps and the farm-labor unions. Obviously, the recruitment of membership into mass organizations was closely connected with Mao's thinking on organizational goals and strategy. Mao felt that the primary goal of an organization was both to arouse revolutionary consciousness and recruit energy for the cause of revolution and to provide concrete programs such as direct participation in the confiscation and redistribution of land or in the administrative processes of local soviet government. The appeal of Mao's organization was carefully designed to have as many people as possible participate in the administrative process of committee work, council meetings, or mass rallies.

The central concept of Mao's organizational theory, therefore, was the soviet system of government. The soviet became the basic organizational form by which Mao and his followers attempted, in the late 1920s and the 1930s, to attain the revolutionary goals of creating new political institutions, accomplishing the equal distribution of land, and throwing off KMT rule. The underlying concept of the soviet was that of "mass line" which helped the leaders initiate and develop a closer relationship between themselves and the masses of people and thus win their support and active participation. The success of the Chinese revolutionary effort, as Chou En-lai stressed in 1959, "was inseparably connected with the fact that the Party has persisted in the Marxist-Leninist working method of the mass line." [24]

The primary elements of the "mass line," as John Lewis succinctly observed, "were the leadership of the party combined with broad mass movement." [25] The organizational techniques of "mass line" grew out of the Chinese Communist leaders' persistent search for organizational form and strategy in their effort to reorient and restructure the Chinese revolution from an elitist and intellectual movement to a mass political movement. As early as August 20, 1927, Mao was firmly convinced of the need for the soviet and had already advocated its establishment as an organizational alternative to the KMT-influenced peasant organization, a means to achieve

[24] Chou En-lai, "A Great Decade," *Ten Glorious Years* (Peking, Foreign Language Press, 1960), pp. 56–57.
[25] John Lewis, *Leadership in Communist China*, p. 71.

the goals of mass political movement. It is, however, uncertain whether Mao himself originated the idea on the basis of his own experience as the leading organizer of the peasant associations or whether he was directly influenced by the theoretical debates being waged by Stalin and Trotsky.

At any rate, to Mao Tse-tung the soviet was definitely the organizational form by which the peasant associations could be transformed and the broadest possible masses won over from the KMT side. "The content of China's revolution," Mao asserted in the fall of 1928, "consists in overthrowing the rule of imperialism and its warlords' tools in China so as to complete the national revolution, and in carrying out the agrarian revolution so as to eliminate the feudal exploitation of the peasant by the landlord class." [26] In this statement Mao explicitly outlined his revolutionary goals, his organizational strategy, and his program of action. In the course of "deepening the agrarian revolution, extending the organizations of the people's political power, and expanding the Red Army and the Red Guards," Mao was fully convinced that "the policies of the Communist Party organizations (local and army) in the Hunan-Kiangsi border area were correct." [27] When the Ninth CCP Conference of the Fourth Red Army convened in Ku-t'ien, Fukien, in December 1929, Mao was not only able to present his thoughts on the "mass line" style of work but also, as the Party's representative, to draft the resolution of the Conference. This resolution later became the guideline for the Red Army in adopting the "mass-line" style of work, in which two important tasks were assigned: the expansion of the Red Army and the construction of the revolutionary base. Hu Hua, the contemporary historian of the Chinese revolution, therefore was able to assert that "the historical significance of the resolution adopted by the Ninth CCP Conference of the Fourth Army was the fact that Mao personally wrote it," [28] and that it systematically outlined his theories and principles, on the basis of which the Party and government organizations were to be constructed. This resolution was selected by the CCP Central Committee as one of the key documents for the ch'eng-feng movement of 1942 in Yenan and was widely distributed among Red Army personnel as a text for ideological indoctrination.[29]

In Nung-ts'un tiao-ch'a, Mao reported on a series of surveys that he

[26] Quoted in Stuart Schram, Mao Tse-tung, p. 109.
[27] Mao Tse-tung, "Why is it that Red Political Power Can Exist in China?" SW, I, 64.
[28] Hu Hua, Chung-kuo hsin min-chu chu-i ko-ming-shih (History of the Chinese Revolution of New Democracy) (Peking, 1952), p. 122.
[29] Only the first chapter of this document, considerably revised, may be found in Mao, SW, I, 105–115.

had systematically conducted, beginning with "An Investigation of Hsing-kuo" in October 1930 and ending with a study of Chang-kang *hsiang* in November 1933. In these surveys, Mao's primary concern was to determine whether his organizational principles and procedures had been effectively implemented at the rice-roots level. The first survey, conducted in October and November 1930, served as the factual basis for the revision of the Draft Land Law of September 1930 and for the Land Law of the Chinese Soviet Republic which was finally proclaimed in November 1931. The second phase, conducted in Ts'ai-hsi *hsiang* in August 1933, was intended to determine whether the land distribution was being carried out according to the procedures established in the Land Law of the Chinese Soviet Republic, and furthermore to lay the groundwork for the Land Investigation Movement. The aim of the third phase, carried out in Changkang *hsiang* in December 1933, was to verify the current status of the Land Investigation Movement at the *hsiang*-level soviet government. What emerges from these reports is that, in addition to his primary concern with class analysis, Mao paid particular attention to the problems of closing the gap between theory and practice and between principles and procedures in the administration of laws and regulations. He thus developed his theory of organizations on the basis of empirical analysis as well as of his own perception of the existing realities in rural China.

Mao's important *Guide to the Land Investigation Movement* differentiated the social groups into five classes: the landlords, the rich, middle, and poor peasants, and the workers. "The exploitation by the small landlords," according to Mao, "is by far the worst." Therefore, he asserted that "the landlord class is the main enemy of the land revolution" and that "The policy of the soviet government toward the landlords is to confiscate all of their land and properties as well and to eliminate the landlord class." No such strong statement appeared, however, in the revised edition of his rural survey published in Yenan, because his policy in Yenan was designed to eliminate the small landlords as a "class" but not as "human beings," and moreover the hope was to reform the small landlords rather than eliminate them. In contrast, the policy of the soviet government toward the landlords and the rich peasants was consistent during the period between 1931 and 1934, inasmuch as the agrarian policy of the central soviet government, as will be seen later, was to confiscate all land of the landlords and rich peasants, and only the latter were entitled to receive inferior land in the redistribution. The basic policy of the central soviet government toward the middle peasants, according to Mao's *Guide to the Land Investigation Movement*, was to establish a solid alliance between the poor and middle peasants, who together constituted more than 75 percent of China's rural population. The land of the middle peasants was not confiscated if they volunteered to surrender it to the soviet government. The middle peasants, like the poor peasants and the farm laborers, were entitled to redistribution of land if they needed it. However, in the course of implementing Mao's guidelines, the local administrators of the Land Investigation Movement violated the established principles and committed some errors, especially with regard to the treatment of the well-to-do middle peasants. Hence Mao called on the Second Soviet Congress in January 1934 to revise the constitution of the Chinese Soviet Republic, and in its first article he stipulated his basic policy line — alliance with the middle peasants.

Mao's criteria for the recruitment in the Party and government were based by and large on his analysis of class structure, which was the core of his organization theory. Mao's report on "The Work of the Central Executive Council and the People's Commissariat" to the Second Soviet Congress on January 24–25, 1934, systematically incorporated his criteria of class analysis which had been established in his report "How to Differentiate the Classes." The revised Constitution of the Chinese Soviet Republic adopted at the Second Soviet Congress incorporated Mao's theory of organization when it declared that "The Chinese Soviet Government has the goals of eliminating the feudal system and of thoroughly improving the livelihood of the peasants under the land law which proclaims the confiscation of the land of the landlord class and its redistribution to farm laborers, poor peasants, and middle peasants. It has the further goal of eventual nationalization of all land." What emerges from Mao's extensive writings and reports for the period between 1927 and 1934 is that his theory of organization minimized elaborate, specialized bureaucratic structures, and was thus contrary to the Western notion of structural differentiation and functional specificity in modern organization. It also combined the functions of government and mass organization into one "mass line" style of work, as a solution to administrative problems, and it mobilized the masses to participate in the policy-formulation process at the basic level of government. The greatest mobilization, such as the Land Investigation Movement, occurred in the policy-execution process.

Experience in the Kiangsi soviet indicated that organization, more than programs and policies, was most important for the success of the revolution, hence Mao's primary concern was always with the development of organization based on his concept of "mass line." From his point of view, new organizations were always needed to bridge the gap between theory and practice as well as between principles and procedures. The strength of new organizations during the Kiangsi period lay in the basic administrative bodies: the *hsiang* soviet governments (administrative units comprising several villages) and the village soviet governments. The concepts which underlay the establishment and operation of these organizations, and which had broad appeal, were a land-reform program and mass participation in the process of local administration. When the political instruments through which the peasants could voice their discontent were established, and when an ideology appealed to the peasant masses, they became a dynamic political force that the Kiangsi political system could mobilize in building the base of political power.

Although the institutional form of the soviets was abandoned in 1937, during the Second United Front period, and gradually evolved into the people's council or people's congress, the underlying concept of "mass line" never changed throughout the revolutionary period and still continues in the People's Republic of China as the basis of the governing principles and procedures of the political system. The Kiangsi experience of governing and managing revolutionary society presents, in a fundamental sense, a vivid case study of the peasant masses caught up in the struggle between the forces of revolutionary change and the forces of maintenance of the status quo. The forces of tradition were represented by the landlords and local-gentry class; the revolutionary forces were represented by the administrative cadres of the soviet government and the impoverished peasants who joined the Red Army and the soviet organizations in order to overthrow the traditional political order. The balance of power in the rural areas of China in the late 1920s and early 1930s was shifting toward revolutionary change, and Mao's concept of "mass line" as the organizational technique of the soviet system of government provided further impetus for such a change.

II

STRUCTURE AND FUNCTION OF THE
SOVIET GOVERNMENT IN KIANGSI

The province of Kiangsi, traditionally known as "Kan," lies south of the Yangtze River. It is surrounded by the provinces of Anhwei and Hupeh in the north, Hunan in the west, Kwangtung in the south, and Fukien and Chekiang in the east. The Kan River, which flows through Kiangsi province, is an important commercial artery in the region between Canton and Yangtze, and in addition there is a river route linking Kiangsi and Chekiang. Kiangsi is one of China's leading rice-producing areas; two crops are harvested annually in the Kan River valley and Poyang basin. Aside from rice, the main cash products of the province are cotton (in the north), tea (in the hills of the northwest and northeast), ramie (in Wantsai), tobacco, sugar cane, and oranges. The province also produces much of China's tungsten and mines high-grade coking coal and kaolin, which supplies the porcelain industry of Fowliang (Kingtenchen).[1]

The Chinese Maritime Customs estimated the population of Kiangsi in 1931 to be 24,467,000 (a figure somewhat lower than that of the 1885 census). In the early 1930s, the majority of the population of the province was engaged in agricultural work; "industrial workers" in the province at that time totaled, according to one estimate, only 8,995 persons, of whom 6,882 were concentrated in Nanch'ang, the capital city of the province, and 2,113 in the city of Kiukiang.[2]

The population of the surrounding provinces was also overwhelmingly agrarian; in those areas, industrial workers were estimated to account for no more than 10 to 20 percent of the 1931 working force. Of course, in 1931, China as a whole was a predominantly agricultural country, with probably 70 to 80 percent of her people engaged in farm-

[1] *The Columbia Lippincott Gazetteer of the World* (New York: Columbia University Press, 1961), p. 942.

[2] The 1885 census gave the population of Kiangsi as 24,500,000. These statistics are drawn from the following sources: *The China Year Book 1933*, edited by H. G. W. Woodhead, 2–3; George Cressey, *China's Geographic Foundations: A Survey of the Land and Its People* (New York: McGraw Hill, 1934), p. 55; and Tōa Keizai Chōsa-kyoku, ed., *Shina Sovetō Undō no Genkyū* (*Study of the Chinese Soviet Movement*), (Tokyo: East Asia Economic Research Bureau, 1934). Classified.

ing. In the country as a whole, farmers and farm laborers, together with their families, may have totaled 300,000,000 persons.

Against the background of the agrarian nature of Kiangsi province this chapter will attempt to describe the development of the soviets and their administrative problems. Roy Hofheinz having already demonstrated in an important piece of research the scope of Communist influence in Kiangsi province, our analysis here will not duplicate the indices he used to measure the patterns of Communist influence in Kiangsi province. "The remarkable growth rates of 1928–34 are due to two separate trends," Hofheinz stated. "First, a sizable portion of the new members of the movement during the early period were defectors from the KMT cause." He therefore concluded that "From 1931 on, the growth of the army and the Party resulted mostly from intensive recruitment within areas already occupied or newly occupied."[3]

The soviet movement in south-central China was expanding under the leadership of Mao Tse-tung and Chu Te from 1928 to 1931, when the central leadership of the CCP was preoccupied with problems of policy-making as well as factionalism within the Party. The CCP organization in south-central China, subsequent to the Sixth Party Congress and until the convocation of the Conference of the Delegates from the Soviet Area in May 1930, sought two major goals: the reorganization and strengthening of the Red Army as it grew rapidly, and the establishment and expansion of the soviet areas under its protection. These activities, of course, were subordinated to the overall policy of Li Li-san.

The theory and practice of the soviet government emerged in the late 1920s during the long period of the peasant movement and the revolutionary experience in rural China. Therefore, the development of the concept of the soviet system of government and Mao's intuitive understanding of the importance of mass organizations cannot be separated. As early as August 1927, Mao began to realize the importance of an organization that would involve peasant masses in local politics. He saw the peasantry as an essential force in Chinese society for carrying out the revolution, and this led him subsequently to develop the soviet for integrating the peasant masses into the political processes of the Chinese Soviet Republic.

Mao's Attitudes toward the Soviets in Kiangsi

Drawing on several years' experience as a peasant organizer during the KMT-CCP collaboration, Mao developed his own concept of "soviet"

[3] Roy Hofheinz, Jr., "The Ecology of Chinese Communist Success: Rural Influence Patterns, 1923–1945," in A. Doak Barnett, ed., *Chinese Communist Politics in Action* (University of Washington Press, 1969), p. 26.

in southern Kiangsi. His concept stressed the primary role of the peasantry in the rural organizations of the soviets even though Lenin had always emphasized the primary role of the industrial proletariat and assigned only a secondary role to the peasants.

After the breakdown of CCP-KMT collaboration, Mao gradually came to realize that the KMT organization was not an effective instrument for dealing with the problems of the peasant masses. What was now required of the Chinese revolution, in Mao's view, was to establish an organization that would be able to perform the functions of mass mobilization and at the same time carry out the program of land distribution. He proposed the idea of a soviet-type institution, because the China of 1927, Mao analyzed correctly, did not resemble the Russia of 1905; China had long since reached the stage of the Russia of 1917. In this sense, Mao, in many respects, was in general agreement with what Trotsky had said earlier about the situation of China. Nevertheless Mao's views remained fundamentally different from those expressed by Trotsky, for Mao did not advocate "permanent revolution" nor did he believe in the sole-leadership function of the industrial proletariat in China. By this time, however, Stalin also — after having defeated the left opposition's challenge for power — was beginning to adopt the major elements of the program that it had advocated.

Although Mao knew the kind of organization that was needed to fulfill the requirements of the revolution in China, the Central Committee of the CCP under the leadership of Ch'ü Ch'iu-pai was not quite ready to accept what he proposed in August 1927. The Party's central leadership was formulating a policy of "military putschism," later implemented in the Nanch'ang Uprisings (August 1, 1927) and the Canton Commune (December 11, 1927). The Central Committee of the CCP reportedly directed Mao not to call for the establishment of soviets, but to maintain the façade of alliance with the KMT by using the KMT flag as a symbol in his conduct of revolutionary activities even after the collapse of CCP-KMT cooperation in April 1927. Mao nevertheless defied the order from the Central Committee to follow the official policy line, thus failing to promote a modern land program which envisaged confiscating land only from the large landlords. Because of his attitude, Mao reportedly was condemned by the Central Committee as a "left" deviationist.[4]

Mao's position with respect to the establishment of soviet organiza-

---

[4] For the question of whether Mao was a "left" or "right" deviationist, see Stuart R. Schram, "On the Nature of Mao Tse-tung's 'Deviation' in 1927," *The China Quarterly*, No. 18 (April–June 1964), pp. 55–66; *Mao Tse-tung* (New York, Simon and Schuster, 1966), pp. 95–131; and K. A. Wittfogel, "The Legend of 'Maoism,'" part II, *The China Quarterly*, No. 2 (April–June 1960), pp. 16–34.

tion in China was manifested in his letter of August 20, 1927, to the
CCP Central Committee. As he put it:

> A certain comrade has come to Hunan announcing that new in-
> structions from the International propose the immediate estab-
> lishment of soviets of workers, peasants, and soldiers in China.
> On hearing this, I jumped for joy. Obviously, China has long
> since reached 1917, but formerly everyone held the opinion that
> we were in 1905. This has been an extremely great error. Soviets
> of workers, peasants, and soldiers are wholly adapted to the ob-
> jective situation, and we must immediately and resolutely estab-
> lish the political power of the workers, peasants, and soldiers in
> the four provinces of Kwangtung, Hunan, Hupeh, and Kiangsi. As
> soon as established, this political power should moreover rapidly
> achieve victory in the whole country. We expect that the Central
> Committee will without a doubt accept the instructions of the
> International, and we shall moreover apply them in Hunan.[5]

Mao's conflict with the CCP Central Committee was concerned with
the issues of when and how to establish the soviet organization, how
to implement the land-confiscation program, and whether or not Mao's
organizational plan should be adopted, i.e., the concepts that Mao had
begun to develop after the debacle of the 1927 revolution. He was later
relieved of his posts both on the Central Committee and on the Hunan
Provincial Committee, when he ignored the call of the Central Committee to attack Ch'angsha because he disagreed with the strategic
plan of the Party's central leadership. Soon afterward, at the November (1927) Plenum of the CCP Central Committee, Mao was condemned for his "military opportunism" and for his use of new war-
lordism.[6]

Ignoring the instructions from the Central Committee and defying
the policy line adopted by the November Plenum (1927), which also
ousted him from his position of leadership within the Party, Mao began to build up his own revolutionary base in the Chingkang mountain
region. The establishment of an independent soviet base at that time
was, as Stuart Schram has observed, far from what the Central Com-

[5] *Chung-yang T'ung-hsin* (Central Newsletter), No. 3 (August 30, 1927), pp. 42–43
quoted in Schram, "On the Nature of Mao Tse-tung's 'Deviation' in 1927," p. 58.
[6] The policy line adopted by the November Plenum (1927) was similar to the idea
of Trotsky, who advocated a "permanent" or "uninterrupted" revolution. During
the ensuing months an uninterrupted series of military uprisings was carried out
in order to achieve the final victory of the revolution. Another manifestation of the
policy was the establishment of the Hai-lu-feng soviets in November 1927 under
the leadership of P'eng P'ai.

mittee expected. What the Central Committee did expect Mao to do, according to a directive of the Central Committee to Communists of Hunan and Hupeh in early December 1927, was to carry out immediately a complete socialist revolution by "sealing off" a *hsien* here and there, by "killing off" as many bad gentry, reactionaries, and big landowners as possible, and by establishing a revolutionary base.[7] This order, of course, was compatible with the policy line of the CCP Central Committee inasmuch as it had earlier, in August 1927, defined the current stage of Chinese revolution as being advanced toward the stage of socialist revolution.

The institutional theory and organizational methods of the local soviets that Mao began to develop in the spring of 1928 in the area of the Chingkang mountains were his own creation. The terminology Mao used, however, such as the "soviet of workers', peasants', and soldiers' deputies" or "the people's council," was in many respects borrowed directly from the concepts discussed in the Chinese Communist literature of the time. As the news of the establishment of the Red Army under Mao and Chu Te spread widely in the Chingkang mountain regions in 1928, peasant armies, scattered in the area, quickly joined the Chu-Mao forces.

An army corps commanded by P'eng Te-huai was reorganized to form the Fifth Red Army. Several other Red Armies also were organized, and by the end of 1928, the total strength of the Red Army stood at fourteen divisions with more than 75,000 men.[8]

As the Red Army grew, the soviets proliferated. By December 1928, more than 60 soviet bases had been created in the provinces of Hunan, Hupeh, Kiangsi, Fukien, and Kwangtung. An official organ of the Russian Communist Party stated that, by the end of 1929, soviets had already been formed in 173 *hsien* in the provinces of Fukien, Kiangsi, Hunan, Hupeh, Honan, Kwangsi, and Szechwan.[9] By May 1930, soviets were said to have been established in more than 103 *hsien* — and by September of that year, according to reports, they existed in 200 *hsien*.[10]

[7] For the information on Mao's deviation and his conflict with the CCP Central Committee, I relied heavily on Stuart Schram's study, *Mao Tse-tung*, pp. 104–117.

[8] Hatano Ken'ichi, "Shina kyō-san gun no rekishi to gensei" ("History and Present Situation of the Chinese Communist Army"), *Shina* (China), March 1935. This article is collected in his *Gendai Shina no seiji to jinbutsu* (Politics and Personalities of Modern China), (Tokyo: Gaizō sha, 1937), pp. 317–324. Hereafter cited as Hatano, *Shina no seiji*.

[9] *Pravda*, April 28, 1934; quoted in Tōa keizai chōsa-kyoku (East Asian Economic Research Bureau), *Shina sovetō undō no genkyu* (*A Study of the Chinese Soviet Movement*) (Tokyo, 1934), p. 239. Hereafter cited as *Shina sovetō undō*.

[10] *Shina sovetō undō*, p. 239.

A Kuomintang general reporting to the KMT's Central Executive Committee in May 1931 on the situation in the soviet areas affirmed that 300 *hsien* were affected by the "red menace." [11] It is quite possible that the KMT military leaders exaggerated the extent of the soviet areas in order to obtain more funds to use in military campaigns against them. A report to the League of Nations in July 1931, however, estimated that soviets had already been established in more than 183 *hsien*.

On November 7, 1931, when the First Soviet Congress convened in Juichin, Kiangsi, the central soviet government reported to the CCP Central Committee in Shanghai that the central soviet government consisted of seven large soviet areas: Central Area, West Fukien, Hunan-Anhwei Border, Hunan-Kiangsi Border, Northeast Hunan–Hupeh–Kiangsi, Western Hunan–Hupeh Border, and Hainan Island.[12] (See the adjoining map.) Estimates of the size of the territorial bases and the population within them vary from source to source. An official report of the Chinese Soviet Republic at the time of its First Congress gave an exaggerated estimate, probably for the sake of propaganda. It claimed that the territorial bases of the soviet comprised approximately 300 *hsien*, scattered in eleven provinces of the eighteen provinces of China at that time. This was estimated at one-sixth of the area of China proper. The total population within the soviet areas, according to the same source, was more than sixty million.

One could, however, conservatively estimate that approximately 100 *hsien* were under soviet rule and that about twelve million people lived within the soviet districts. The Communist reports usually implied that an entire *hsien* was under soviet rule even if only a small portion of it was occupied by the Red Army and affected by the soviet system of government. Once a village or *hsiang* soviet was formed in a *hsien*, it became the task of the Red Army to "pacify" neighboring villages and *hsiang* and extend the soviet rule over the whole *hsien*. Hence, if even a couple of village or *hsiang* soviets were established, the CCP leaders considered the entire *hsien* to be under soviet rule.

Organizational Patterns of Soviet Governments

No set pattern for the establishment of soviet governments evolved during the period from 1928 to 1931. One can, however, draw a general picture of the organizational composition of the local soviets by

[11] *Ibid.*

[12] See the text of a telegram dispatched by the First National Soviet Congress to the Central Committee of the CCP on November 15, 1931; reproduced in Hatano, *Chūkyō-shi*, I, 595–596.

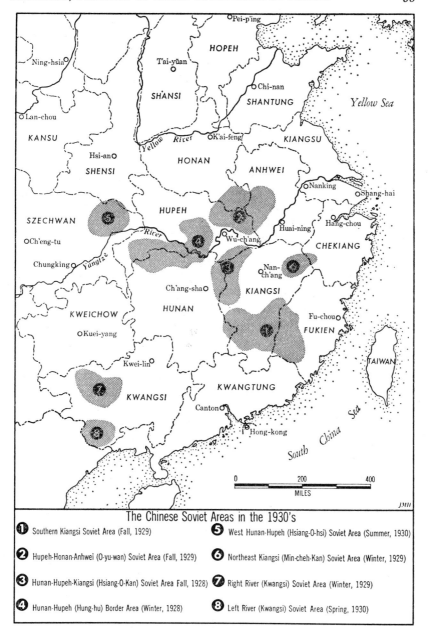

The Chinese Soviet Areas in the 1930's

1 Southern Kiangsi Soviet Area (Fall, 1929)

2 Hupeh-Honan-Anhwei (O-yu-wan) Soviet Area (Fall, 1929)

3 Hunan-Hupeh-Kiangsi (Hsiang-O-Kan) Soviet Area Fall, 1928)

4 Hunan-Hupeh (Hung-hu) Border Area (Winter, 1928)

5 West Hunan-Hupeh (Hsiang-O-hsi) Soviet Area (Summer, 1930)

6 Northeast Kiangsi (Min-cheh-Kan) Soviet Area (Winter, 1929)

7 Right River (Kwangsi) Soviet Area (Winter, 1929)

8 Left River (Kwangsi) Soviet Area (Spring, 1930)

analyzing eyewitness reports and reminiscences of former participants in the operations of the local soviets.[13]

The general procedure of establishing soviet apparatus in a rural area after the Red Army had occupied a village or city began to take shape when Red Army officers started organizing "revolutionary committees" with the direct participation of the local population. Such committees usually abolished all previous bureaucratic organizations, barred traditional leaders from participation, and eliminated such oppressive measures as the land tax and high interest rates on loans. These revolutionary committees in villages or cities were formed with the active participation of the CCP members in the area, but when there was no CCP member who could lead the committee, "progressive elements" of the society such as labor-union leaders, organizers of the peasant movement, or dependents of Red Army members were recruited to provide leadership.

The revolutionary committees generally comprised three to five active members who, after proclaiming the establishment of their committee, published a political program usually prepared by or transmitted from the Party leadership of the Red Army. The committee often enacted new laws and regulations to destroy the material basis of "oppressive elements" and to prevent counterrevolution. It sometimes freed prisoners from the jails, organized revolutionary courts to try subversive elements, and formed police forces. As a rule, such police were armed with the weapons seized from the previous regime.

The revolutionary committees also organized labor unions, peasant associations, and other mass organizations, besides building the Red Army and guerrilla units for the locality. After the groundwork for the establishment of a local soviet government had been solidly laid, the revolutionary committee usually set a date for a general election of representatives to the *hsiang* soviet government in the region. The electoral process became a highly developed mechanism through which the soviet government attempted to create a sense of participation on the part of the masses and the rural population.[14]

There were, admittedly, mistakes in recruiting local cadres and establishing revolutionary committees. Sometimes the Red Army leaders,

[13] For example, see *Hui-i Ching kang shan-ch'ü ti toucheng* (*Reminiscence of the Struggle in the Chingkang Mountain Area*); Yang Shang-kuei, *The Red Kiangsi-Kwangtung Border Region* (Peking: Foreign Language Press, 1961); and a series of articles in *Hung-ch'i P'iao-p'iao* (*Red Flag Fluttering*) (Peking: China Youth Press, 1957–1960), vols. I–XIII.

[14] See "Ch'üan-kuo ti-i-tz-u Su-wei-ai ch'ü tai-piao ta-hui hsuan-ch'üan kang-yao" ("A Summary of the Declaration of the All-China Conference of Delegates from the Soviet Areas"), *Hung-ch'i* (*Red Flag*), No. 112 (June 21, 1930), reproduced in Hatano, *Chūkyō shi*, I, 388–394.

it was said, had no way of understanding the local situation, and picked unsuitable persons for the revolutionary committees, thereby antagonizing the majority of local people. Therefore, the Conference of Delegates from the Soviet Areas, held in May 1930, called on the delegates to adopt regulations that would enable the local people of the newly liberated areas to elect their own representatives to the revolutionary committees rather than have them appointed by Red Army officers. It was stressed that the revolutionary committees were to prepare immediately for general elections of the local delegate council (soviet) by mobilizing the entire population of their regions.

Traditionally the peasant masses in rural China were remote from the central authority and did not have significant opportunities to participate in local government. As a result, there was usually a wide gap between the ruling elite in the urban centers and the rural peasant population. The representatives of the central or provincial governments in rural China were frequently unable to establish two-way communication with the peasant population. The Communists hoped to close this gap by establishing the soviet system of government, which was to provide immediate opportunities for each and every member of a locality to participate in the political process of local government. In practice, however, the Communist leaders in the Kiangsi soviet base did not have sufficient time to implement their project, because the base areas were under constant attack by the KMT forces and were in a state of military siege.

The newly organized soviet governments in rural China had some success in recruiting local people and training them as leaders of the local soviet governments, and the majority of these people were also faithful followers of Mao Tse-tung; this later strengthened Mao's power position. All industrial workers, artisans, and Red Army men and officers, regardless of religion or nationality, upon reaching the age of sixteen, had the right to participate in the electoral processes of the soviet government, and the soviet administrators succeeded, more than past regimes, in mobilizing and controlling most of the population in certain parts of rural China through the mechanism of representative councils (soviets).

The soviet governments served as local administrative agencies as well as legislative bodies, in keeping with the role of the soviet government as defined by Mao Tse-tung. They had two major tasks: to administer and control Chinese society at the grass-roots level and to serve as channels of communication between the CCP organizations and the masses.

It was in the area around Tung-ku and Hsing-kuo in southern Kiangsi that Mao and Chu, after leaving the Chingkang mountain area, on January 14, 1929, began to build up the revolutionary base and install soviet governments, which eventually became the foundation on which the Chinese Soviet Republic was established, with its capital at Juichin. By amalgamating the scattered local soviets in southwest Kiangsi, Mao Tse-tung succeeded in forming a southwest Kiangsi provincial soviet government in February 1930.[15]

Wherever the Red Army conducted guerrilla warfare and seized territory, a revolutionary committee was installed, and later it served as the basis for a soviet government. The small Chu-Mao forces in southern Kiangsi first occupied an inaccessible and readily defensible location in the border areas of the province and then began to create the provincial soviet government. The southwest Kiangsi soviet government, northeast Kiangsi soviet government, and Fukien-Kiangsi border soviet government (known as the central soviet area) provide an excellent case study of how the Chinese Communist leaders attempted to create the soviet system of government in the formative stage of their institution building, how they sought to resolve the organizational problems of ruling and administering the occupied territories, and how they operated the soviet system in response to the requirements and needs of the revolution.

The Southwest Kiangsi (Kan-hsi-nan) Soviet Government

The origin of the southwest Kiangsi soviet government may be traced back to the military insurrection of Wan-an *hsien* in 1927.[16] Subsequent to this uprising the guerrilla forces occupied a number of rural villages and finally succeeded in establishing a base area. This early success can be attributed primarily to the CCP's determined leadership and also to its winning the broadest possible support of the masses in the area. It also enabled the Chu-Mao forces to consolidate the scattered guerrilla bases and transform them into a "red base area." This was the origin of the 24th Army Corps of workers and peasants which later became the Third Red Army.[17]

After the establishment of the southwest Kiangsi provisional gov-

[15] Edgar Snow, *Red Star Over China*, pp. 174–175.

[16] *Chiang-shi ch'üan-sheng ti-i tz'u kung-nung-ping su-wei-ai tai-hui-tui su-wei-ai kung-tso pao-kao* (Resolution of the First Kiangsi Provincial Congress of the Council of Workers, Peasants, and Soldiers on the Report of the Soviet Work), May 6, 1932. Collected in *SSCM*, Reel 10. This resolution hereafter cited as *Resolution of the First Kiangsi Provincial Congress*.

[17] The Third Army was created by the amalgamation of the Second, Third, and Fourth Corps in southwest Kiangsi and was commanded by Ts'ai Shen-hsi, a graduate of Whampoa Military Academy. Tseng Lu-po served as political commissar. This army had about 5,400 men, the majority of whom were poor peasants of the region. See Hatano, *Chūkyō-shi*, I, 284.

ernment in 1930, Mao proposed a new slogan: "Mobilize the masses and take Kian." The new tasks were to seize political power, increase the size of the Red Army, and distribute land. There is no way of knowing how these programs were implemented in 1930, but it was claimed that they helped the newly established southwest Kiangsi government acquire more territory and further consolidate the base areas. The impetus for greater expansion and a large recruitment of army personnel, however, came when the KMT army began its attack on the base area in late October 1930.[18]

The southwest Kiangsi soviet government, in its formative stage, was nothing but a mass organization in which the workers and peasants could join and demonstrate their support of the Red Army. Because the base area was created in a warfare situation, the newly organized soviets were instructed to establish and maintain a close relationship with the masses by giving them the opportunity to take part in local politics. The primary task of the soviet system in southwest Kiangsi, therefore, was to arouse the masses and generate their enthusiasm for the revolution.

The newly established soviets attempted to eliminate "bureaucratic formalism" by instituting a broadly based representative system and also by setting up numerous committees, both permanent and *ad hoc*, in which as many persons as possible participated, thus avoiding the concentration of administrative power in the hands of a few individuals. Various administrative tasks ranging from land confiscation and redistribution to the mobilization of logistical support for the Red Army were handled by the local soviet. Those who took part in the councils (soviets) or their committees became the most politicized group of people in the village. They served both as the link between the rural population and the Red Army's party officials and as the local activists for political education of the masses.

The basic unit of the soviet at the *hsiang* level of southwest Kiangsi comprised one delegate from every fifty peasants and one delegate from every ten members of the proletariat who had reached the age of sixteen. The migrant workers in the village were classified as poor peasants and given the opportunity of taking part in the election of the *hsiang* soviet government. When the *hsiang* delegate council was elected, it in turn elected the seven-member executive committee that functioned as the soviet government of the *hsiang*. The executive committee elected a standing committee or presidium, consisting of a chairman, a vice-chairman, and a secretary, which functioned as the administrative agency of the *hsiang*. The same pattern of organization was repeated

[18] *Resolution of the First Kiangsi Provincial Congress.*

at the *ch'ü* and *hsien* level, although the number of committees and staff personnel varied, depending on the size of the local population.

According to a comprehensive report concerning the activities of the CCP and the soviet government in southwest Kiangsi (the Hunan-Kiangsi border area), submitted by the Party's Provincial Committee to the CCP Central Committee in Shanghai on January 12, 1932, the party's primary task after the conclusion of the Provincial Party Congress of November 1931 was to develop a mass political movement by restructuring the existing organization and also by forming a new one.[19] Such mass organizations as the Red Labor Union, farm-labor union, mutual-aid society, antiimperialist league, poor-peasant corps, and women's organization were being established from the *hsien* to the *hsiang* level by November–December 1931. Many of these mass organizations, however, had only a meager membership list. No attempt was made to recruit members by means of arousing revolutionary consciousness at a mass struggle. Consequently, the mass organization in the region was unable to carry out independent work and the Red Labor Union was criticized as having been "quite unsatisfactory" in its conduct of mass work.[20] The attitude of the workers toward the labor union became so indifferent that the union failed to extend its power and influence among them. The labor law passed by the First National Soviet Congress in November 1931 was just beginning to be put into effect, but only in the industrial plants and printing shops owned and operated by the provincial soviet government, and it was not even implemented by the *hsien*-level government. The reason for this error was simply that the local government continued to maintain a rich-peasant mentality.

The report asserted that the soviet work in the region did not actually begin until the provincial soviet government was established in November 1931. Even though the provincial soviet government paid special attention to central policy in the region, many directives were not put into effect. At each level of government, the soviets failed to accomplish independent work because the staff lacked creative imagination or administrative skill and tended to look to the party officials in the region or even to the central soviet government for policy guidance and executive instructions. Sometimes the party office in the region

[19] "The Report on the General Situation in the Hunan-Kiangsi Border Soviet Area," submitted by the CCP Committee of the Hunan-Kiangsi Soviet Area to the CCP Central Committee in Shanghai on January 12, 1932. This document is translated by Himori Torao and collected in *Mantetsu Chōsa Geppō*, XII, No. 9 (September 1932), 109–121. Hereafter cited as *The Report on the Hunan-Kiangsi Soviet Area*.

[20] *Ibid.*, p. 110.

managed all of the soviet activities. In P'ing-hsiang and Shu *hsien*, for example, "one gets an impression that the soviet government is nothing but an extension office of the Party." [21] Therefore, the provincial soviet government continued to urge the *hsien* to correct such erroneous tendencies by establishing an independent work system.

The report also stressed that such functional departments as land, finance, labor, and education were organized under the executive committee of the provincial government, but that their work too had many defects. Some staff members were unable to conduct independent work because they were unfamiliar with anything but the work of their own departments. Many staff personnel concentrated their work only in the provincial offices and never left their offices to go to the *hsien* or *ch'ü* level to offer assistance. Even in the offices of the provincial government, not all were familiar with the administrative procedures and only two or three people carried out the administrative duties. For the purpose of solving such organizational problems, the provincial government of Southwest Kiangsi convened on January 5, 1932; it was an enlarged conference of the executive committee, to which all the chairmen and executive-committee members of each *hsien* government were invited. After evaluating and discussing soviet work in each *hsien*, the conference adopted a decision to implement a new method of work based on Mao's "mass line" approach to the local administration.

The series of reorganization programs implemented in 1931 was, therefore, by no means intended to bring the southwest Kiangsi soviet areas under Party control, as some scholars have interpreted, but was chiefly designed to replace the old cadres, assigned to the offices during the days of revolutionary committee, with newly recruited and trained personnel. This was precisely the program that the central soviet government carried out immediately after its establishment under the leadership of Mao Tse-tung. Even the Party organization in southwest Kiangsi was devised so as not to eliminate the Mao supporters but to eliminate the influence of Li Li-san and his policy. Thus "we began to transform our own method of work and establish a new system of conducting party activities when we reorganized the Party structure and set up such programs as the revolutionary contests, the illiteracy program, reading the documents, and utilizing the Lenin library effectively every Saturday," the report asserted.[22] After the reorganization, the Party's branch organizations increased their effectiveness by stimulating the creativity of the Party members.

The Party's most serious problem in the region, however, according

[21] *Ibid.*, p. 111.
[22] *Ibid.*, p. 119.

to the same report, "was the inability of the lower Party organizations to respond to the higher Party organization in implementing the Party's resolutions and directives more rapidly and effectively." The Party committees in "certain *hsien* like the ones in P'ing-hsiang, Shu, Sui-ch'üan, and Ling *hsien* continued their opportunistic tendencies by ignoring the directives coming from the provincial committee," the report continued.[23] Added to such problems was the shortage of trained cadres at the local level, which inevitably slowed down party activities. To obviate such shortcomings, the provincial committee actively recruited and trained new cadres from the workers and peasants and also instituted a short-term training program in the provincial headquarters. Soon the program graduated more than one hundred new cadres each month, and emphasized the study of such important documents as the resolutions and directives of the Comintern as well as those of the CCP Central Committee. The provincial graduates were sent to the *hsien* level to establish the *hsien* cadres' training program. Such programs were already in operation in Ch'a-lung, Yung-hsin, Shu *hsien*, An-fu, and Ning-kang *hsien*, according to the report, and were being extended to the other *hsien* of the region.[24] What emerges from this report is a constant struggle of the central leadership in Juichin to close the gap in the structural difference between the organization created in the 1928–1930 period and those set up after the establishment of the central soviet government in November 1931. Consequently, the determined effort to restructure such existing institutions as the Party, soviet governments, and mass organizations must be understood and analyzed in the light of the goal of the central government, which was to establish a uniform pattern for the soviet system of government.

The Northeast Kiangsi (Kan-tung-pei) Soviet Government

In contrast to southwest Kiangsi, the northeast Kiangsi soviet government was rather well developed and had fewer administrative problems. Even Mao recognized northeast Kiangsi as one of the most highly developed base areas under soviet rule. "The comrades in northeast Kiangsi are doing the most creative work in building soviet institutions," Mao said in his "Report on the Work of the Central Soviet Government" to the Second National Soviet Congress in January 1934. "They are certainly the model soviets," he continued. From Mao's point of view, institution-building in the northeast Kiangsi soviet area was

[23] *Ibid.*, p. 120.
[24] *Ibid.*, p. 121.

as important as the model soviet he was trying to create in the Hsing-kuo *hsien* of the central soviet area. As Mao put it:

The comrades in Hsing-kuo *hsien* as well as those in northeast Kiangsi link the political life of the masses with the revolutionary effort. At the same time, they are able to resolve the problems of the goals and methods of the revolutionary activities. They are exemplary organizers of revolutionary war and of mass political life.[25]

Two documents "The Situation in the Northeast Kiangsi Soviet Area," written by Ma Lo, a party representative in the northeast Kiangsi soviet base, and submitted to the CCP Central Committee in Shanghai on July 20, 1931, and "Report on the Work of the Northeast Kiangsi Soviet Area," written by Tu Chen-nung, another party representative in northeast Kiangsi, submitted to the CCP Central Committee in Shanghai in December 1932 — provide some interesting insights into the administrative processes of the regional soviet government.[26]

The geographic area of the northeast Kiangsi soviet government, as described in these two reports, comprised a total of sixteen *hsien* (ten in Northeast Kiangsi, three in Fukien, one in southern Anhwei, and two in western Chekiang).[27] The northeast Kiangsi soviets emerged

[25] Mao Tse-tung, "Chung-kuo Su-wei-ai kung-ho kuo chung-yang chih-hsieng wei-yüan hui tui ti-erh tz'u ch'üan-kuo Su-wei-ai tai-piao ta-hui ti pao-kao" ("Report of the Central Executive Council and the Council of People's Commissars of the Chinese Soviet Republic to the Second National Soviet Congress") in *Hung-se Chung-hua*, special issue, No. 3 (January 26, 1934) in *SSCM*, Reel 18. Also in Hatano, *Chūkyō-shi*, IV, 106. Hereafter cited as *Mao's Report to the Second Soviet Congress*.

[26] Ma Lo, "Kiangsi tung-pei su-wei-ai ch'ü ti chin-hsiang" ("Recent Situation in the Northeast Kiangsi Soviet Area," collected in *Mantetsu Chōsa Geppō*, vol. XII, No. 8 (August 1932), 57–66. A summary of this report is in Wang Chien-min, *Chung-kung Shih-kao* (A Draft History of the Chinese Communist Party), II, 257–258.

Tu Chen-nung, "Kan tung-pei su-wei-ai ch'ü ti kung-tso pao-kao" ("Report on the Work of the Northeast Kiangsi Soviet Area"), reproduced in Hatano, *Chūkyō-shi*, III, 311–385. Hereafter cited as Tu, *Kan tung-pei pao-kao*.

[27] The northeast Kiangsi soviet government was reported to have administered the following *hsien* in four provinces:

Kiangsi (20 *hsien*) — I-yang, Heng-feng, Shang-jao, Kuei-chi, Yü-shan, Kwang-feng, Ch'ien-shan, Teh-hsing, Le-p'ing, Wan-nien, Fou-liang, P'o-yang, Yü-kan, Yü-kiang, Tou-chiang, Hu-kou, P'eng-tse, Tung-hsiang, Tse-chi, Chin-chi.

Fukien (12 *hsien*)—Ch'ung-an, Chien-yang, Chien-ch'ü, Shao-wu, Kwang-tse, Po-cheng, Fu-t'ing, Fu-an, Shou-ning, Ping-nan, Tu-yuan, Cheng-ho.

Chekiang (13 *hsien*) — Kiang-shan, Kai-ho, Ch'ü *hsien*, P'ing-yang, Yün-shan, Chu-chiang, Yün-ho, T'ai-hsun, Ying-cha, Ching-t'ien, Jui-an, Ching-yuan, Ching-ning.

Anhwei (7 *hsien*) — Wu-yuan, Ch'i-wen, Tung-liu, Ch'iu-po, Hsiu-ning, T'ai-p'ing, Ching *hsien*.

For this information, see "Chung-kuo Kung-ch'an tang tsai chung-nan ti-ch'ü

under the leadership of Fang Chih-min, a native son of northeast Kiangsi and an outstanding revolutionary leader.[28] After the failure of the Nanch'ang Uprising in 1927, Fang Chih-min returned to his native village in I-yang *hsien* of northeast Kiangsi and in the early fall started organizing agrarian revolution and armed uprisings. He was aided by two veteran leaders of the Chinese Communist movement in the region: Shao Shih-p'ing and Huang Tao.[29] When he returned to his native village, Fang tried to reorganize the peasant associations of northeast Kiangsi with an eye to separating the Communist-affiliated associations from those controlled by the KMT. He also reorganized all the CCP committees and created a peasant militia so that the CCP organizations might maintain independence from the KMT. Fang Chih-min initiated antilandlord struggles by recruiting poor peasants and demanding distribution of land, reduction of rent, and abolition of all debts. By September 1927, Fang's "armed struggle unit" had drawn about 200 active cadres from the poor-peasant corps of the region.[30]

In November 1927, Fang called a conference attended by the leaders of the local party organization.[31] There the representatives of the local CCP organizations of northeast Kiangsi learned for the first time of the breakdown of CCP-KMT collaboration and the new policy line of the CCP; therefore, they had not heard the outcome of the August 7 (1927) Emergency Conference, which had already established the Party's new direction and policy line. The task of the CCP, as Fang explained to the representatives of the local party, was first to carry out the agrarian revolution in the rural areas and then to attempt to seize political power through armed insurrection. At the conclusion of this conference, an "Operational Committee" (*Kung-tso wei-yüan-hui"*) was established, consisting of seven key leaders of the local CCP organizations.[32] Fang Chih-min became executive secretary of the committee

ling-tao ko-ming tou-cheng ti li-shih tse-liao" ("Historical Material on the CCP Leadership of the Revolutionary Struggle in South-Central China"), edited by Wuhan City's Evening School of Marxism-Leninism in 1951, pp. 203–204. See also Hatano, *Chūkyō-shi*, III, 145.

[28] Hujita Shōten, "Ho Chi Min tō Min-Setsu-Kan Sovetō Ku" ("Fang Chih-min and the Fukien-Chiekiang-Kiangsi Soviet District") *Ajia Kenkyū* (Asian Studies), 6, No. 4, 1–38.

[29] Kiangsi jen-min ch'u-pan she, ed. *Chung-kuo Kung-ch'an tang Kiangsi ti-ch'ü ling-tao ko-ming tou-cheng ti li-shih tsu-liao (Historical Documents on the CCP Leadership in the Revolutionary Struggle of the Kiangsi Area)* (Kiangsi, Jen-min Ch'u-pan-she, 1958). 3 vols., I, 253–254. Hereafter cited as *Documents on Kiangsi*.

[30] *Ibid.*, p. 247.

[31] The Party representatives came from five *hsien* in the region: I-yang, Heng-feng, Shang-jao, ch'ien-shan, Teh-hsing.

[32] The operation committee was organized with Fang Chih-min, Huang Tao, Shao Shih-p'ing, Fang Chih-shun, Wu Hsien-min, Shao Tang, and Fang Yün-hui.

which was to function as the "supreme leadership organ" of the region until communication with the Party's central organ was instituted. This was probably the first conference in northeast Kiangsi which drew CCP representatives from various localities. It laid the organizational foundation for the provincial Party committee of northeast Kiangsi.

Within a month Fang organized seventy or eighty peasant associations in northeast Kiangsi, on the basis of which he created a new political institution, namely, the government of the workers and peasants (soviet). These institutions were originally established in I-yang and Heng-feng *hsien* but were gradually introduced in other regions, with two important programs: distribution of all land (owned by the local gentry, who were frequently bullies) and the abolition of all debts. The newly recruited peasants were also trained to form guerrilla units, and these were amalgamated in December 1927 into two independent regiments of the Red Army, later called the First Red Army Corps of northeast Kiangsi. Fang also served as chairman of the military-affairs committee of the region and by May 1928 was able to create a new government institution by linking the CCP and the soviet organizations that had been in existence in I-yang and Heng-feng *hsien*.

The turning point in the growth and development of the soviet institutions in the base area of northeast Kiangsi, however, was the Fang-sheng Hill Conference in June 1928. More than twenty leaders of the CCP organizations in I-yang and Heng-feng met at the border of the two *hsien* to formulate future revolutionary policy. Fang obtained a resolution to establish a revolutionary base area similar to the one Mao and Chu were creating in the Chingkang mountains. After this conference the Party and soviet organizations of northeast Kiangsi began to emerge, and Fang later represented the Party committee of northeast Kiangsi at the Party conference of the entire province in Hu-kuo in October 1928. The rapid growth of the base area was in fact promoted by the defeat suffered by the KMT Army during its campaign against the soviet base.

The official Communist source claimed that the Red Army in northeast Kiangsi had increased its manpower by 50 percent and that the soviet government had also spread to include eight other *hsien* of the region, increasing the population of the base area to 40,000.[33] Pulling these base areas together and establishing them as a foundation for the creation of the provincial soviet government, Fang organized the Hsin

[33] Huang T'ao, *Chung-kuo jen-min chieh-fang chün ti san-shih nien (Thirty Years of the Chinese People's Liberation Army)* (Peking, Jen-min ch'u-pan she, 1958), II, 589–590.

chiang (Hsin River) soviet government which maintained a 33-member executive committee. The Hsin *chiang* soviet government was so named simply because all the component *hsien*, except Te-hsing *hsien*, were located along the banks of the Hsin River. This government under the able leadership of Fang Chih-min actually laid the organizational base on which the northeast Kiangsi soviet government was created in August 1930. Until the First National Soviet Congress convened in November 1931, Fang Chih-min continued to serve concurrently as chairman of the northeast Kiangsi revolutionary committee and as chairman of the northeast Kiangsi soviet government, and Chou Chien-p'ing commanded the reorganized Tenth Red Army.[34]

The northeast Kiangsi soviet area became one of the most important base areas because it was located in the region through which communication flowed constantly between the CCP central organs in Shanghai and the CCP central bureau of the soviet area in Juichin. The significance of this region was also manifested in the election of Fang Chih-min to the Central Executive Council (CEC), a 62-member policy-making body, when the Chinese Soviet Republic was proclaimed in November 1931.

The organizational structure of the northeast Kiangsi soviet, like the southwest Kiangsi soviet apparatus at the provincial level, was consolidated on the basis of what had already emerged under the leadership of Fang Chih-min. However, the organizational pattern of the rural soviets that were formed prior to the formal adoption of the "Provisional Organic Law of Local Soviet Government" on November 27, 1931, varied from region to region, and there was no uniform pattern of soviet organization — except that all the soviet organizations followed the general principle of mass participation.

One of the most serious problems that the northeast Kiangsi soviet government encountered in conducting its work, according to Ma Lo's report, was the persistence of "bureaucratic formalism" just as in the case of the southwest Kiangsi soviet base. Because of official red tape, government organizations were unable to respond to the directives sent down from the central government. The Party's central bureau in Juichin had assigned new and important tasks to the northeast Kiangsi soviet; the consolidation and expansion of the base area after breaking through the encirclement of the KMT Army and the positive promotion of the Party's mass-line policy in order to link the northeast Kiangsi base with the scattered base areas of Hunan, Hupeh, and

---

[34] After the Second National Soviet Congress, however, Liu Ch'ou-hsi became the Commander of the Tenth Red Army.

Kiangsi. But the party organizations were slow in responding.[35] This lag was explained by Ma Lo in terms of the deficiency in the operational methods of the party and soviet organizations. The executive-committee members of the northeast Kiangsi soviet government simply issued their directive letters and executive orders to the lower-level governments and then stayed in their offices. They failed to go to the villages and *hsiang* to help conduct the work of political mobilization and mass uprisings for the support of the central directives. "The local people's attitude toward the *hsiang* and village soviet governments was passive and acquiescent at best; the rich peasants had even sneaked into the *ch'ü-* and *hsien*-level governments," Ma Lo asserted. "Therefore, the basic-level government under the influence of the upper-level governments like the *ch'ü* and *hsien* continued to follow the rich-peasant policy line."[36]

Another administrative problem was the wide gap between written reports and actual performance. All reports filed by the lower-level government described a high quality of work, but this was true only on paper, and the actual performance had not been checked by the inspection cadres. In solving the problems of land distribution, for example, the soviet government paid no attention to the resolution concerning equal distribution, which was to be implemented throughout the base area. They simply confiscated all the land of the peasants regardless of their class status and distributed it without following the guidelines established in the resolution. These errors, it was admitted, were caused by the ambiguity of the resolution, for it did not stipulate the amount of land that was to be confiscated from designated peasants, nor the division of the confiscated land among specific recipients. No specific stipulation having been made as to whether the rich peasant would receive good or inferior land, the rich peasants, because of their economic status and political influence, usually acquired almost all the good land, the report charged. Although the resolution stipulated that land distribution to the poor and middle peasants should be based on the number of individuals in the family and on the number of its members who had been able to cultivate the land for the rich peasants, these principles were not followed by the local organizations. In certain areas the local government had even failed, Ma Lo charged, to redistribute confiscated farm implements quickly when they were needed for cultivation.[37]

The most pressing administrative problem at the *hsien* level of gov-

[35] Ma Lo, "Recent Situation in the Northeast Kiangsi Soviet," p. 57.
[36] *Ibid.*, p. 59.
[37] *Ibid.*, p. 60.

ernment, Ma Lo claimed, had to do with coordination between the Party, the soviet government, and the military-affairs committee. In some areas the Party's *hsien* committee and the *hsien* soviet government had frequent disagreements over policy issues of a local nature. The three elements of power in the *hsien* failed "to cooperate with each other because the party, the soviet government, and the military-affairs committee knew only their own work and were concerned only with their own affairs in carrying out their organizational activities." [38] As in the case of the southwest Kiangsi base, these problems were caused primarily by the shortage of trained cadres at the *hsien* level. There-fore, Ma Lo specifically recommended that the party organizations in the northeast Kiangsi soviet base should recruit more cadres and train them in a new program so that they might coordinate the three organizations.

In order to overcome such administrative problems, the northeast Kiangsi soviet government launched a new political movement based on Mao's concept of "mass line" and carried out a series of mass strug-gles in late 1932 and early 1933, after which the young and en-thusiastic activists were quickly identified and recruited into the train-ing program of new cadres. Thus the organizational structure of the northeast Kiangsi soviet area, like the soviet apparatus in the southwest Kiangsi soviet base, was consolidated and strengthened only after the new offensive line was implemented by mass political movement and mass struggle in every aspect of administrative work.

The Kiangsi Provincial Soviet Government

The provincial soviet government of Kiangsi (commonly known as the central soviet area), unlike the southwest or northeast Kiangsi soviet areas, was the political and administrative nerve center of the Chinese Soviet Government that was established in the town of Juichin in November 1931. Its territorial jurisdiction was said to have extended to more than twenty-two *hsien* in the southern part of Kiangsi as well as in the border areas of western Fukien. In this base area were in-cluded such *hsien* as Hsing-kuo, Kung-lüeh, Yung-feng, Ning-tu, Kan, Hsin-wu, Wan-t'ai, An-yuan, and Sheng-li in Kiangsi province, and Chien-ning, T'ing-chou, and Wu-p'ing in Fukien province.[39]

[38] *Ibid.*, p. 63.
[39] *Kiangsi Sheng-Su Pao-kao (Report of the Kiangsi Soviet)*, part 1, in *Hung-se Chung-hua (HSCH*, November 21, 1932), p. 5. Part 2 may be found in *HSCH*, November 28, 1932, p. 7. This two-part report is one of the most comprehensive on such activities of the provincial government as (1) General Survey of Land Dis-tribution; (2) Overall Picture of Internal Affairs, which includes everything from

This soviet area, created in April 1928, was guarded by the Fourth Army under the command of Chu Te, and Mao Tse-tung served as political commissar. Within two years, the Red Army's strength increased to more than fourteen armies, with 75,000 men.[40] By the spring of 1932, while Mao Tse-tung continued to serve as political commissar, the First Front Army under the command of Chu Te was formed to safeguard the central soviet area. Lin Piao's First Army Corps consisted of the Fourth Army (under Lin's command), Tso Ch'üan's Fifteenth Army, and Lo Ping-hui's Twelfth Army, as well as P'eng Te-huai's Third Army Corps and Tung Chen-t'ang's Fifth Army Corps; these were under the direct command of Chu Te's First Front Army to safeguard the central soviet areas.[41]

The patterns of organizational development in south Kiangsi varied from region to region, especially during the 1927–1931 period. A certain organizational pattern began to emerge however, after the First National Soviet Congress of November 1931. One of the most striking aspects of this pattern was the uniformity of governmental structures established throughout the base areas on the basis of the "Provisional Law Governing the Administrative Districts of the Chinese Soviet Republic."[42] Whereas the soviet governments of the period between 1927 and 1931 had no clear-cut functional divisions, and there was no structural differentiation between the CCP, the Red Army, and other mass organizations because the leadership responsibilities overlapped, the organizations that emerged in the 1931–1934 period established definite divisions between the component institutions, although they had numerous problems of coordination. The soviet government was thus set up at each level parallel to the structure of the Party organization, and even the leadership positions were held by different people.

Following the general election in preparation for the First National Soviet Congress in November 1931, a council of workers, peasants, and soldiers (soviet) was established at each level, and it elected in turn the executive committee that functioned as the soviet government. The delegate councils of soviet government at each level dealt with the

road construction to the breakdown of population by *hsien*; (3) The Rules of How to Treat the Red Army; (4) The Sale of Public Bonds; (5) The Laborers' General Condition; (6) Statistics on Culture and Education. The report, however, included only nine *hsien* (Hsing-Kuo, Kung-lüeh, Yung-feng, Ning-tu, Kan, Hsin-wu, Wan-t'ai, An-yuan, Sheng-li) in Kiangsi province.

[40] For a brief history of each army from the First to the Fourteenth, see Hatano, *Chūkyō-shi*, I, 284–287.

[41] For a detailed order of battle in southern Kiangsi, see Hatano, *Chūkyō-shi*, I, 622–623, and II, 7–9.

[42] See *Chung-hua su-wei-ai kung-huo-kuo hua-fen hsing-cheng ch'ü-yü tsan-hsing t'iao-li* (*Provisional Law Governing the Administrative District of the Chinese Soviet Republic*), collected in Wang Chien-min, *Chung-kung shih-kao*, II, 328–330.

problems of their own regions and elected executive committees to which they delegated power when the councils were not in session. Those committees usually carried out the major administrative and governmental functions, and the councils at each level served simply as legislative bodies. A *hsien* delegate council, for example, was composed of the delegates elected by each council of the *ch'ü* and the *hsiang* of the *hsien*, as well as a certain number of delegates elected by the labor unions or the Red Guard units.

The organizational principle and its operation can also be illustrated by the practices in the central soviet areas of Kiangsi. The Kiangsi council was composed of delegates who were elected by the councils of each *hsien*, *ch'ü*, and *hsiang* of the province, and anyone who had reached the age of sixteen had the right to be elected to office and participate in the general election. The councils at all levels of Kiangsi province were composed of workers, peasants, soldiers, and revolutionary students of the region. If a member of the council failed to represent the majority will, the electors had the right, in theory at least, to recall him and choose a new delegate. This procedure was usually followed at mass rallies held in the region to create a sense of mass struggle and participation as well as to awaken political consciousness on the part of the local population. In the event that a member of the executive committee (government bureaucrat) showed negligence, he could be replaced by another member at the general meeting of the delegate council. This provision was necessary, it was said, to avoid the bureaucratic formalism that had existed in China for centuries. This was the reason for the worker-peasant inspection department, which investigated abuses of bureaucratic power, misuse of public funds, and corruption of government officials.

There exist a number of documents that shed an interesting light on political and administrative processes in the provincial-level government of Kiangsi.[43] These materials show that the Kiangsi provincial government was simply a subsidiary agency of the central soviet government and that it merely executed centrally directed programs and policies and did not play an independent role in local government.

The Kiangsi provincial government, like the southwest and northeast

---

[43] "The Directive Letter of the CCP Central Bureau for the Soviet Area to the CCP Provincial Committee" (January 19, 1932) and "The Kiangsi Provincial Committee's Resolution on the Acceptance of the CGSA's Directive Letter" (February 11, 1932) in *SSCM* Reel 14. "Resolution of the First Provincial Soviet Congress Concerning the Work Report" (May 6, 1932) in *SSCM* Reel 10. "Summary of the Six-Month (May–October 1932) Work Plan of the Kiangsi Provincial Soviet Government" (October 28, 1932) in *SSCM* Reel 10. "The Summary of Daily Proceedings of the Second Soviet Congress of the Kiangsi Province" (December 21–29, 1933) may be found in *Ta-hui jih-kan* (incomplete), collected in *SSCM* Reel 9.

Kiangsi governments, maintained such administrative departments as finance, economy, labor, culture, social insurance, health, military, and worker-peasant inspection, and the heads of these departments constituted the provincial executive committee. The standing committee or the presidium of the executive committee was headed by Tseng Shan as chairman, and Ch'en Cheng-jen and Hu Hai were vice-chairmen. Although Tseng Shan was criticized at the Second Provincial Soviet Government in December 1933 for his lack of self-criticism, he was reelected to head the provincial government of Kiangsi.

This governmental organization had been in operation for two or three years before the convocation of the First Provincial Soviet Congress of May 1932 — in other words, even before the First National Soviet Congress convened in November 1931. One of its shortcomings, mentioned in the criticism made by the First Provincial Congress, was that it had been very slow to carry out internal structural reforms and reorganization programs. At the level of *hsiang* and city soviet government, no changes had been made even though the central soviet government had called for structural reform immediately after the First National Soviet Congress. Even at the provincial level, the government leadership was alleged to have failed to carry out the reorganization program simultaneously with the mass struggle. The provincial government was unable to implement the structural changes, it was claimed, simply because it did not know how to mobilize the masses and generate their enthusiasm in support of government work. The government officials were so afraid of criticism at mass meetings that they dared not call any mass rallies or organize mass struggle.

The government officials were also charged with being too arbitrary — ordering the people rather than having them voluntarily carry out the work — and with being too punitive. Moreover, the provincial government was responsible for fostering the idea that the Red Army was more powerful than the soviet government, because the government permitted the Red Army to launch the reorganization of the government system, thus failing to take the initiative in its own reform work. The tendency to rely solely on the Red Army extended to every sphere, even to such simple work as the relief of the poor. In almost all aspects of its work it had lost touch with the masses of people. It tended to look to the leadership of the central government rather than go to the people and win their support.

To rectify this deficiency the First Provincial Congress called on each department of the executive committee, from the province to the *hsiang* soviet, to institute a conference system. By means of holding committee meetings as often as possible, the soviet system of government could be solidly established. The congress also suggested that the committee-work system should be implemented in every department of the executive committee. The committee-work system was thus designed to draw as many people as possible into administrative activities that would eventually help to counteract the alienation of the people from administrative work. This committee system would operate to mobilize as many people as possible to participate in the government's work and would also enable the government and the mass organizations to establish close relations.

"The Summary of the Report of the Six Month (May–October 1932) Work Plan," written by the leadership of the Kiangsi provincial government, indicates that it had already established a system of planning and inspecting work in the various departments of the provincial government as well as in all the executive committees. The departments of finance, labor, internal affairs (police), land, culture, and education all formulated their own planning systems and mapped out the work six months in advance. In pursuance of this plan, daily meetings of the department were held to discuss methods of implementation. The executive committee of the provincial soviet government met more than twenty times each month, and such functional departments as finance held fifteen meetings each month. When these meetings were called, the chairmen of the functional departments of the *hsien, ch'ü,* and *hsiang* governments were invited to participate and then return to their localities to carry out decisions reached at the meetings. The department head of the provincial government went to the lower-level departments *(hsien, ch'ü, hsiang)* to inspect their work at least once a month. This system of having upper-level administrators go to the lower level to inspect the work as well as to provide leadership was actually initiated by the central government. The regular meetings of the People's Commissariat (cabinet), for example, usually started with a cabinet member's report on his inspection tour of a certain locality. At the eighth session of the People's Commissariat meeting on March 1, 1932, Mao Tse-tung himself made a report on his inspection tour of the entire province of Kiangsi and surveyed the work of each finance department from the *hsien* to the *hsiang.* Mao's report was followed by discussion of the problems of finance management at each level of government. The People's Commissariat, on the basis of Mao's report, recommended that the finance commissar should (1) start to train more cadres for better finance management; (2) eliminate corrupt government officials; (3) issue a proclamation to call the masses of Kiangsi province to participate in checking the work of the finance departments and helping the inspection department eliminate corrupt bureaucrats;

and (4) urge the working masses to participate actively in the manage-ment of cooperatives owned and operated by the provincial soviet gov-ernment.[44] The resolution adopted by the People's Commissariat was immediately sent on to the provincial governments of Kiangsi in the form of an executive order.

In direct response to the executive order of the central government concerning possible steps by the provincial government to improve the management of the finance department, a series of conferences took place in each department to discuss ways in which they could imple-ment it. The finance administration was apparently one of the two most important organs (the other being the military-affairs committee) in the soviet system of government, because it was primarily concerned with the collection of revenues for government operation, the admin-istration of economic policies (until the creation of the People's Com-mission for National Economy in January 1933), and the management of banks and cooperatives in the soviet bases.[45]

The importance of the finance department in Kiangsi was indicated both by Mao's direct involvement in it and by a joint conference of the finance-department chairmen at the *hsien* and *ch'ü* levels of govern-ment, convened by the Kiangsi provincial government in October 1933.[46] The work of the finance department became far more crucial after the central soviet government declared war on Japan in February 1932 and intensified its military operations and total mobilization of economic resources to cope with the KMT's economic blockade. As the volume of work increased, so did the problems of administration. The joint conference of the finance-department chairmen asserted that their central task was to adopt a new method by replacing the old practices at each level in order to make a significant contribution to the work of economic construction and to recruit more cadres and train them to work in the finance administration. The shortage of trained cadres was greater at the *hsien* level, especially those recruited recently, who had no experience. The establishment of a close working relationship between the upper and lower departments of finance, the routinization of work reports, and the improvement of the cadres' training program

[44] See *HSCH*, No. 12, March 2, 1932, p. 5, for the announcement of the Eighth Session of the People's Commissariat's regular meeting.

[45] See "Tsai-cheng jen-min wei-yüan pu i-nien lai kung-tso pao-kao" ("The Re-port of the Finance Commissariat's One Year Work") in *HSCH*, No. 39, Novem-ber 7, 1932. This report was to summarize the work of the finance department in the central government since its establishment on November 7, 1931.

[46] "Kiangsi sheng ko-hsien chih chung-hsin ch'ü ts'ai-chang lien-hsi hui-i" ("The Joint Conference of the Finance Department Chairmen of Each *hsien* and Central District of the Kiangsi Province") in *SSCM*, Reel 10.

were three fundamental tasks that should be executed immediately after the joint conference.

To implement these programs, the finance departments agreed to recruit more cadres to staff the finance administration, to establish the division of labor, and to call regular departmental meetings. Each department was also asked to initiate a system of regular reports on their work to be sent to the upper-level finance department. The finance department of the *ch'ü* government was to submit at least one report every two weeks to the *hsien*, and the *hsien* finance department was to send a monthly report to the provincial finance department, which in turn would report each month to the finance department of the central soviet government.

In recruiting the cadres of the finance administration, the joint conference stressed, the aim was to find individuals who had at least one skill, such as mathematics, accounting, or bookkeeping, to help in the land distribution. When the older cadres were assigned to work in the finance management, they should be given definite and appropriate instructions as well as ideological retraining in advance of their assignment. In the work of finance management the upper-level cadres were told to take the full responsibility of teaching the lower-echelon cadres and to try to establish a model *hsiang* in the management of finance.

The regular meetings, the routine system of work reports, and the advance planning were part of the restructuring and reorganizing program launched by the central soviet government at the level of provincial government in early 1932 to coincide with the new offensive policy line. In this way a thorough structural reorganization of the Kiangsi provincial government was carried out before October 1932, and the reform of the district-level government followed it in December 1932, thus establishing a precedent for other provincial governments.

It is difficult to generalize about the structure and function of the Kiangsi soviet governments. The three soviet areas of southwest, northeast, and southern Kiangsi maintained their own unique patterns of institution-building — which depended on the needs and requirements of revolutionary war and the style and method of mobilizing and arming the masses of the population — while administering and managing the newly acquired territorial base. However, these three soviet areas shared the problems of mass mobilization for the support of revolutionary war and economic construction in a rural population.

A uniform pattern of governmental structure began to emerge after the establishment of the Chinese Soviet Republic in November 1931, but the task of institutionalizing administrative procedures was by no means easy. The central soviet government, under the leadership of Mao Tse-tung, attempted to persuade as many people as possible to participate in the administrative processes at the local political level. Therefore, the reapportionment programs of the administrative district throughout the base area were designed chiefly to broaden the participation of the rural population.

Although the provincial governments of the southwest, northeast, and central soviet areas were formed parallel to the CCP's provincial committees immediately after the First National Soviet Congress, the leadership personnel of the Party and the government overlapped a great deal because of the shortage of trained cadres. The party committees of the *hsien* and *ch'ü* were the most active and powerful organizations at the local level, overshadowing the soviet governments in the region. The party fraction (*tang-tuan*), organized in every government unit where there were two or three CCP members, controlled the administrative procedures of the soviet-government personnel.

The process of building a new soviet government in the province of Kiangsi may be characterized as highly centralized, because local institutions were either initiated by the party committees or built from the top to the bottom. The provincial soviet congresses, like those held in the province of Kiangsi, were not preceded by the First National Soviet Congress but followed by it, contrary to the principle of "democratic centralism." This practice was intended to implement the centrally adopted resolutions and policies through the mechanism of congresses and conferences rather than by generating policy ideas from the masses. The convocation of the provincial soviet congress was simply an occasion when the local delegates representing every village assembled in the provincial capital to listen to political reports and patriotic speeches and reaffirm their enthusiasm for revolutionary change. The *hsien*-level congress of the soviet government, usually followed by the provincial congress, became a process of ratifying the policies already formulated by the provincial congress, but it also served as an occasion for creating grass-roots organizations by identifying and recruiting activists to lead the mass struggle and revolution in the villages. At the same time, the rural delegates were tested on their ability to conduct administrative work in executing the centrally formulated policies after the *hsien* congress.

The structure of the soviet government in Kiangsi was therefore highly centralized in the sense that all institutions were centrally created and all policies centrally controlled and supervised through the mechanisms of the party fraction, through the conferences at each level of government, and by the reporting and inspection systems. At the same time, the masses of people were mobilized and organized to take part in the implementation of policies which met, to a certain degree, the aspirations of the local masses. This represented the main thrust of mass-line politics. The persistent conflict between, on the one hand, the centrally created institutions such as the party fraction and the soviet government, and on the other, the needs and aspirations of the local population for revolutionary change was the key to the solution of organizational problems in the Kiangsi soviet base. There was also conflict between the Party leadership, which emphasized the centralization of control over the government and mass organization, and the government bureaucracy, which pressed for a certain degree of decentralization of policy implementation. This conflict was settled when they agreed to adopt a compromise solution of the mass-line approach to policy implementation.

III

LEADERSHIP STRUCTURE AND
ADMINISTRATIVE CONTROL

One of the most crucial problems that the Chinese Communist leadership had to solve was how to overcome intraparty factionalism and establish institutional stability under a strong leadership within the Party organization. Factional alignments and intergroup conflicts weakened the effectiveness of the Party leadership and also had a tremendous impact on the CCP's control over the government and mass organizations. The conflicts between the contending power groups usually arose because of differing opinions with regard to the contemporary revolutionary situation and also the strategy by which to attain revolutionary goals.

Following the Fourth Plenum of the CCP Central Committee in Shanghai (January 1931), at which the returned-student group took over the leadership, a balance was carefully maintained between the three major elements of power: the returned-student group, the leaders and organizers of the soviets and the Red Army units who staffed the complex organization of the government bureaucracy, and the veteran leaders of the CCP. The tensions among these three groups contending for power seem to have persisted throughout the Kiangsi soviet period and to have reached a peak during the power struggle in early 1933 when Mao Tse-tung was relieved of his leadership of the Red Army. However, the power struggle and the conflict of policy issues did not reach the point of complete political breakdown in Kiangsi.

This chapter will analyze the structural characteristics of the leadership and organization of the Kiangsi political system in terms of the Party's control over the government and its administrative system for restraining bureaucratic behavior. Because the returned students played a significant role in the policy-making processes, though not a dominant one, this chapter will first take up their emergence as a political group and then analyze the techniques by which they seized power and the procedures by which they attempted to exert control over the government in the Kiangsi soviet base. It is the thesis of this chapter that neither an individual leader nor a single group wielded absolute power or dictated the political processes during the Kiangsi period (1931–1934), so that a situation existed in which the concept of collective leadership was fully worked out and the balance of power between the contending groups was carefully maintained.

The Structure of the Leadership Group

In order to describe and analyze the emergence of the returned-student group (the so-called 28 Bolsheviks) [1] which took over the Party's leadership positions at the Fourth Plenum in January 1931, one must go back to the conflict and factional struggles of the Chinese students at Sun Yat-sen University in Moscow. According to various sources, including Chang Kuo-t'ao's personal memoir, the Stalin-Trotsky controversy over the strategy of the Chinese revolution, coupled with the breakdown of KMT-CCP cooperation in the spring of 1927, inevitably split the Chinese students in Moscow into a number of factions.[2] There emerged, however, a dominant power group led by Ch'en Shao-yü (alias Wang Ming), Ch'in Pang-hsien (alias Po Ku), and Chang Wen-t'ien (alias Lo Fu), which triumphed over the other groups. They gained the upper hand partly because they were supported by Pavel Mif, who succeeded Karl Radek as president of Sun Yat-sen University in the spring of 1927, and partly because they were dedicated Stalinists during the power struggle between Stalin and Trotsky.

The Chinese delegation accredited to the Communist International (Comintern) included Ch'ü Ch'iu-pai, Teng Chung-hsia, and Chang Kuo-t'ao, men who disagreed over who should control the Chinese students in Moscow and who took an active part in the rectification campaigns of Sun Yat-sen University. Ch'ü and Teng put their support behind the anti-Wang Ming group because they objected to Pavel Mif's involvement, but Chang Kuo-t'ao seemed to favor the Mif–Wang alliance, though he insists in his recent memoir that he maintained a

[1] Wang Chien-min lists the so-called 28 Bolsheviks as follows: Chang Ch'in-ch'iu, Chang Wen-t'ien, Ch'en Ch'ang-hao, Ch'en Shao-yü, Ch'en Yüan-tao, Ch'in Pang-hsien, Chu A-ken, Chu Tzu-hsün, Ho Tzu-shu, Hsia Hsi, Kuo Miao-ken, Li Chu-sheng, Meng Ch'ing-shu, Shen Tse-min, Sheng Ch'ung-liang, Sun Chi-min, Tu Tso-hsiang, Tu Yen, Wang Chia-hsiang, Wang Hsiu, Wang Pao-li, Wang Sheng-jung, Wang Sheng-ti, Wang Yün-ch'eng, Yang Shang-k'un, Yin Chien, Yüan Chia-yung, and Yün Yü-jung. See Wang Chien-min, *Chung-kuo Kung-ch'an tang shih-kao* (*A Draft History of the Chinese Communist Party*), (Taipei 1965), II, 100. Hereafter cited as Wang, *Chung-kung shih-kao*.

[2] *Ibid.*, 81–94.

neutral position in the disputes.[3] Japanese sources reporting from China in the 1930s, on the basis of information provided by ex-Communists who had either defected to or been captured by the KMT police in Shanghai, asserted that Chang Kuo-t'ao was in the Mif-Wang Ming group from the beginning.[4] Because of their hostility to the Mif–Wang Ming group in Moscow, veteran leaders such as Ch'ü and Teng as well as many of the Chinese students in Moscow were discredited by both the Mif–Wang Ming group and the Comintern officials. Many of the anti-Wang Ming leaders were either expelled from the CCP branch at Sun Yat-sen University or voluntarily quit the Chinese Communist movement.

It is difficult to apply rational criteria in evaluating the leadership style and techniques of the returned-student group, for the only description of the so-called 28 Bolsheviks was written by the anti-Wang Ming group which later defected to the KMT side. So far the information available on the student leadership comes either from hostile sources or from those with axes to grind, hence the statements about the leadership that took over the policy-making machinery of the CCP at the Fourth Plenum are unreliable. Even later accounts, such as Mao's, of the role of the returned students in the Chinese Communist movement have not yet clarified many issues or answered the fundamental question as to what was really taking place in the leadership structure and the policy-making circles of the Kiangsi soviet base.[5]

The returned-student group, like the younger-generation leaders in many parts of the world today, had ideals that they hoped to put into practice when and if they seized control of the policy-making machin-

[3] See Chang Kuo-t'ao, "Wo-ti Hui-i" ("My Reminiscence"), *Ming Pao Monthly*, No. 30 (June 1968), 91–94, for his discussion of Sun Yat-sen University and Pavel Mif's role. In an interview with me in Hong Kong in December 1964 Mr. Chang also characterized the Wang Ming-Po Ku group as "small men."

[4] For example, see *Tzu 1931 nien chih 1933 nien liang-nien-lai chih Chung-kuo Kung-ch'an-tang* (*Two Years of the Chinese Communist Party from 1931 to 1933*). This booklet was made available to the top-ranking cadres of the KMT by its central organ in 1933 as a reference guide for the conduct of the anti-Communist campaign in China, and was classified as "top secret." The information contained in it had been gathered by the KMT intelligence people after the interrogation of several Communist leaders who were arrested in Shanghai and other areas during the early 1930s. The booklet is available at the Bureau of Investigation Archives of the Ministry of Justice, Ch'ing-tan, Taiwan. Hereafter cited as KMT, *The CCP from 1931 to 1933*. See also *Chung-kuo Kung-ch'an tang chih T'ou-shih* (*Perspectives on the Chinese Communist Party*), edited by the Kuomintang's Investigation Section of the Organization Department and published by Wen-hsing shu-t'ien in 1962. Hereafter cited as *Chung-kung T'ou-shih*. Hatano Ken'ichi collected considerable information on the so-called 28 Bolsheviks in his *Gendai Shina no seiji to jinbutsu* (*Politics and Personalities of Modern China*), Tokyo, Kaizo Sha, 1937.

[5] For Mao's own account of the Russian-returned students, see "Resolution on Some Historical Problems," Mao, *SW*, vol. IV.

ery. Power was, in their view, the key to their goals. However, when they took over the top positions of the CCP, they had to cope with numerous problems, such as leadership change (the replacement of veteran leaders with the younger generation), structural reform (the establishment of the routinized procedure of collective leadership at all levels of the Party), and institutionalization of the policy-making processes (the creation of a procedure by which all interested or contending groups could participate in the decision-making processes).

The organizational techniques employed by the returned-student group in its seizure of power were in many respects similar to those used by Stalin in the late 1920s to win control of the CPSU and the soviet government. By first seizing control of the CCP central apparatus, the returned-student group was able to gain control of the key positions in the machinery of government and finally replace the Party's veteran leaders with the younger leaders who supported them. By January 1931, the returned-student leadership had defeated the so-called leftist opposition of Ch'ü Ch'iu-pai, and Li Li-san, after which it then adopted major portions of the program of the leftist opposition and turned on the so-called rightist opposition of Ho Meng-hsiung, Lo Chang-lung, and Wang K'o-ch'üan. One is struck by the similarities between these techniques and those that Stalin used during the late 1920s in his rise to power. By 1927 Stalin had defeated the "leftist opposition" of Trotsky, Zinoviev, and Kamenev. Then, adopting significant portions of the programs of the "leftist opposition," he attacked the "rightist opposition" of Bukharin, Tomsky, and Rykov.

Faced with constant attack by the "right opposition" group led by Ho Meng-hsiung and Lo Chang-lung after the Fourth Plenum, the new leadership of the returned-student group could not possibly afford to alienate completely the support of such veteran leaders as Hsiang Chung-fa, Chou En-lai, Hsiang Ying, and Jen Pi-shih. Therefore, Hsiang Chung-fa persuaded the new leadership of the CCP to retain certain members of the Politburo who were not totally supported by or sympathetic to the Li Li-san leadership and its policy line. Of the 16-member Politburo elected by the Fourth Plenum, a majority of ten could be easily identified as the Party's veteran leaders, and the rest, including Wang Ming (Ch'en Shao-yü), Po Ku (Ch'in Pang-hsien), Shen Tse-min, and K'ang Sheng could be identified as either members of the returned-student group or men sympathetic to their policy positions.[6]

[6] There has been no official list of the members of the Politburo elected by the Fourth Plenum in January 1931, but various sources have identified those who may have been elected at that time. For various listings of such members, see Warren

In discussing the power relations between the returned-student leadership and the leadership of the soviet base in the Kiangsi period, Hsiao Tso-liang argued that the returned students had begun to extend power and authority to the soviet base through the central bureau of the soviet area (CBSA), and he interpreted the sending of *A Directive Letter of the Central Politburo to the Soviet Area* in September 1931 as "the beginning of the power struggle between Ch'in and Mao during this period."[7] To support his contention, Hsiao selected a number of pertinent documents published by the returned students and summarized them in his study.[8]

Nevertheless, the initial techniques of the returned-student leadership, immediately after the Fourth Plenum, in the process of establishing and extending its influence to the soviet area did not involve a direct confrontation with the leaders of the soviet government and the Red Army in the rural hinterland. The organizational techniques employed by the returned students were calculated to establish, at least in the initial period, a cordial relationship between the central leadership and the leaders of the soviet areas through such third parties as Hsiang Chung-fa, Hsiang Ying, or Chou En-lai, all of whom already had good relationships with some leaders of the soviet areas.

When the new leaders took over the CCP Politburo and established control of the Party's leadership positions, they did not immediately attempt to take over the post of general secretary of the Party. The leadership structure of the CCP after the Fourth Plenum, unlike its predecessor was highly diffused and greatly differentiated among the contending power groups in the sense that veteran leaders constituted the majority of the Politburo members and that the returned students,

Kuo, *Analytical History of the Chinese Communist Party* (Taipei: The Institute of International Relations, Republic of China, 1968), II, 233–236; Hatano, *Chū-kyō-shi*, I, 560–561; Wang, *Chung-kung shih-kao*, II, 99–102. The Politburo of the CCP after the Fourth Plenum consisted of sixteen members (both the full members and candidate members). They were Hsiang Chung-fa, Hsiang Ying, Ch'en Yün, Lo Fu-t'an, Ch'en Yü, Hsü Hsi-ken, Ho K'o-ch'üan, Lo Teng-hsien, Kuan Hsiang-ying, K'ang Sheng (alias Chao Yün), Ku Shun-chang, Chou En-lai, Chang Kuo-t'ao, Ch'en Shao-yü (alias Wang Ming), Jen Pi-shih, Ch'in Pang-hsien (alias Po Ku). The Standing Committee of the Politburo consisted of Hsiang Chung-fa (General Secretary); Ch'en Shao-yü (Secretary of the Provincial Party Committee of Kiangsu); Chou En-lai (Chairman of the Party's military affairs committee); K'ang Sheng (alias Chao Yün) (Head of the Organization Department); and Ch'in Pang-hsien (Secretary of the Chinese Communist Youth League). Although Chang Wen-t'ien was not a member of the Politburo, he was in charge of the Party's publication committee and headed the peasant department. Later Chang Wen-t'ien took over the propaganda department when Shen Tse-min died.

[7] Tso-liang Hsiao, *Power Relations within the Chinese Communist Movement, 1931–1934*, p. 159.

[8] *Ibid.*, p. 169.

Ch'en and Ch'in, for example, could control the Standing Committee of the Politburo only with the support of the veteran leaders, notably Chou En-lai and Hsiang Chung-fa. Thus, the leadership structure was based on the concept of collective leadership in the strict sense of the term. "As a result of the election held by the Fourth Plenum," Hsiang Chung-fa confessed, "I remained general secretary of the Party, but a division of labor was already in effect; thus Shen Tse-min took the propaganda post, Chou En-lai the military affairs post, and K'ang Sheng the organization post. Each person took care of his own duty and I managed only a portion of the Party's affairs." [9] All except Hsiang Chung-fa, Chou En-lai, and Hsiang Ying were key members of the returned-student group who had been ardently opposed to Li Li-san and the veteran leaders, not because of differences in their policy views but because of their wish to bring about the transfer of leadership from the old to the new generation.

It is difficult to explain why Chou En-lai was reelected. Even though closely associated with the Li Li-san faction and its policy, he was not only elected again to the Party's Politburo but also reelected at the Fourth Plenum to the important post of chairman of the Party's military-affairs committee. Subsequent events lead one to speculate on two possible explanations. First, Chou may already have switched his support to the Mif-Wang leadership during his trip to Moscow in the spring of 1930. At that time he had been sent by Li Li-san to mediate in the power struggle between the Chinese delegation headed by Ch'ü Ch'iu-pai and Pavel Mif over control of the Chinese student leadership in the Soviet Union. The second possibility is that the returned-student leaders foresaw the difficulties they would encounter in establishing their authority and control over the Party organization and the leadership in the soviet areas, and may have decided to try to utilize Chou as their intermediary in dealing with the already strongly entrenched political and military leaders of the soviet region. In support of the latter assumption, it is worth noting that a majority of the Red Army commanders in the soviet areas — with the exception of Chu Te, P'eng Te-huai, and Huang Kung-lüeh — had been closely associated with Chou En-lai at the Whampoa Military Academy.[10] Perhaps Chou retained an important

[9] *Chung-kuo Kung-ch'an tang chih t'ou-shih*, p. 120. See also Wang, *Chung-kung shih-kao*, II, 159–164. The office of General Secretary of the Party was held by Hsiang Chung-fa after the Party Congress, but it never regained the prestige lost when Ch'en Tu-hsiu was deposed from that post. Therefore, the activities of the Party's central body were undertaken largely by Li Li-san himself.

[10] The Red Whampoa group included the commanding general (Hsu Chi-shen) and the chief of staff (Ch'en Yi) of the First Red Army; the commanding general of the Third Red Army (Wu Chung-hao); the commanding general of the Tenth Red Army Corps (Liu Ch'u-hsi); the commanding general of the Sixth Route Army (Chou

leadership position because of his association with this group; in any case he was able to retain his post as chairman of the military-affairs committee of the CCP, to which he had first been elected in 1928 at the Sixth Party Congress in Moscow.

The choice of Hsiang Ying to become secretary of the Party's central bureau for the soviet area when it was created in early 1931 may have been due at least in part to his earlier personal relationship with Hsiang Chung-fa, who continued to serve as general secretary of the Party after the Fourth Plenum. Hsiang Chung-fa was said to have recognized the organizational talents of Hsiang Ying as early as 1926. At that time, Hsiang Ying organized the labor movement and conducted a strike campaign in Hupeh, and he also served as secretary of the CCP committee in the Hupeh federation of labor unions when Hsiang Chung-fa was chairman of the Hupeh provincial party committee. Later, in 1927, Hsiang Ying was transferred to Shanghai and became the Party secretary of the Shanghai federation of labor unions, where he worked with Li Li-san's group.

At any rate, Hsiang Ying was assigned to the post of secretary of the central bureau for the soviet area (CBSA) after the Fourth Plenum. The problems of operating the CBSA were further complicated when the Party's leadership personnel in Shanghai, having escaped mass arrest during the raid of the KMT police in May–June of 1931, moved into the soviet area one by one. At this time the Party's general secretary, Hsiang Chung-fa, was arrested and executed by the KMT police. Although a clandestine office known as the Shanghai bureau of the party was established and continued to operate, the key leaders, including the majority of the newly elected Politburo, went to the Kiangsi soviet in order to avoid the KMT's police terror as well as to prepare for the First National Congress of the Soviets in Juichin on November 7, 1931. The leadership structure had consequently now become much more complex as the result of the migration of leadership personnel from Shanghai to the Kiangsi soviet area.

The members of the Central Committee left Shanghai in the course of the summer and fall of 1931 to avoid mass arrest by the KMT police and frequent raids on the headquarters of the Central Committee in

Yi-ch'ün); the commanding general of the Fourteenth Red Army (Chang Ho-k'un); the commanding general of the Thirteenth Red Army (Ho Kung-mien); the commanding general of the Southeast Route Army in Kiangsi (Chung Ch'ih-hsien); and the chief secretary of the Central Military Affairs Committee of the CCP (Nieh Jung-chen). For this information, see Ozaki Hotsumi, "Shu On-rai no chi-i" ("The Position of Chou En-lai"), *Chūō Kōron*, 52, No. 12 (November, 1937), 97–105; Hatano Ken'ichi, "Shu On-rai ten" ("Biography of Chou En-lai"). *Kaizō*, 19, No. 7 (July 1937), 86–91. This group was later known as the Red Whampoa group, and its members emerged as powerful military leaders in the soviet areas.

Shanghai. Some of these fugitives followed inland routes and others traveled by boat on the Yangtze River. Still others were hiding out in the suburbs of the city of Shanghai. The transit of the members of the Central Committee from Shanghai to Juichin may therefore have taken longer than they anticipated. When the move was completed in January 1933, the Central Bureau of the Soviet Area and the Central Committee were amalgamated into one Party committee, the top policy-making machinery in the Kiangsi soviet base. Shanghai retained a reorganized Party bureau, still called *Chung-yang-chü* (central bureau), under the direction and management of Wang Yün-ting, Lo Fu-t'an, and Li Chu-sheng, all of whom were arrested by the KMT police in 1932 or 1933.

The members of the Central Committee who arrived first in Juichin were returned students such as Yang Shan-k'un, Chang Wen-t'ien, and Ch'in Pang-hsien. At about this time, K'ang Sheng left for Moscow to join the Chinese representatives assigned to the Comintern. The CCP continued to use the title *Chung-yang-chü* (central bureau) even after the completion of their move and also continued to publish their directives and resolutions under the same title. The apparent changes in the Party structure were evidenced by the leadership personnel as well as the titles of the official journals published by the CBSA.

The power structure and policy-making processes were now concentrated in the hands of less than a dozen members of the Party's Politburo and Secretariat. The standing committee of the Politburo consisted of Ch'in Pang-hsien, Chang Wen-t'ien, Chou En-lai, Hsiang Ying, and Ch'en Yün. The nine-member Secretariat of the Central Committee included Ch'ing Pang-hsien, Chang Wen-t'ien, Chou En-lai, Hsiang Ying, Ch'en Yün, Mao Tse-tung, Chu Te, Wang Chia-hsiang, and Jen Pi-shih. In all probability these two important organizations of the CCP were the center of power and policy-making. If one takes these nine leaders into account in analyzing policy perspectives and policy positions, one can easily discern the careful balance between the returned-student group (Ch'in Pang-hsien, Chang Wen-t'ien, Wang Chia-hsiang), the leaders of the soviet base and the Red Army (Mao Tse-tung, Chu Te), and the veteran leaders of the CCP (Hsiang Ying, Ch'en Yün, Jen Pi-shih). Perhaps Chou En-lai played the pivotal role. In many respects the leadership structure established after the Fourth Plenum seemed to indicate that neither the returned-student group nor the veteran leaders of the CCP controlled the machinery of the Party and the government. That structure was characterized by a coalition of three important power elements.

After the move of the CCP Central Committee, the two official journals published by the CBSA, *Shih-hua* (*True Story*) and *Tang-ti chien-She* (*Party Reconstruction*), were merged, forming a new journal, *Tou-cheng* (*Struggle*), which began to appear on February 4, 1933. Even the official newspaper of the central soviet government, *Hung-se Chung-hua* (*Red China*), had now become an organ jointly sponsored by the party fraction in the government unit, the central soviet government, and the labor union, and beginning February 7, 1933, the paper, which had been a weekly, was published every three days.[11]

The Mechanisms for Administrative Control

To learn how the new leadership extended its control over the soviet base area and what kind of control mechanism was devised, it is necessary to analyze the organizational structure of the Central Bureau for the Soviet Areas (CBSA) and its relationship with the Central Soviet Government as well as with the organization of administrative control in the Kiangsi soviet base. The Party's Central Bureau for the Soviet Areas may be conveniently divided into three stages: (1) the pre-Fourth Plenum period, in which the General Front Committee (*Tsung-ch'ien-wei*) performed a function similar to that of the Party's CBSA; (2) the period from the establishment of the CBSA on January 15, 1931, to the completion of the move of the CCP Central Committee from Shanghai to Juichin in January 1933; and (3) the period from February 1933 to the beginning of the Long March in 1934. Between January 1931 and January 1933, the CBSA, in contrast to the five subbureaus of the CCP organization in China,[12] was the most active and important center of Party activities in the soviet base.

After its establishment, the CBSA sent out its first Circular Letter to announce that fact and to set forth the tasks of the Party organizations in the soviet area.[13] Its content clearly reflected the intentions and programs of the Party's central leadership as well as those of the CBSA. The basic task of the Central Bureau, the circular declared, was to establish correct strategy and tactics for the revolutionary effort and to

[11] The announcement in the first issue of *Tou-cheng* stressed that in the past the Party's CBSA had published two different journals — *Shih-hua* (*True Story*) and *Tang-ti chien-shih* (*Party's Construction*) — but that neither could function as the Party's official organ because of their irregularity and other defects. Therefore, the Party's Central Bureau decided to amalgamate these two periodicals into one, this being the new journal, *Tou-cheng* (*Struggle*). They also attempted to improve its contents. See the announcement in *Hung-se Chung-hua*, February 4, 1933.

[12] Five subbureaus were operating in the following regions: 1) Hupeh-Honan-Anhwei (O-Yu-Wan) Area; 2) West-Hupeh (Hsiang-O-Hsi) Area; 3) Fukien-Kwangtung (Min-Yüeh) Area; 4) Chihli-Hopei (Shunchih) Area; and 5) Manchuria. The CCP maintained a Special Party Committee in Harbin, Manchuria, and four provincial committees in Honan, Shensi, Kwangtung, and Anhwei provinces.

[13] "Chung-kung su-ch'ü chung-yang-chü t'ung-kao ti-i-hao, Su-wei-ai ch'ü Chung-yang-chü ti ch'eng-li chi ch'i jen-wu" ("Circular No. 1 of the CCP Central Bureau

lead the bourgeois-democratic revolution to an ultimate victory. Therefore, "all other activities of the Party — such as strengthening the Red
Army, expanding the soviet base areas, and establishing the soviet system of government — should be directed to that ultimate goal." [14] The
political goals of the CBSA, the circular asserted, were to carry out
resolutely the land-reform struggle by implementing the program of
"equal distribution of land," to broaden the base of mass support in
the soviet area, and to establish new soviet governments as well as to
reform the existing ones at each level.

Almost eight months after the establishment of the CBSA, the Party's
Central Committee in Shanghai sent its directive letter to the CBSA
and assigned new tasks to the Bureau. [15] Was there a change in the
policy of the central leadership during those eight months? Both Hsiao
Tso-liang and Tsao Po-i stressed that this directive letter constituted
a deliberate attempt on the part of the returned-student leaders to extend their authority and control over the Party organization of the
soviet base, which was alleged to have been under the control of Mao
Tse-tung and Chu Te. [16] Hsiao and Tsao therefore attempted to detect
certain differences in content and tone between the circular letter of
January 1931 and the directive letter of September 1931. Hsiao Tso-
liang argued that the idea of establishing the CBSA was originally conceived by the Third Plenum in the aftermath of the failure of the Li
Li-san line, therefore Hsiang Ying was considered to be unsympathetic
to the returned-student leadership.

One of the most significant factors that might have influenced the
policy-makers' analysis of the situation was the strength of a formidable
enemy force that was constantly raiding the CCP headquarters in
Shanghai and also organizing itself to direct its military attacks against
the soviet area. To win the support of the masses, the new leadership
needed to reorganize the existing government and Party structure;
therefore, the returned students used their attack on Li Li-san and his
policy line as a means to justify their execution of the reorganization
programs of the Party and government at all levels. It is evident that
the returned students did not really change the basic elements of Li's
program and revived once again Li Li-san's well-known policy, "The

of the Soviet Areas — Establishment of the Central Bureau of the Soviet Areas and
Its Tasks"), in SSCM, Reel No. 14. Hereafter cited as Circular Letter No. 1.
    [14] Ibid.
    [15] "Chung-yang tui su-ch'ü chih-shih-hsin" ("A Directive Letter of the Central to
Soviet Areas"), SSCM, Reel No. 14. Also in Wang, Chung-kung shih-kao, II, 507–515.
    [16] For Tso-liang Hsiao's argument, see his Power Relations, I, 159–162. For Tsao
Po-i's argument, see his Kiangsi su-wei-ai chih chien-li chi peng-k'uei (The Rise and
Fall of the Chinese Soviet in Kiangsi) (Taipei, Kuo-li cheng-chih ta-hsüeh tung-ya
yen-chiu-so, 1969), p. 453.

initial victory in a province or several provinces" in January 1932. Li's policy therefore was implemented when the slogan, "The Initial Victory in Kiangsi Province and Several Other Provinces," was adopted. The new leadership was careful to direct its attack and criticism against Li Li-san's method of operating the CCP and his way of conducting revolutionary tactics, and not against the strategic aspect of his policy, which could actually be traced back to the Comintern.

One of the most complex situations in this analysis of the structure of power and leadership organization has to do with the role of Hsiang Ying and Chou En-lai in the CBSA and their relationship with Mao Tse-tung and Chu Te. Although Hsiang Ying was appointed to the post of secretary of the CBSA, the real power was in the hands of Chou En-lai in the early months of 1931. The precise date when Chou En-lai reached the Kiangsi soviet cannot be established, largely because of conflicting information emanating from such former participants in the soviet movement as Kung Ch'u and Yang Yüeh-pin.[17] However, one should be able to reach certain conclusions on the basis of published reports that Chou probably left Shanghai in the spring of 1931 and went to the soviet base sometime in the summer of that year to participate in the Red Army campaign as director of the Party's military-affairs committee, during the KMT's second encirclement campaign launched in April 1931. He was also laying the groundwork for the convocation of the First National Congress of the Soviets in November of that year. In the spring of 1931 the KMT police carried out a mass arrest of Communists in Shanghai, on the basis of information supplied by a former member of the CCP Central Committee, Ku Shun-chang. Chou, who reportedly escaped arrest and slipped into the soviet area,[18] was possibly the only veteran leader who had been fully trusted by the Party's new leadership headed first by Wang Ming and then by Ch'in Pang-hsien. The latter had succeeded Wang Ming as the Party's

---

[17] Kung Ch'u was chief of staff of the First Front Red Army in the Central Soviet Area and wrote his memoir, *Wo yü hung-chün* (*I and the Red Army*). Yang Yüeh-ping was a Red Army general and director of army mobilization in the Central Soviet Area. Yang's memoir appeared in *Juichin shou-fu chi-shih* (*Report on the Recovery of Juichin*), a magazine published by the Special Department of the KMT in the Nationalist Fourth Division in January 1935, collected in Hatano, *Chūkyō-shi*, V, 537–586. Hereafter cited as Yang Yüeh-ping, *Juichin Shou-fu chi-shih*.

[18] Some of the Party leaders who were arrested in Shanghai at that time included Hsiang Chung-fa, the Party's General Secretary; Ku Shun-chang, Huang P'ing, Hu Ta-hai, Hsu Hsi-k'en, Yü Fei, Hu Chün-ho, and Lo Teng-hsien. Three top Communist leaders who were trained in the Soviet Union were Wang Yün-ting, Sun Chi-ming, and Wang Sheng-chiu. The information came from the interrogation of these and other leaders of the CCP and is collected in a KMT booklet, *The CCP from 1931 to 1933*; see note 4 above. Some of the public confessions of these people and the report on the events leading to their arrest are collected in *Chung-kuo Kung-ch'an-tang chih T'ou-shih*, 312–392.

general secretary when Wang relinquished his post to serve as one of the CCP representatives to the Comintern.

At any rate, Chou En-lai seems to have played an important part in establishing a closer relationship between the leaders of the soviet base area (i.e., Mao and Chu) and the Party's newly organized leadership in the Central Committee. Chou transmitted the policy line of the Party's new leadership to the soviet areas, and also reported back to its new leadership in Shanghai the revolutionary situation of the soviet base as well as the current attitudes of the soviet leaders.

Thanks to Chou En-lai's effectiveness in bridging the gap between the Party's Central Committee and the leaders of the soviet movement, especially Mao and Chu, the actual policy of the CCP in late 1931 reflected in some ways a juxtaposition of ideas provided by Mao and Chu with the theoretical rationale infused by the returned-student leaders. Mao gradually won the support of certain members of the returned-student group, including Chang Wen-t'ien and Wang Chia-hsiang, by suggesting new ideas and policies based on his practical experience in involving the peasant masses in the operations of the soviet and Red Army organizations.

The organizational goals of the Party's new leadership from January to September 1931 were, therefore, first to eliminate the loyal supporters of Li Li-san from the local Party apparatus and the soviet organizations, and then to reorganize the existing Party and soviet institutions so as to gain the support of the masses. This particular technique was manifested in the series of reorganization programs that the new leadership implemented in the soviet area in 1931 and 1932. The political tasks of the CBSA were as broad and comprehensive as the policy objectives established by the Party's central leadership. Therefore, Circular Letter No. 1 of the CBSA declared that the main tasks were to carry out resolutely the land struggle by equal distribution of land, broaden the base of mass support in the soviet area, and reform the structure of the existing soviet government at each level while expanding new soviet bases into other areas. All these programs were solidly based on the policy goal of winning more support from the peasant masses that Li Li-san was charged with having alienated.

The power relationships of the leaders of the Chinese Communist movement in the Kiangsi soviet period were further complicated by the fact that communications between the Party's Central Committee in Shanghai and the Party's Central Bureau in the Soviet Area were not as normal as one might have expected, because the Party's office in Shanghai was frequently raided by the KMT police, who arrested some of the members of the Central Committee, including returned students. Word of the Party's new policies, sent out by the Shanghai office did not even reach the soviet area until several months later, and often these dispatches were intercepted by the KMT intelligence network. Moreover, by the time they reached the soviet area, the leaders of the soviet base had already formulated their own policy on the basis of what they perceived to be the broad policy line established by the central leadership as well as what they thought to be best for the soviet base. The power to formulate new policy for the Kiangsi base seems therefore to have centered in the hands of the leaders of the soviet base, at least in the first half of 1931 following the Fourth Plenum. When the central bureau was created in January 1931, the leadership was composed of such veterans as Hsiang Ying, Chou En-lai, Mao Tse-tung, Chu Te, Jen Pi-shih, and younger-generation leaders such as Yü Fei, Tseng Shan, Wang Shu-tao and Ku Tso-lin, all of whom were either members of the returned-student group or sympathetic to their policy positions.[19]

The composition of the CBSA itself reflected the careful balance among the three elements of power. Mao Tse-tung and Chu Te probably represented an important element of the soviet government, whereas Tseng Shan and Yü Fei seem to have represented the interests of the returned students. Chou En-lai, Hsiang Ying, and Jen Pi-shih controlled the third element of power — the veteran leaders of the CCP and the Red Army units.

Interactions of power between the Party's central leadership and the leaders of the soviet base changed, of course, with shifts in the leadership positions of the CBSA. Yang Yüeh-pin, a Red Army general and one-time director of army mobilization in the Kiangsi base, has asserted that Chou En-lai's power was further strengthened in the CBSA when he succeeded in winning the full support of Mao Tse-tung and Chu Te at a certain point when he was in conflict with Hsiang Ying and struggling to consolidate his power.[20] Hsiang Ying was beginning to lose status during the period between the successful repulsion of the Second KMT Encirclement Campaign and the Third Campaign in the fall of 1931. This was also a turning point for Chou En-lai, because Mao was reported to have played an important role in organizing support for Chou against Hsiang Ying and helping him to be elected to the Party's leadership position in the CBSA.

In return for their assistance, the same source recounts, Chou En-lai fully supported Mao Tse-tung and Chu Te, not only to become members of the Party's military-affairs committee but also to be elected,

[19] See Tso-liang Hsiao, *Power Relations*, I, 150. See also Tsao Po-i, *Kiangsi Su-wei-ai*, 453.

[20] Yang Yüeh-pin, *Juichin shou-fu chi-shih*.

respectively, to the posts of chairman of the Central Executive Council of the Chinese Soviet Republic and chairman of the Central Revolutionary Military Commission when those two important institutions were created after the First National Congress of the Soviets in November 1931. Chou supported Mao simply because at this particular juncture Chou agreed more often with Mao in his policy lines, based on his experience of rural administration, than with anyone else in the CBSA. Chou also seems to have recognized that Mao and Chu had the broadest support from the peasant masses among leaders in the base area.

The development and operation of the Party organizations were, of course, intimately related to the process of establishing and administering the soviet system of government. After exploring ways and means of carrying out the soviet movement more effectively, the First Party Congress of the Soviet Area, held in November 1931, declared that the southwest Kiangsi soviet area was the most important base where a strong central soviet government could be founded. The central soviet government, therefore, was to be established only after the new Party leadership restored the "Revolutionary Committee" and held general elections to choose members of it at each level.

After several months of preparation, the First Congress finally convened on November 7, 1931, in Juichin, Kiangsi. According to a telegram dispatched by the Congress to the CCP Central Committee, more than 249 delegates representing various soviet areas assembled there to proclaim the establishment of the Chinese Soviet Republic.[21] A breakdown of the delegates by their social background showed that 30 were workers, 24 were from the Red Army, 5 were poor peasants, and 190 were peasants. Of the 249 delegates elected by the eight soviet areas, 195 were therefore considered to be peasant representatives. A total of 610 delegates representing various soviet areas, the Red Army units, and a number of labor unions, as well as a Korean delegation, participated in the proceedings of the Congress.

The Congress discussed and adopted unanimously a constitution for the Chinese Soviet Republic, a labor law, and a land law, all of which had been drafted by the Central Preparatory Commission in February of that year. It also passed the Declaration of the Congress, a political resolution, a resolution on the Red Army, and statements on economic policies and national minority policies.[22]

[21] Chung-hua Su-wei-ai Tai-piao ta-hui kei Chung-kung chung-yang tien (Telegram from the Chinese Congress to the CCP Central Committee), signed by the Presidium of the Congress on November 8, 1931; reproduced in Hatano, Chūkyō-shi, I, 595–596.

[22] For the constitution, land law, labor law, and resolutions of the First Soviet Congress, see Wang, Chung-kung shih-kao, chapters 16 and 17 (pp. 355–448); and also

The sixty-three-member Central Executive Council, elected by the First Soviet Congress in November 1931,[23] had a legislative function. In theory, the National Soviet Congress had absolute power to formulate policy and pass upon all matters related to the soviet areas. In practice, the CEC was expected to function as the legislative body of the Chinese soviet government, and the National Soviet Congress became little more than a sounding board for mass participation. Actually, the CEC, because of its large size and infrequent meetings, could not serve as a very effective policy-making organ. In fact, power to legislate and administer the policy of the Chinese soviet government rested in the hands of the thirteen-member People's Commissariat (cabinet), in which the top leaders of the Party's CBSA were strongly represented. (A list of the Central Executive Council members elected at the First National Soviet Congress, November 1931, constitutes appendix A of this chapter.)

The CEC called its first meeting on November 27, 1931, and elected Mao Tse-tung as chairman and Hsiang Ying and Chang Kuo-t'ao as vice-chairmen. It also organized a cabinet, known as the People's Commissariat (Jen-min wei-yüan-hui), patterned on its counterpart in the Soviet Union. The commissioners responsible for various commissariats were Wang Chia-hsiang, foreign affairs; Chu Te, military affairs; Hsiang Ying (who served concurrently as a vice-chairman), labor commissariat; Teng Tzu-huai, financial affairs; Chang Ting-ch'eng, land commissariat; Ch'ü Ch'iu-pai, education; Chou Yi-su, internal affairs; Chang Kuo-t'ao (who served concurrently as a vice-chairman), judicial commissariat; Ho Shu-heng, workers and peasant inspection; and Teng Fa, state security bureau.[24]

The adjoining chart outlines the overall organizational structure of the central soviet government as of November 7, 1931.

Intense competition between the Chinese soviet government and the KMT and the effort to seize political power and rule all China had just begun, and the new leadership was eager to obtain mass support for and participation in the newly created soviet system of government.

Inasmuch as the underlying principle of the soviet system in the

Hatano, Chūkyō-shi, I, 595–596. Five draft resolutions were prepared by the CCP Central Committee and submitted to the First Soviet Congress for adoption: (1) Question of the Red Army; (2) Land Law; (3) Labor Law; (4) Economic Policy; and (5) Task and Organizational System of the Workers' and Peasants' Inspection Bureau; these may be found in SSCM, Reel 20.

[23] Kuan-yü i-ch'üan ta-hui hsüan-chü chung-yang wei-yüan yü jen-min wei-yüan (The election of members of the central executive council and the council of People's commissars at the First Soviet Congress) lists the members of both bodies. This proclamation also appears in HSCH, initial issue, December 11, 1931. SSCM, Reel 16.

[24] For the composition of the People's Commissariat of the Central Executive Council of the Chinese Soviet Republic, see Wang, Chung-kung shih-kao, II, 313–314.

THE CENTRAL GOVERNMENT OF THE CHINESE SOVIET REPUBLIC
(NOVEMBER 7, 1931)

The People's Commissariats (13)

	Chairman: Mao Tse-tung
	Vice-chairmen: Hsiang Ying, Chang
State	Kuo-t'ao
Security	*Foreign Affairs*: Wang Chia-hsiang
Bureau:	*Military Affairs*: Chu Te
Teng Fa	*Internal Affairs*: Chou Yi-su
	Labor: Hsiang Ying
	Finance: Teng Tzu-hui
	Land: Chang Ting-ch'eng
	Education: Ch'ü Ch'iu-pai
	Judicial: Chang Kuo-t'ao
	Workers and Peasant Inspection: Ho Shu-heng

The Central Executive Council (63)

Chairman: Mao Tse-tung
Vice-chairmen: Hsiang Ying
Chang Kuo-t'ao

The First National Soviet Congress (106)

Kiangsi base was to assure mass involvement in policy-making and policy execution it will be useful here to analyze the Central Executive Council (CEC) as it performed dual legislative and administrative functions. The chief function of the CEC, elected by the First Soviet Congress in November 1931, was to serve as the policy-making body, and its standing committee (known as the People's Commissariats) acted as an important executive body when the CEC was not in session. At the plenary session on November 27, 1931, Mao Tse-tung was elected chairman of the CEC, thus becoming *ex officio* chairman of the People's Commissariats, the administrative center of the Chinese Soviet Republic. This office was equivalent to that of premier in the present-day political structure of the People's Republic of China.

Why was Mao Tse-tung elected Chairman of the Chinese Soviet Republic? The circumstances that led to his election were described to me by Chang Kuo-t'ao, who had been one of the two vice-chairmen of the Chinese Soviet Republic, in an interview in Hong Kong in December 1964. Chang stated that Mao Tse-tung was chosen because he was the most respected person closely linked to the peasant masses of the soviet areas, as a result of his organizational talent in the peasant movement. No Party leader was so widely known and, in fact, his name already circulated among the peasants "as if history were a legend." It was to enhance the popular prestige of the Chinese soviet government and to maintain the unwavering support of the peasant masses in the soviet area that Mao was elected to head the Chinese Soviet Republic in November 1931.

The three elements of power were unmistakably represented in this policy-making machinery of the central soviet government. The first on the list of the CEC's sixty-three member's was Mao Tse-tung, followed by a number of the Party's veteran leaders, including Hsiang Ying, Chang Kuo-t'ao, Chou En-lai, Chu Te, and Ch'ü Ch'iu-pai. The returned-student group was represented by such prominent leaders as Wang Chia-hsiang, Ch'en Shao-yü (Wang Ming), and Shen Tse-min. (Ch'in Pang-hsien is missing from this list.) Moreover, the original members of the CEC, particularly Mao Tse-tung, Chou En-lai, Chu Te, Wang Chia-hsiang, Lin Piao, Teng Tzu-hui, Liu Shao-ch'i, and Ch'en Yi, to name only the most prominent ones, continued to serve in important positions throughout the Yenan period and even after the establishment of the People's Republic of China on the mainland.

On June 8, 1933, only a year and a half after the establishment of the Chinese Soviet Republic, the CEC passed a resolution to convene the Second National Congress of the Soviets.[25] Its purpose was to strengthen the leadership of the revolution and to sum up the achievements and experiences of the soviet movement during the two-year period, as well as to formulate new policies and to reelect the members of the Central Executive Council. The CEC called on the Directors of the Internal (police) Departments in the Kiangsi, Fukien, and Fukien-Kiangsi border regions to convene a joint meeting to discuss the forthcoming election. It also instructed the leaders of mass organizations and the representatives of the press corps to hold joint meetings for discussions and preparations for the forthcoming Congress of the Soviets. The CEC also directed the People's Commissariats to prepare a comprehensive report on the work of each commissariat during the past two years.

Two of the most significant political events in connection with the convocation of the Second Congress were the Land Investigation Movement (Ch'a-t'ien yün-tung) and the reapportionment of the administrative districts, both under the administrative leadership of Mao Tse-tung. During the three-month period from July to September 1933, these two tasks were completed, and between September and November 1933, the soviet government at each level, from the township (hsiang) to the province (sheng), elected new soviets. The delegates from each level of soviets then assembled in the Provincial Congress of the Soviets to elect the delegates to the Second National Congress. The

---

[25] For this resolution, see Hung-se Chung-hua (HSCH), June 17, 1933.

provincial congresses of the soviets, according to instructions from the CEC, were held between October 1 and 15, 1933.[26]

After six months of intensive preparation, the Second Congress of the Soviets convened in Juichin on January 22, 1934, the delay of a month having been caused by the beginning of the fifth KMT encirclement campaign in October 1933. More than 700 delegates and 1500 observers were present at the Congress. It was opened by Mao Tse-tung, and congratulatory remarks were delivered by Ch'in Pang-hsien (Po Ku), representing the CCP, Liu Shao-ch'i, representing the All-China Federation of Trade Unions, Kai Feng (Ho K'o-ch'üan), representing the Communist Youth League of China, and Chu Te, representing the Red Army. The Congress's most important event was the long and comprehensive report "On the Work of the Central Executive Council and the People's Commissariats for the Two-Year Period," delivered by Mao Tse-tung himself.[27] Mao began his 42,000-word report on the afternoon of January 24 and completed it on the morning of January 25, 1934. This report and Chang Wen-t'ien's on the work of the soviet government during the two-year period, delivered earlier to the Fifth Plenum of the CCP Central Committee, should be considered the most important documents, in view of the controversy over whether or not Mao had completely lost his power. A careful analysis of these two documents clearly indicates that Mao was beginning to reassert his power, if indeed he had lost it, sometime between the Ningtu Conference of August 1932 and the spring of 1933, and that he was in full command, as before, of the government bureaucracy and its policy-making processes.

At any rate, the Second Congress elected the 211-member Central Executive Council (with 175 full members and 36 alternate members) on February 1, 1934. (See appendix B for a list of the members.) This time the Party's general secretary, Ch'in Pang-hsien (Po Ku), headed the list, followed by Wang Ming, Ho K'o-ch'üan, Liu Shao-ch'i, and Mao Tse-tung.[28] Was this order an indication of rank in power? Had Mao's standing slipped from first to fifth? Confusion also arises when one tries to understand why Chang Wen-t'ien was 117th on this list when elected chairman of the People's Commissariats by the new CEC at its first plenary session on February 3, 1934. Therefore the order of names on the list obviously did not mean much so far as the exercise of actual power was concerned. In any case, there certainly was a marked change in the organizational structure of the central soviet

[26] HSCH, No. 90, June 30, 1933.

[27] The text of this report may be found in HSCH, special editions on the Second Congress, No. 3 (January 26, 1934), pp. 1–12.

[28] HSCH, No. 148 (February 3, 1934).

government following the Second Congress, by which new power align-ments were created.

At the Second Congress, the Central Executive Council more than tripled in size, from 63 members to 211. The expanded CEC included almost every *bona fide* delegate elected by the provincial conferences of the soviets. Inasmuch as the CEC had now become too large to conduct any meaningful discussions and as it met only once every six months, its function as a policy-making body seems to have diminished. Consequently, the CEC created the seventeen-member presidium (*chu-hsi-tuan*), a top policy-making body in the government, and this served as the supervisory and decision-making apparatus of the central soviet government, whereas the CEC had become a mere rubber stamp for the presidium. More importantly, the presidium of the CEC had now acquired direct jurisdiction over the correct and prompt execution of the Constitution of the Republic and the implementation of the laws and resolutions adopted by the CEC. The presidium had the power to cancel or amend the laws and regulations adopted by each commissariat (cabinet department) as well as those implemented by the provincial soviet governments. The CEC, on the other hand, possessed its own right to pass laws and issue executive orders. It also was responsible for mediating disputes between the various administrative agencies and resolving conflicts between commissariats within the central soviet gov-ernment or between the provincial soviet governments. In short, the presidium of the CEC functioned as an intermediary between the CEC, a legislative body, and the People's Commissariats, which were admin-istrative bodies, hence the presidium was not only responsible for re-flecting the wishes of the CEC to the People's Commissariats but also for reporting the work of the People's Commissariats to the CEC.[29]

The presidium, which included all the members of the Politburo's Standing Committee, was set up parallel to the People's Commissariats (cabinet) after the Second Congress and was headed by Mao. Whereas the seventeen-member presidium performed policy-making and super-visory functions, the sixteen-member People's Commissariats, which were headed by Chang Wen-t'ien, carried out daily administrative rou-tines. The presidium, like the State Council of the People's Republic of China, functioned as the top policy-making body and its member-ship overlapped that of the Party's central bureau for the soviet area

[29] See "Chung-hua su-wei-ai kung-ho-kuo chung-yang su-wei-ai chu-chih-fa" ("Organic Law of the Central Soviets of the Chinese Soviet Republic"), passed by the Central Executive Council on February 17, 1934. Collected in Wang, *Chung-kung shih-kao*, II, 333–338. Also in *Chung-hua su-wei-ai kung-ho-kuo Ti-erh tz'u ch'üan-kuo tai-piao ta-hui wen-hsien* (Documents of the Second Soviet Congress of the Chinese Soviet Republic), published by the People's Commissariat, March 1934. See *SSCM*, Reel 16.

(CBSA). At least eight members of the Party's Politburo were represented in the presidium. When Chinese Communist sources refer to the "enlarged" meeting of the Party's Politburo, in all probability they include the members of the seventeen-member presidium, the nine-member secretariat, and the five-member standing committee of the Politburo. However, the enlarged Politburo meetings actually comprised only eighteen persons, and it was they who made the important decisions, because thirteen of them had interlocking positions in the three important organs of decision-making. It is also possible that the presidium of the CEC served as the Party's fraction (*Tang-tuan*) in the central soviet government, as all of them were Party members. The Party's fraction was organized in every unit of the soviet government from the central to the village government. At any rate, the presidium of the CEC performed wide-ranging functions of policy-making and policy execution and also supervised the work of the People's Commissariats. (See the adjoining chart for the structure and membership of the presidium and the People's Commissariats.)

The People's Commissariats, headed by Chang Wen-t'ien after the Second Soviet Congress, had a rather limited administrative function. They carried out the daily routines within the limits established by the presidium, headed by Mao Tse-tung. The chairman of the People's Commissariats (modern equivalent of premier) was directly responsible to the presidium in his supervision of the work of each central administrative commissariat (department) and of the departments of each provincial executive committee. All the resolutions and executive orders adopted or issued by the People's Commissariats were reported in advance to the presidium, and any resolutions or executive orders concerned with government policy were examined (*shen-ch'a*) and approved (*p'i-chun*) by the presidium beforehand. Even emergency matters had to be reported to the presidium in order to obtain its solutions. Thus the People's Commissariats, at least in principle, were subservient to the administrative jurisdiction of the presidium of the CEC.

The Patterns of Administrative Control

The methods of political control in the Kiangsi soviet base were established through the mechanism of interlocking positions held by the top leaders of the Party and government, through the machinery of the Party fraction (*Tang-tuan*) organized in every unit of government and in the mass organizations where two or three Party members worked, and through the system of worker-peasant inspections that existed at every level of the soviet government. The extent to which

THE CENTRAL GOVERNMENT OF THE CHINESE SOVIET REPUBLIC
(FEBRUARY 1, 1934)

The Presidium
of the CEC
(17)

The People's Commissariats
(16)

Chairman: Mao Tse-tung
Vice-chairmen: Hsiang Ying, Chang
Kuo-t'ao
Members: Chu Te, Chang Wen-t'ien,
Ch'in Pang-hsien, Chou En-lai, Ch'ü
Ch'iu-pai, Liu Shao-ch'i, Ch'en Yün,
Lin Po-ch'ü, Teng Chen-hsün, Chu
Ti-yüan, Teng Fa, Fang Chih-min,
Lo Mei, Chou Yüeh-lin

Chairman: Chang Wen-t'ien
Foreign Affairs: Wang Chia-hsiang
Military Affairs: Chu Te
Labor Affairs: Teng Chen-hsün
Land Affairs: Kao Tzu-li
Finance Affairs: Lin Po-ch'ü
Grain Foods: Ch'en T'an-ch'iu
Judiciary: Liang Po-t'ai
Internal (Police): Tseng Shan
Education: Ch'ü Ch'iu-pai
Workers and
  Peasant Inspection: Hsiang Ying
Central Auditing: Yüan Shao-hsien
Provisional
  Supreme Court: Teng Pi-wu
Revolutionary
  Military Affairs
  Commission: Chu Te (chairman)
      Wang Chia-hsiang
      (vice-chairman)
People's Commission
for National
Economy: Wu Liang-p'ing

The Central Executive Council (211)   (175 full members)
                                      (36 alternates)

Chairman: Mao Tse-tung
Vice-chairman: Hsiang Ying, Chang Kuot'ao

The Second National Soviet Congress (211)   (175 full members)
                                            (36 alternates)

the Party augmented its control over the government machinery
through the Party fractions was succinctly expressed in the CCP Central Committee's Directive Letter of instructions for the Party fraction
of the Second National Soviet Congress:

The party must strengthen further the leadership functions of the
cadres working in each department of the central soviet govern-

ment and also in the provincial governments. Therefore, the party
unit in each level of the soviet government should assist the government agencies in recruiting and mobilizing the cadres of
excellent quality and of workers' and peasants' background to the
rank of the party by assisting each and every comrade in the
government agencies to understand fully that the soviet system
of government can be developed and consolidated only by the
CCP, and the party must bear full responsibility for every success
or failure of the soviet work.[30]

The Party was also able to extend its control over the government
bureaucracy, in addition to the interlocking positions of the top leaders
and the machinery of the Party fractions, by creating a special agency,
the worker-peasant inspection department, from the central government to the *ch'ü* level government. A case study of the inspection department as a control mechanism will shed some light on the structure
and functions of a cabinet department. The worker-peasant inspection
(*Kung-nung chien-ch'a*) system was introduced in the central soviet
government in November 1931 as one of the nine People's Commissariats, and its first commissioner was Ho Shu-heng, later replaced by
Hsiang Ying after the Second National Soviet Congress. The worker-
peasant inspection department was also instilled in the provincial and
hsien soviet governments along with other functional departments, and
at the *ch'ü* and city levels it was called simply the worker-peasant inspection section (*Kung-nung chien-ch'a k'o*) and was under the jurisdiction of the *ch'ü* and city executive committee. The commissioner
in the central soviet government, according to "Organizational Regulations of the Worker-Peasant Inspection Department," [31] was elected
by the Central Executive Council (CEC) like other members of the
People's Commissariats. However, the directors of the provincial, *hsien*,
and *ch'ü* inspection departments were first nominated by the inspection commissioner of the central government and appointed by their
executive committees. The ultimate authority for recruiting and appointing the inspection directors, from the provincial government to
the *ch'ü* level, lay in the hands of the inspection commissioner of the

[30] For this Directive Letter, see Wang Chien-min, *Chung-kung shih-kao*, II, pp.
523–537. Also in *Chung-hua Su-wei-ai kung-ho kuo ti erh-tz'u ch'üan-kuo tai-piao
ta-hui wen-hsien* (Documents of the Second National Soviet Congress of the Chinese
Soviet Republic), published by the People's Commissariat in March 1934. Collected
in *SSCM*, Reel 16. This collection of documents hereafter cited as *Documents of the
Second National Soviet Congress.*

[31] "Kung-nung chien-ch'a pu tsu-chih t'iao-li" (Organizational Regulations of the
Worker-Peasant Inspection Department), passed by the First National Soviet Congress in November 1931; collected in *SSCM*, Reel 10.

central soviet government. There was vertical control of the inspection department because the lower departments were responsible directly to the upper-level directors.

In many respects, the worker-peasant inspection system was one of the most pervasive control mechanisms available to the Party and government leadership to check the administrative behavior and bureaucratic conduct of local-government officials. According to the "Draft Resolution on Organizational System and Tasks of the Worker-Peasant Inspection Office," [32] the aim of the inspection system was to protect the interests of the workers, peasants, farm laborers, and poor people during the land confiscation and redistribution. Actually the inspection system was designed to induce the people to participate in supervising government officials in such policies as the confiscation and redistribution of land, finance, and revenue collections, and all other economic programs to increase productivity. The inspection department was responsible for ensuring honest election of the delegate council at each level and also a good relationship between the upper and lower levels of government. It paid special attention to an investigation of bureaucratic formalities, corruption, and red tape. The inspection department also had wide power to investigate malpractice by government officials as well as to help government officials establish rational procedures for better operation of government institutions.

The worker-peasant inspection department was, in a sense, a special government agency that had a broad range of responsibilities and the power to supervise and investigate the political, economic, and cultural activities of the government institutions, as well as the right to look into the conduct of state enterprises and economic institutions. However, it had no authority to investigate or supervise the CCP and the Red Army organizations; its investigative power extended only to government-related institutions. Its primary function therefore was to supervise the government and its auxiliary agencies as well as to ascertain whether they had violated any government regulations and whether they were implementing the government's policies properly. "The worker-peasant inspection department of the central government," Proclamation No. 1 of the department asserted, "is a supervisory organ which carries out the supervision and investigation of the soviet government's administrative behavior and bureaucratic conduct. It is also responsible for the correct and thorough implementation of every

---

[32] "Kung-nung chien-ch'a ch'ü-ti tz'u-chih hsi-t'ung yü jen-wu" (Draft Resolution on Organization System and Tasks of the Worker-Peasant Inspection Office"); collected in *Ch'üan-kuo su-wei-ai ti-i-tz'u tai-piao ta-hui ts'ao-an* (*Draft Resolutions of the First National Soviet Congress*). SSCM, Reel 16. This resolution was prepared by the CCP Central Committee and submitted to the Congress for adoption.

aspect of the laws and policies proclaimed by the central soviet government." [33]

Under each inspection department were two subunits: the appeals bureau (kung-kao chü), which received complaints registered by the workers and peasants, and the surprise-attack unit (tu-chi-tui), which usually uncovered bureaucratic corruption and administrative misconduct by carrying out unannounced raids on government agencies and state economic institutions. The appeals bureau of the ch'ü soviet government usually provided appeals boxes in towns and villages, where the citizens could drop their complaint letters. Those peasants unable to write their complaints were invited to speak confidentially to a member of the surprise-attack unit or an informer (t'ung-hsin-yüan) maintained by the inspection department in towns and villages.

The cadres of the inspection department were specially trained to listen carefully to the workers and peasants and also to scrutinize thoroughly the letters dropped in the appeals box. When and if bureaucratic misconduct or administrative corruption was uncovered, the inspection cadres were told to turn the cases over to the "mass trial court" to be judged by the masses of people. The mass trials at the local level were also calculated to create a sense of participation on the part of the local population in the administration of justice. The inspection cadres therefore had only the responsibility of uncovering the misconduct and corruption of local officials; the right to pass judgment or impose punishment lay in the hands of the court. The trial court was set up under the judiciary department of the soviet government at each level, independently of the worker-peasant inspection department. According to "The Work of the Judicial Commissariat for a Year Period" (from November 7, 1931 to November 7, 1932), the judicial decisions on political crimes were about 70 percent of the total, and on civil crimes, 30 percent.[34] This was an indication of the extent to which the government officials were tightly controlled by the worker-peasant inspection cadres, since "political crimes" meant bureaucratic misbehavior and abuses of power.

In the course of its inspection work, the provincial and hsien inspection department regularly sent its own team or surprise-attack unit to the ch'ü, hsiang, and village governments to investigate the work of the officials and determine whether they were following policy directives correctly or violating administrative procedures. An interesting

[33] See "Proclamation No. 1 of the Worker-Peasant Inspection Department Concerning the Rights and Jurisdiction of the Inspection Committee," dated March 28, 1934. SSCM, Reel 10.
[34] "Szu-fa jen-min wei-yüan pu i-nien lai kung-tso" (The Work of the Judicial Commissariat for One Year Period), HSCH, No. 39, November 7, 1932, p. 7.

case showing how the *hsien*-level inspection department conducted its work was reported in the official newspaper of the Communist Youth League, *Ch'ing-nien Shih-hua*.[35] A detailed report of a surprise-attack unit dispatched by the inspection department of the Kiangsi provincial government to conduct an inspection of the Juichin *hsien* soviet government disclosed that the *hsien*-government officials overspent 236 *yüan* in September and an additional 850 *yüan* in October, which exceeded the monthly budget appropriated by the *hsien* delegate council (soviet). The government officials spent the money to purchase their own lunches. To end such a waste of resources and mismanagement of public funds, the surprise-attack unit and *hsien* inspection department jointly called a mass rally to conduct a political-struggle session. At the mass meeting the government officials of Juichin confessed their own crimes of misappropriating public funds, thus arousing the masses' indignation, and the masses were invited to criticize the administrators and suggest methods of preventing such misconduct.

Following this example, the inspection department carried out its own house-cleaning job at the *hsien* government offices as well as at each *ch'ü* office. An inspection was set in motion by the surprise-attack unit and spread throughout the *hsien* of Juichin. This was carried out in compliance with Directive No. 2 of the Inspection Commissioner of the central soviet government and "cleaned out the lazy and passive element and the corrupt bureaucrats with undesirable class origin from the soviet government and military installations."[36] "On February 7, 1933, a Joint Conference of all *ch'ü* inspection directors was called to evaluate the inspection movement of the *hsien*. I personally went down to take part in the conference, but I found that many serious mistakes were being committed in the course of the investigation," asserted Chou Yüeh-lin, a member of the Inspection Commissariat, who later became a presidium member of the central soviet government.[37] These defects not only existed in Juichin *hsien* but were also widespread in other regions of Kiangsi, asserted Chou Yüeh-lin. "Therefore, I wrote this short report with the hope that other regions may take these shortcomings seriously and correct them." Criticisms of the inspection movement were that its cadres failed to arouse the political enthusiasm of the masses because the masses were unable to grasp the central issues of the movement. What was needed in the inspection movement, Chou

[35] *Ch'ing-nien Shih-hua Chou-kan* (The Youth's Weekly of True Story), December 17, 1933. Collected in *SSCM*, Reel 19. This publication hereafter cited as *Ch'ing-nien Shih-hua*.

[36] (Chou) Yüeh Lin, "Juichin hsien ko-ch'ü chien-ch'a kung-tso ti chüeh-t'ien (The Shortcomings of the Inspection Work in Various Ch'ü in Juichin Hsien), *HSCH*, No. 52, February 13, 1933, p. 4.

[37] *Ibid.*

Yüeh-lin recommended, was an analysis of the class origins of the government officials being investigated and an evaluation of their performance in the light of their class background.

The *hsien*-level inspection departments of Kiangsi province concentrated on the misuse of public funds, bureaucratic tardiness, passive attitudes, corruption, and waste of resources, rather than working to arouse the political consciousness of the masses to participate in the mass struggles of the investigation movement. The primary task therefore, was to mobilize as many people as possible to take part in the execution of the policies decided upon by the central government. In the course of this mass mobilization, the problems of administrative misbehavior, bureaucratic corruption, tardiness, and red tape could all be rectified. The inspection system was, in many ways, a special mechanism through which the party and the central government attempted to exercise political control over the conduct of the government officials working at the local level.

A cabinet member or a member of the central inspection commissariat usually left his office to visit the local level in order to verify the work report of the inspection cadres. For example, Liang Po-t'ai, a member of the central inspection commissariat and later Commissioner of the Judicial Commissariat, went to Ningtu *hsien* to verify a report submitted by the Ningtu *hsien* inspection department. After verifying the report, Liang made specific recommendations to improve the inspection procedures. Upon his return to the central government, Liang also made a comprehensive report to the People's Commissariat concerning his investigation tour of Ningtu *hsien*. Having discussed and evaluated Liang's report, the People's Commissariat decided to send a specific directive on the conduct of inspection to all *hsien* and *ch'ü* governments.[38]

The worker-peasant inspection system, however, encountered enormous problems of communication and coordination in 1933, when its activities suddenly increased along with the intensified activities of the land-investigation movement, the cooperative movement, and the economic-reconstruction movement, all of which were directed by Mao Tse-tung as head of the central soviet government. In his "Preliminary Summary of the Land Investigation," Mao charged that some inspection departments were committing numerous errors because they did not know what they were doing. "Many of our comrades in the worker-peasant inspection department," Mao stressed, "have failed to recognize that the land investigation is to develop the ideological struggle, to

[38] Liang Po-t'ai, "Ningtu-hsien su-wei-ai kung-tso chih i-pan" (The General Condition of the Soviet Work in Ningtu-hsien), *HSCH*, No. 18, April 21, 1933. The specific directive to Ningtu *hsien* based on Liang's report may be found in the same issue of *HSCH*.

oppose bureaucracy, corruption and passivity. It should also become an opportunity to exclude the undesirable class element from the soviet government, but this work has not been carried out sufficiently." [39]

Mao charged that some cadres had shown their own passivity, bureaucracy, and formalism in the conduct of their work. The director of the Juichin inspection department, for example, failed to disclose the corruption of the director of the judicial department, after the latter took one thousand *yüan* for private use.[40] In certain regions the inspection department was criticized for not taking an active part in the land-investigation movement, and in other regions the inspection work failed to generate self-criticism and to promote the class struggle. "Needless to say, those staff members who have been committing serious errors for a long time," Mao suggested, "should be eliminated." [41] For these shortcomings Ho Shu-heng, the first commissioner of the Worker-Peasant Commissariat, took the blame and was replaced by Hsiang Ying after the Second Soviet Congress in February 1934.

After his appointment, Hsiang Ying issued his department's Proclamation No. 1, in which he stressed that the department would continue to investigate the administrative conduct of the government agencies, from the central to the basic level, but the inspection cadres were instructed to "listen to the opinions and suggestions of the workers and peasants concerning the conduct of government agencies." The inspection offices throughout the soviet base were urged to open their doors to the workers and peasants so that they could come in at any time and register their complaint about the local bureaucrats' behavior.[42] The inspection cadres were, in turn, supervised by the CCP member who served either a deputy director or a member of the inspection department and the Party member usually represented the Party's control commission (*chien-ch'a wei-yüan-hui*). In this way a pattern of administrative control over the government bureaucracy was fully realized by means of the interlocking positions held by a dozen or so leaders in top-level positions of the Party and government, the establishment of the Party fractions in every unit of the government, and the system of worker-peasant inspection committees at each level of government from the central soviet government to the basic administrative unit.

[39] *Mao Tse-tung chi (Collected Writings of Mao Tse-tung)*, supervised by Takeuchi Minoru (Tokyo, Hokubōsha, 1970), vol. III, p. 351.

[40] *Ibid.*, p. 352.

[41] *Ibid.*

[42] See "Proclamation No. 1 of the Worker-Peasant Commissariat Concerning the Rights and Jurisdiction of the Inspection Committee," dated March 28, 1934. *SSCM*, Reel 10.

APPENDIX A
ALPHABETICAL LIST OF THE CENTRAL EXECUTIVE COUNCIL (CEC) MEMBERS ELECTED AT THE FIRST NATIONAL SOVIET CONGRESS, NOVEMBER 1931*

41 Chang Hua-hsien	11 Hsü Hsi-ken	26 Lo Teng-hsien
3 Chang Kuo-t'ao	53 Hsü T'eh-li	5 Lu Fu-t'an
8 Chang Ting-ch'eng	52 Hu Chün-ho	51 Lu Teh-kuang
49 Chang Yün-yi	44 Hu Hai	1 Mao Tse-tung
31 Ch'en Cheng-jen	22 Huang P'ing	37 P'eng Kuei
38 Ch'en Fu-yüan	43 Huang Su	14 P'eng Te-huai
13 Ch'en Shao-yü	55 Hung Tau-ch'ing	54 Shao Shih-p'ing
48 Ch'en Yi	18 Jen Pi-shih	20 Shen Tse-min
25 Ch'en Yü	63 Juan Hsiao-hsien	21 T'an Chen-lin
4 Chou En-lai	36 Ko Yao-shan	9 Teng Fa
50 Chou Yi-li	39 Ku Ta-ts'un	28 Teng Tzu-hui
6 Chu Te	15 Kuang Hsiang-ying	45 T'eng Tai-yüan
7 Ch'ü Ch'iu-pai	16 K'ung Ho-ch'ung	23 Tseng Shan
34 Ch'ü Teng-kao	60 Li Tsung-po	33 Ts'ui Ch'i
12 Fan Lo-ch'un	24 Lin Piao	35 Tuan Te-ch'ang
17 Fang Chih-min	59 Liu Chien-chung	10 Wang Chia-hsiang
19 Ho Lung	56 Liu Kuang-wan	62 Wang Yung-sheng
42 Ho Shu-heng	29 Liu Shao-ch'i	40 Wai Pa-ch'ün
27 Hsia Hsi	61 Liu Sheng-yüan	58 Wu Chih-min
2 Hsiang Ying	30 Liu Ta-ch'ao	57 Yü Han-chao
46 Hsiao Heng-t'ai	47 Lo Ping-hui	32 Yüan Teh-sheng

*This list is from an original copy of the *Chung-hua su-wei-ai kung-ho-kuo chung-yang chih-hsing wei-yüan-hui pu-kuo, ti-i-hao* (Announcement No. 1 of the Central Executive Council of the Chinese Soviet Republic), dated December 1, 1931, to be found on the SSCM, Reel 16; also printed in *Hung-se Chung-hua (Red China)*, No. 1 (December 11, 1931), p. 2. The numbers represent the order in which the names were listed on the announcement, and probably indicate the relative numbers of votes received.

APPENDIX B
ALPHABETICAL LIST OF ALL FULL AND ALTERNATE MEMBERS OF THE CEC ELECTED AT THE SECOND NATIONAL SOVIET CONGRESS, FEBRUARY 1934*

79 Chan Yi-chin	59 Chang Kuo-t'ao	109 Ch'en Hsiang-sheng
Chang Ai-p'ing (18)	121 Chang Ta-ho	55 Ch'en Hung-shih
31 Chang Chih-chih	92 Chang Teh-san	49 Ch'en Kuang
130 Chang Chin-lou	123 Chang Ting-ch'eng	2 Ch'en Shao-yü
69 Chang Ch'in-ch'iu	117 Chang Wen-t'ien	133 Ch'en Shou-ch'ang
175 Chang Ch'un-ch'ing	120 Chang Yün-hsien	128 Ch'en T'an-ch'iu
74 Chang Jan-ho	61 Ch'en A-chin	151 Ch'en Tau-ch'ien
86 Chang Kuan-yi	58 Ch'en Ch'ang-hao	54 Ch'en Yi

126 Ch'en Yün
87 Chang Chen-fen
89 Chang Wei-san
90 Ch'eng Fang-wu
Chia Yüan (14)
76 Chiang A-san
10 Chin Wei-ying
1 Ch'in Pang-hsien
(Po Ku)
116 Ch'iu Hsien-ying
Ch'iu Shih-feng (3)
51 Chou Chien-p'ing
30 Chou En-lai
140 Chou Kuang-k'un
Chou Kuei-hsiang
(33)
52 Chou K'un
131 Chou Shao-wan
106 Chou Yi-k'ai
9 Chou Yüeh-lin
94 Chu Chao-hsiang
78 Chu Ch'i
66 Chu Jui
Chu Jung-sheng (13)
29 Chu Te
165 Chu Ti-yüan
93 Chu Wei-yüan
8 Ch'ü Ch'iu-pai
23 Chung Ch'ang-t'ao
25 Chung Hsün-jen
108 Chung Kuei-hsin
19 Chung Pao-yüan
105 Chung Shih-pin
Chung Yi-chin (26)
112 Fan Lo-ch'un
Fang Chen-hua (28)
161 Fang Chih-min
Fang Ching-ho (24)
Feng Hsüeh-feng (15)
96 Fu Ts'ai-shiu
34 Ho Ch'ang
35 Ho Ch'ang-kung
132 Ho Chen-wu
3 Ho K'o-ch'üan
60 Ho Lung
157 Ho Shu-heng
148 Ho Wei

71 Hsia Hsi
6 Hsiang Ying
65 Hsiao K'o
15 Hsiao Shih-pang
Hsieh Chen-fu (2)
23 Hsieh Hsien-szu
14 Hsieh Ming-jen
Hsieh Ping-huang
(25)
12 Hsieh Yü-ch'in
107 Hsiung Hsien-pi
137 Hsiung Kuo-ping
63 Hsü Hsiang-ch'ien
Hsü Ming-fu (10)
Hsü Shun-yüan (9)
21 Hsü Ta-chih
168 Hsü T'eh-li
67 Hsü Yen-kang
40 Hsün Huai-chou
111 Hu Hai
Hua Hsin-hsiang (32)
17 Huang Ch'ang-chiao
129 Huang Chia-kao
11 Huang Fa-kuei
Huang Fu-wu (27)
141 Huang Kuang-pao
37 Huang Su
103 Huang Tao
162 Huang Wan-sheng
122 Huang Yi-chang
82 Hung Shui
145 Jen Pi-shih
159 Juan Hsiao-hsien
K'ang K'o-ch'ing (36)
170 K'ang Sheng (Chao
Yün)
88 Kao Chün-t'ing
167 Kao Tau-li
77 Ku Ta-ts'un
101 Ku Tso-lin
164 Kuan Ch'un-hsiang
70 Kuan Hsiang-ying
163 Kuan Ying
K'uang Chu-ch'üan
(34)
144 K'uang Piao
56 K'ung Ho-ch'ung

104 K'ung Shu-an
91 Kuo Shu-shen
174 Lai Mei-yü
150 Li Ch'eng-chia
124 Li Chien-chen
26 Li Cho-jan
13 Li Fu-ch'ün
139 Li Hsien-nien
Li K'o-nung (17)
Li Mei-ch'ün (7)
Li Tz'u-fan (20)
138 Li Wei-hai
99 Li Wei-han (Lo Mai)
Li Yi-meng (16)
158 Liang Po-t'ai
Liao Han-hua (30)
16 Lin Mao-sung
44 Lin Piao
100 Lin Po-ch'ü
24 Liu Ch'i-yao
57 Liu Ch'ou-hsi
110 Liu Ch'ün-hsien
95 Liu Hsiao
27 Liu Kuang-ch'en
98 Liu Kuo-chu
97 Liu Hing-hui
33 Liu Po-ch'eng 46
46 Liu Po-chien
4 Liu Shao-ch'i
143 Liu Shih-chieh
Liu Yen-yü (23)
Liu Yi (6)
50 Lo Jui-ch'ing
Lo Jung-huan (19)
81 Lo Ping-hui
172 Lo Tzu-ming
20 Lou Meng-hsia
Lung Ch'un-shan (31)
5 Mao Tse-tung
38 Nieh Hung-chün
45 Nieh Jung-chen
119 P'an Han-nien
85 P'an Shih-chung
135 P'eng Jen-ch'ang
42 P'eng Te-huai
64 Pi Shih-t'i
102 Shao Shih-p'ing

72 Sung Pai-min	125 Wu Pi-hsien	156 Yang Ch'i-hsin
142 T'an Yü-pao	136 Wu Teh-feng	Yang Ping-lung (1)
166 Teng Chen-hsün	36 Tung Chan-t'ang	43 Yang Shang-k'un
118 Teng Fa	160 Tung Pi-wu	173 Yang Shih-chu
Teng P'ing (35)	39 Wan Yung-ch'eng	63 Yeh Chien-ying
Teng Tzu-hui (12)	134 Wang Chen	Yeh Teh-kuei (11)
Teng Yao-shang (4)	32 Wang Chia-hsiang	Yen Li-chi (21)
169 Teng Ying-ch'ao	153 Wang Chin-hsieng	Yin Jen-kuei (22)
41 T'eng Tai-yüan	80 Wang Feng-ming	154 Yü Chen-nung
18 Ts'ai Ch'ang	171 Wang Hsien-hsüeh	152 Yü Han-chao
83 Ts'ai Kan	146 Wang Hsiu-chang	84 Yü Hung-wen
47 Ts'ai Shu-fan	48 Wang Ju-ch'ih	147 Yü Hung-yüan
113 Tseng Hung-yi	127 Wang Sheng-jung	62 Yüan Kuo-p'ing
149 Tseng Kuang-lan	75 Wang Shih-t'ai	53 Yüeh Shao-hsien
22 Tseng Shan	73 Wang Wei-chou	
Tsou Chung-ts'ai (8)	115 Wu Lan-fu	
Tsou Tua-hou (29)	7 Wu Liang-p'ing	
Tung Ch'ang-shang	114 Wu Tzu-yüan	
(5)	155 Wu Yü-chang	

*This list is taken from an original text of the *Chung-hua su-wei-ai kung-ho-kuo chung-yang chih-hsing wei-yüan-hui pu-kao, ti-i-hao* (Announcement No. 1 of the Central Executive Council of the Chinese Soviet Republic), dated February 5, 1934, to be found on the *SSCM*, Reel 16; also printed in *HSCH*, No. 148 (February 12, 1934), p. 1, dated February 3, 1934.

APPENDIX C
LIST OF PERSONNEL ON THE 1934 CEC KNOWN TO HAVE SURVIVED UNTIL 1936

Chang Ai-p'ing	Feng Hsüeh-feng	Kuan Hsiang-ying
Chang Ch'in-ch'iu	Ho Ch'ang-kung	Kuo Shu-shen
Chang Kuo-t'ao	Ho K'o-ch'üan	Li Chien-chen
Chang Ting-ch'eng	Ho Lung	Li Cho-jan
Chang Wen-t'ien	Ho Wei	Li Fu-ch'ün
Ch'en Ch'ang-hao	Hsia Hsi (killed in 1936)	Li Hsien-nien
Ch'en Kuang	Hsiang Ying	Li K'o-nung
Ch'en Shao-yü	Hsiao K'o	Li Tz'u-fan
Ch'en T'an-ch'iu	Hsü Hsiang-ch'ien	Li Wei-han
Ch'en Yi	Hsü T'eh-li	Li Yi-meng
Ch'en Yün	Huang Tao	Lin Piao
Cheng Wei-san	Jen Pi-shih	Lin Po-ch'ü
Ch'eng Fang-wu	K'ang K'o-ch'ing	Liu Hsiao
Ch'in Pang-hsien	K'ang Sheng	Liu Ming-hui
Chou En-lai	Kao Chün-t'ing	Liu Po-ch'eng
Chu Jui	Kao Tzu-li	Liu Shao-ch'i
Chu Te	Ku Ta-ts'un	Liu Yi

Lo Jui-ch'ing
Lo Jung-huan
Lo Ping-hui
Lo Tau-ming
Mao Tse-tung
Nieh Hung-chün
Nieh Jung-chen
P'an Han-nien
P'eng Te-huai
Shao Shih-p'ing
T'an Yü-pao

Teng Chen-hsün
Teng Fa
Teng Tzu-hui
Teng Ying-ch'ao
T'eng Tai-yüan
Ts'ai Ch'ang
Ts'ai Shu-fan
Tseng Shan
Tung Pi-wu
Wang Chen
Wang Chia-hsiang

Wang Chin-hsiang
Wang Shih-t'ai
Wang Wei-chou
Wu Liang-p'ing
Wu Teh-feng
Wu Yü-chang
Yang Shang-k'un
Yeh Chien-ying
Yüan Kuo-p'ing

IV

POLICY-MAKING AND
LEADERSHIP BEHAVIOR

During the Kiangsi soviet period (between the Fourth Plenum of
January 1931 and the Fifth Plenum of January 1934), the leadership
structure, as described earlier, was neither dominated by a single group
nor controlled by a powerful individual. Relations between the three
elements of power (the Party, the government, and the Red Army)
were complex and diffused at best, and the power alignments within
the Chinese Communist movement continued to shift with the changing policy-making and implementation processes.

Policy formulation and execution during the Kiangsi soviet period
may be conveniently divided into three important stages, the first
beginning with the Fourth Plenum of January 1931 when the returned-
student group took over the Party's policy-making machinery and
issued a series of directives. At that time the Party's work in Shanghai
was carried on at great risk because of the KMT police. It consisted,
in the main, of dispatching policy directives or instructions. The policy-
making was not based on the realities of the revolutionary situation and
the directives tended to be ideological or rhetorical in tone. In the first
stage of policy formulation a struggle for control of the party leadership was also waged between the CCP leaders in Shanghai and those
in the rural hinterland under the leadership of Mao and Chu Te.

The second stage was initiated with the formal establishment of the
Chinese Soviet Republic (CSR) in November 1931. From that time
on, the central soviet government began to formulate important policies for the administration of the revolutionary society in the Kiangsi
soviet base. During that period the forward and offensive policy line
was adopted, with the revival of the slogan, "The initial victory in a
province or several provinces" (January 1932), and the central soviet
government formally declared war on Japan in April 1932. The most
dramatic of all the policy changes that took place at this stage followed
the Ningtu conference of August 1932, when the debate between the
supporters of Mao and the returned-student leadership was temporarily
settled by a division of policy-making tasks between the government

and the military. At that time, Mao was replaced by Chou En-lai as political commissar of the First Front Army.

The third stage of policy-making in the Kiangsi soviet base involved the completion of the move of the CCP Central Committee from Shanghai to Juichin in early 1933 and the establishment of collective leadership which included both Mao's supporters and the returned-student leaders. That stage ended with the Fifth Plenum and the Second National Soviet Congress in January–February 1934.

Changes in policy of any organization are greatly influenced by such variables as shifts in the power alignment; changes in the policy perspectives of the key policy-makers usually are based on reevaluation of their assessment of current situations and the introduction of new organizational techniques to implement the policies as well as to cope with such external threats as military attack or economic blockade. Therefore, the survival of the system becomes the most important factor in the formulation and implementation of policies in any complex organization. Obviously the policy-makers of the Kiangsi soviet base were influenced by their own assessment of the revolutionary situation, especially when they faced the KMT Army's persistent attack and economic blockade. The policies always incorporated the ideological aspect of sustaining the revolutionary war and the practical aspect of developing new organizational techniques of winning the support and loyalty of the masses.

This chapter will first take up the policy-making machinery of the central soviet government in connection with the Party's policy-making center, the CBSA, and will analyze some of the policy issues of the time; it will then examine the perspectives of the key policy-makers in both the Party and government. (The views and positions of the key policy-makers were often expressed in their directives or signed articles published in such Party publications as *Tang-ti chien-she, Shih-hua,* and *Tou-cheng,* as well as in the official journal of the central soviet government *Hung-se Chung-hua.* The chapter will also attempt to explain the changing attitudes of the key leaders in the process of policy implementation. Its thesis is that the relationship between Mao and the returned-student leaders in the Kiangsi soviet base was not one of hostility but was motivated by mutual necessity, because Mao needed the theoretical justification that the returned students had acquired in Moscow and their leaders required Mao's support and influence in the soviet base area in order to sustain their leadership positions in the Party. The returned students also needed Mao's practical experience in directing the rural-based revolution, as well as the organizational techniques he had learned from his experience with the peasant movement, and were dependent upon the support of Mao and his associates when the revolutionary strategy was being shifted from the cities to the rural hinterland. The vital element in the policy processes of the Kiangsi period, especially after the returned-students' move to Juichin in 1933, was the union of Mao's practical strategy of revolution with the student leaders' ideological rationale in order to meet the requirements of the Comintern policy line.

In terms of power, Mao still held an important position in the Party and government, though it was shared with other elements, and he participated in every aspect of policy formulation and implementation. Mao was chairman of the People's Commissariat (the cabinet) and of the Central Executive Council (CEC), an important policy-making body of the central soviet government; he was elected chairman of the seventeen-member presidium of the CEC, the most powerful policy-making group within the central government, following the Second National Soviet Congress in February 1934, when the CEC's plenary session was called to choose the presidium. Mao also continued to serve as a member of the Politburo of the CBSA, and there is clear evidence that he continued to take an active part in every aspect of its policy-making. For example, prior to the formal adoption of the "Resolution of the Central Bureau on the Land Investigation Movement" in June 1933, Mao Tse-tung, as chairman of the CEC and of the People's Commissariat of the central soviet government, accompanied by a cabinet member, Hu Hai (the acting land commissioner since January 1933), took part in the policy deliberation of the CBSA. Mao and Hu made a comprehensive report on the land-investigation movement with which they were experimenting in certain districts (ch'ü) of Juichin hsien.[1] "After listening to the reports of Comrades Mao Tse-tung and Hu Hai the Central Bureau has now become convinced," the Resolution asserted, "that the land-investigation movement has just taken a first step." [2] Mao's preliminary study based on his empirical analysis of land distribution as well as on his survey of experimental programs of land investigation seems to have strongly influenced the final decision of the CBSA to pass a resolution calling for a land-investigation movement. Mao's analysis and report might be characterized in modern terms as the input of the policy-making process.

Mechanisms of Policy Formulation

To understand the policy-making processes in the Kiangsi soviet base one must explore the question of how the CCP leaders maintained a functional relationship among the major centers of policy formulation — on the one hand, the Party's Politburo, Secretariat, and Military

[1] See the introduction to the resolution in HSCH, No. 87, June 20, 1933, p. 2.
[2] Ibid.

Affairs Committee, and on the other, the central government's policy-making machinery such as the People's Commissariat (*Jen-min wei-yüan hui*) in the first and second stages, and the Presidium of the Central Executive Council (*Chung-yang chih-hsing wei-yüan hui chu-hsi-tuan*) and the Central Revolutionary Military Commission (*Chung-yang k'o-ming chün-shih wei-yüan hui*) in the third stage. An analysis of the structure and function of the mechanisms of policy-making in terms of their relationship and of the part that Mao Tse-tung and the returned-student leaders played in them throws light on the questions of who was formulating what kind of policies and how the political institutions were operated in the Kiangsi soviet base.

If one looks closely at the organizational structure of the Kiangsi policy-making system, he will quickly identify the three major centers of policy formulation: (1) the standing committee of the CBSA, which was incorporated into the CCP Politburo when the CCP Central Committee completed its move from Shanghai to Juichin, thus becoming the center of the Party's policy-making; (2) the People's Commissariat (cabinet) in the 1931–1933 period, and after the Second National Soviet Congress, the Presidium of the CEC; and (3) the Military Affairs Committee (MAC) of the CCP and the Central Revolutionary Military Commission (CRMC) of the central soviet government, which seem to have maintained a close and active relationship for the formulation of military strategy. It is therefore evident that policy formulation in the Kiangsi soviet base was divided into two important spheres of influence: one dealing with the formulation of socioeconomic policies of the central soviet government and the other dealing exclusively with the formulation of military strategy.

The policies for the administration and management of the revolutionary society in the Kiangsi soviet base were formulated by the joint session of the fourteen-member Politburo of the CBSA and the thirteen-member People's Commissariat during the first and second stages, between the establishment of the central soviet government and the adoption of a new and offensive policy line in January 1932. The membership of these two organs, as in the case of the standing committee of the CCP Politburo and of the standing committee of the State Council in the present day People's Republic, overlapped. However, an important change in the Party's policy-making machinery took place in mid-1931 and early 1932 when CCP Politburo members Hsiang Chung-fa, Hsü Hsi-k'en, Lo Fu-t'an, Lo Teng-hsien, Kuan Hsiang-ying, and Ku Shun-chang were arrested by the KMT police, Ch'en Shao-yü (Wang Ming), the Party's general secretary, left Shanghai for Moscow to serve as the CCP representative to the Comintern, and Chang Kuo-t'ao went to the O-Yü-Wan soviet area to serve as chief of the Party's subbureau (*Chung-yang fen-chi*). Only half of the sixteen-member Politburo and only two of its five-member standing committee (Ch'in Pang-hsien and K'ang Sheng) were left in Shanghai to take part in the Party's policy-making process. Two of the remaining eleven members of the Politburo, Hsiang Ying and Chou En-lai, had gone to the Kiangsi soviet base to formulate military strategy to cope with the KMT's encirclement campaigns. At about the same time, K'ang Sheng had gone to Moscow to serve in the CCP delegation to the Comintern. It was therefore necessary for the CCP Politburo to restructure itself or recruit new members to replace those who were no longer able to participate in the Party's policy deliberations.

During the fall of 1931 and the early months of 1932 the Party's policy-making machinery was beginning to change, with the appointment of such new Politburo members as Chang Wen-t'ien, Liu Shao-ch'i, and Kai Feng (Ho K'o-ch'üan). In the reorganized Politburo, Ch'in Pang-hsien replaced Ch'en Shao-yü as the Party's general secretary, and Chang Wen-t'ien took over the propaganda post from Shen Tse-min, who left for the O-Yü-Wan soviet area to work under Chang Kuo-t'ao. Liu Shao-ch'i was promoted to the directorship of the reorganized Shanghai bureau after Lo Fu-t'an's arrest by the KMT police. Kai Feng succeeded Ch'in Pang-hsien as secretary of the Youth League, the post that Ch'in had held since April 1931. As soon as they gained control of the Party's policy-making machinery, the Politburo, Ch'in Pang-hsien and his colleagues began to send a number of policy directives to the subordinate units of the party organization. Their new and aggressive policy, embodying a hard line, was clearly reflected in the Directive Letter of September 1, 1931, to the leaders of the Kiangsi soviet. That letter criticized the Central Soviet Area for having been too lenient toward the rich peasants in its agrarian policy, among other things, and for being too much disposed to guerrilla tactics in its military strategy. As will be seen later, however, the conflicting policy lines, the ones established by the returned-student leaders in Shanghai and the ones implemented by the Mao-Chu forces in the base area, coexisted in the Kiangsi soviet throughout the period (1931–1934). The political struggle between the returned-student group in Shanghai and Mao's supporters in the Kiangsi soviet base was beginning to emerge in the fall of 1931, as Hsiao Tso-liang asserted on the basis of this letter, but the coexistence of the conflicting policy lines was fully reflected in the policy-implementation processes in Kiangsi.

When the nine-member standing committee of the Party's CBSA was established in January 1931, it included Hsiang Ying, Chou En-lai, and Jen Pi-shih, who were concurrently members of the CCP Politburo in Shanghai. It is quite possible that the remaining eight-member Politburo in Shanghai and the nine-member standing committee of the

CBSA were merged when the Politburo was reorganized and Ch'in Pang-hsien took over the Party's general secretaryship from Ch'en Shao-yü in the fall of 1931. One might therefore be able to identify only a dozen or so key policy makers who operated the policy-making machinery of the Party in Shanghai as well as in the Kiangsi soviet. Until the move of the CCP Central Committee from Shanghai to Juichin in early 1933, the policy lines were laid down by Ch'in Pang-hsien and Chang Wen-t'ien in Shanghai, but the actual formulation of specific policies was done by the reorganized Politburo of the CBSA in the Kiangsi soviet base. This group included Mao Tse-tung, Hsiang Ying, Chou En-lai, Ch'en Yün, Chu Te, Jen Pi-shih, Kai Feng (Ho K'och'üan), Tseng Shan, Wang Shou-tao, Ku Tso-lin, and Ch'in Pang hsien.

The nine-member standing committee of the CBSA also included Mao, Hsiang Ying, and Chu Te, who represented the policy positions of the soviet government in the Party's policy-making center.[3] These men performed the input functions for the government's side when the CBSA formulated the Party's policies. When the thirteen-member People's Commissariat of the central soviet government was established in November 1931, fewer than half the commissioners (the cabinet members) represented the CBSA's viewpoints in the government's policy-making process. However, when the returned-student leaders moved from Shanghai to Juichin at the time of the transfer of the CCP Central Committee in early 1933, an important change in the policy-making machinery of the Party and the central soviet government took place. It consisted of the establishment of a collective-leadership system in the Party's and the government's policy-making machinery.

The concept of collective leadership had already been under discussion as early as the spring of 1932, when such veteran party leaders as Jen Pi-shih, the head of CBSA's organization department, and Teng Ying-ch'ao, wife of Chou En-lai, began to write about the urgent need to establish a collective-leadership system in the process of building the Party organizations.[4] An analysis of the seventeen-member presidium (*Chu-hsi-tuan*) of the CEC, which emerged as the most powerful policy-making organ of the central soviet government subsequent to the Second National Soviet Congress in January–February 1934, indicates that

[3] The nine-member standing committee of the CBSA consisted of Hsiang Ying, Chou En-lai, Mao Tse-tung, Chu Te, Jen Pi-shih, Yü Fei, Tseng Shan, Wang Shu-tao, and Ku Tso-lin.

[4] For Jen Pi-shih's idea of collective leadership, see his article in *Tang-ti chien-she* (*The Party Building*), No. 3, August 5, 1932. For Teng Ying-ch'ao's ideas on collective leadership, see her article in *Tang-ti chien-she* (*The Party Building*), No. 1, June 10, 1932. See particularly the first section, on "Hsin-ti ling-tao fang-shih yü ch'e-ti ch'üan-pien" ("A New Method of Leadership and A Thorough Transformation").

a balance of power was carefully maintained, thus establishing a collective-leadership system involving all three elements of power: the
Party, the government, and the military. The collective-leadership system was continued, with one-third of the Presidium members (Chang
Wen-t'ien, Ch'in Pang-hsien, Chou En-lai, Ch'en Yün, Liu Shao-ch'i,
Chu Ti-yüan) representing the Party elements. This was basically a
coalition of the returned students and certain veteran leaders. Slightly
more than a third of the Presidium members (Mao Tse-tung, Fang
Chih-min, Chou Yüeh-lin, Teng Fa, Teng Chen-hsün, and Lin Po-
ch'ü) seem to have represented the government organizations. The
other third (Chu Te, Chang Kuo-t'ao, Ch'ü Ch'iu-pai, Hsiang Ying,
Lo Mai, and Li Wei-han) represented the military and a segment of
the veteran leaders of the Chinese Communist movement.

The presidium, a new and important instrument of policy formulation, was established in February 1934 at the first plenary session of
the CEC following the Second Soviet Congress. This organ was charged
with the policy-making function because the membership of the CEC
had by then increased from 63 at the time of the First Congress in
1931 to 211. In order to have a better picture of the way in which the
presidium took over the policy-making function from the People's Commissariat one should examine the role of the People's Commissariat
in the policy-making process during the 1931–1933 period and its
metamorphosis after the establishment in 1933 of the superorganization
called the People's Commission for National Economy, under the jurisdiction of the People's Commissariat. At that time supporters of Mao's
policy positions were appointed to cabinet posts. For example, Liu
Shao-ch'i was appointed deputy commissioner of labor, Liang Po-t'ai
deputy commissioner of the judiciary, Kao Tzu-li deputy commissioner
of worker-peasant inspection, Wu Liang-p'ing deputy commissioner of
the national economy. Kao and Liang were later promoted, becoming
full commissioners, and Wu Liang-p'ing succeeded Teng Tzu-hui as
commissioner of national economy.[5]

The function of the People's Commissariats in the policy-making
process was apparent in the regular session (shang-hui) of the Commissariats, which were convened as often as once every week. Although we
do not have a complete record of these sessions, the substance of the
discussions was published regularly in the government paper Hung-se
Chung-hua immediately after the sessions. By skimming the pages of
the newspaper and reading the announcement of each session one

[5] Appointments usually were announced immediately after the regular session of
the People's Commissariat. The main content of the session as well as appointments
to cabinet posts were published in Hung-se Chung-hua (Red China), the daily newspaper of the central soviet government. These papers are to be found in the Ch'en
Ch'eng microfilms, Reels 16 and 17.

should be able to obtain a fairly good idea of what was discussed at the regular meetings of the Commissariat. More than fifty regular meetings of the People's Commissariats were reported in the pages of *Hung-se Chung-hua*. These sessions usually devoted a great deal of time to the evaluation of reports (such as the one presented by Mao on the land-investigation movement) submitted by either a commissioner or the representative of a provincial soviet government. Each session usually began with the presentation of a report, followed by a question-and-answer period, after which came policy deliberations. For example, Teng Fa, director of the state security bureau, made a report to the tenth regular session of the People's Commissariat on March 16, 1932, concerning his inspection tour of soviet work in Hsing-kuo and Yü-tu *hsien* of Kiangsi province. Next to be considered was a specific recommendation to the Kiangsi provincial soviet government about the correction of certain problems of organization.[6] At the thirtieth regular session of the People's Commissariat, on January 11, 1933, Teng Tzu-hui, the finance commissioner, submitted a comprehensive report on his inspection tour of Hui-ch'ang *hsien* and also described his own experience in taking part in the enlarged meeting of the Hui-ch'ang *hsien* executive committee during his tour.[7]

The chairmen or the representatives of the provincial soviet governments, such as Liu Shih-ch'i and Ma Wen-pin of the Hsiang-Kan (Hunan-Kiangsi) soviet government and Chang T'ing-cheng, chairman of the Fukien provincial soviet government, were frequently invited to the regular sessions of the People's Commissariat to make reports and respond to questions concerning the governmental activities of their provinces. The People's Commissariat formulated specific policy directives on the basis of the reports and the discussions at the meetings and conveyed them to the governments concerned. These directives usually served other soviet government leaders as policy guidelines. This indicates clearly how the People's Commissariat kept close contact with the administrative heads of the local governments and also maintained a constant flow of communication between the upper- and lower-level administrative organs by means of policy directives and reports. The regular session of the People's Commissariat thus continued to serve an important function in formulating policy, the input usually depending on the reports by the local administrators or the cabinet members concerning their empirical observations.

Decisions on appointments to cabinet posts in the central soviet government, however, were made by the People's Commissariat on the basis of recommendations proposed by the CEC. For example, the ap-

[6] The announcement of the tenth regular session of the People's Commissariat may be found in *HSCH*, No. 14, March 16, 1932, p. 6.

[7] See *HSCH*, No. 48, January 28, 1932, p. 8.

pointments of Hu Hai as land commissioner and of Tung Pi-wu and Liu Shao-ch'i as members of the Worker-Peasant Inspection Commissariat were made by the People's Commissariat in compliance with the recommendations of the CEC.[8]

Confronted with the fourth encirclement campaign of the KMT forces in the spring of 1933, during which the KMT Army carried out a stringent economic blockade of the soviet base, the leadership of the central soviet government began to discuss and debate the methods by which they should cope with the external threats of military attack and economic blockade. Both the economic and military pressures exerted by the KMT forces were beginning to be felt deeply in the base areas. The survival of the Kiangsi political system was the main question in the policy deliberations, and the Chinese Communist leaders were able to formulate two important strategies of revolution: total mobilization of human resources for the support of the revolutionary war, and maximum mobilization of societal resources for economic reconstruction and development. To carry out this dual strategy they further strengthened the Central Revolutionary Military Council (CRMC) to execute the military strategy and established a new organ, the People's Commission for National Economy, in the central soviet government to implement the economic-mobilization strategy. As a result, there was an important change in the structure of the policy-making machinery within the People's Commissariat in early 1933.

The People's Commission for National Economy was established by the People's Commissariat at its thirty-sixth regular session on February 26, 1933, and the soviet governments, from the province to the *ch'ü* level, were instructed to form departments of national economy.[9] Seven prominent leaders of the central soviet government — Teng Tzu-hui, Chang Wen-t'ien, Hsiang Ying, Wu Liang-p'ing, Hu Hai, Ch'en Ying, and Liu Ping-huei — were appointed to the newly established commission.[10] Teng Tzu-hui was appointed commissioner and Wu Liang-p'ing became deputy commissioner. The commission was not formally organized, however, until April 28, 1933, when the central soviet government issued Executive Order No. 19 over the signature of Mao Tse-tung as chairman of the Republic.[11]

"To increase the productivity of all industry, to expand foreign and domestic trade, and to develop the national economy of the soviet area, as well as to destroy the enemy's economic blockade," Mao asserted, "we must establish the Commission for National Economy in the cen-

[8] See the announcement of the thirty-fifth regular session of the People's Commissariat in *HSCH*, No. 57, March 3, 1933, p. 1.
[9] See *HSCH*, No. 58, March 6, 1933, p. 5.
[10] See *HSCH*, No. 70, April 17, 1933.
[11] See *HSCH*, No. 77, May 8, 1933, p. 5.

tral government and the departments of national economy at the province and *hsien* levels of soviet government, and then by developing the offensive line of the economic front we must rectify the mistakes of neglecting the economic reconstruction of the soviet government at each level." [12] The organizational goal of the Commission for National Economy, therefore, was to solve the economic problems caused by the KMT's economic blockade, to improve the economic situation of the working masses, and to contribute to a decisive victory of the Red Army over the KMT's fourth encirclement campaign. However, the most important task of the Commission, according to Mao, was "to win victory in the revolutionary war by arousing the revolutionary enthusiasm of the masses and by giving logistical support to the Red Army. But the task should be coordinated with the mobilization work of winning the war."

To reach such a goal the soviet government at each level was instructed to concentrate its work on such tasks as the increase of agricultural and industrial production, the distribution of food grains, and the further extension of the cooperative movement. All of the administrative work connected with the economic sphere was transferred from various commissariats and consolidated under the leadership of the Commission for National Economy. For example, the bureau of food-grain circulation, the bureau of the cooperative movement, the external-trade office of the Finance Commissariat, the state printing house of the Education Commissariat, and the labor correction camp of the Judiciary Commissariat, were all transferred to the jurisdiction of the Commission for National Economy.[13] Moreover, the department of national economy of each provincial and *hsien* soviet government was directly responsible to the central commission, thus creating a highly centralized mechanism of policy-making in the economic sphere.

As Chang Wen-t'ien, one of the key members of the commission, explained, the Commission for National Economy was to function as "the command post for economic affairs in the soviet area." [14] Such mobilization programs for economic construction as the land-investigation (*ch'a-t'ien*) movement and the cooperative (*ho-tso-she*) movement were all carried out by the People's Commission for National Economy. Although the maximum mobilization of economic resources was the responsibility of the People's Commission for National Economy, the total mobilization of human resources for the pursuit of the

[12] *Ibid.*

[13] See "Chan-hsing tzu-chih kang-yao" ("Summary of Provisional Organization") in *HSCH*, May 8, 1933, p. 5.

[14] Chang Wen-t'ien, "Prospects for Economic Development in the Soviet Area," *Tou-cheng*, No. 11, August 14, 1933. Translated in Hatano, *Chūkyō-shi*, III, 601–609.

revolutionary war was administered solely by the Central Revolutionary Military Commission (CRMC), beginning in early 1933.

The fifteen-member CRMC was established in December 1931, immediately after the First Soviet Congress, and Chu Te was appointed chairman of the commission, Wang Chia-hsiang and P'eng Te-huai being named to serve as vice-chairmen.[15] Some of the military leaders held overlapping appointments in the CCP's military-affairs committee, headed by Chou En-lai. The policy-making machinery for military strategy therefore was a joint meeting of the Party's MAC and the central government's CRMC. An important change in the mechanism of military policy-making, however, took place when the People's Commission for National Economy was created. Chu Te was appointed to serve as supreme commander of the Red Army as well as of the First Front Army, and Chou En-lai became political commissar of the Red Army as well as of the First Front Army at the forty-first session of the People's Commissariat on May 8, 1933. The People's Commissariat also decided to enlarge the military commission by appointing Hsiang Ying and Ch'in Pang-hsien, thus making up a seventeen-member CRMC. Hsiang Ying was given the post of acting chairman of the CRMC, replacing Chu Te. It was also decided that the headquarters of the CRMC was to be transferred to another place, possibly closer to the front line, where the military commanders were located.[16]

This sweeping change in the structure of military policy-making has been invariably interpreted as evidence of the decline of Mao's power in the Kiangsi soviet and the rise of Chou En-lai's in the military sphere. However, it might be considered as illustrative of how a division of labor was effected between Mao's supporters (Wu Liang-p'ing, Kao Tzu-li, and Chang Wen-t'ien, for example) and Chou En-lai with the backing of a group of the returned students — including Ch'in Pang-hsien and Wang Chia-hsiang — and how the concept of collective leadership that had been developing ever since the spring of 1932 was implemented by the spring of 1933. Some policy disputes and power struggles were said to have been developing in the policy-making machinery of the CCP after the Ning-tu Conference of August 1932. As may be seen from the foregoing, the issues of policy-making were centered around two broad areas: the formulation of military strategy to cope with the KMT's encirclement campaign and the development of mobilization policy to cope with the organizational problems of economic reconstruction and development.

[15] The members of the military commission were Chu Te, P'eng Te-huai, Wang Chia-hsiang, Lin Piao, Tan Chen-lin, Yeh Chien-ying, Kung Ho-lung, Chou En-lai, Chang Kuo-t'ao, Shao Shih-p'ing, Ho Lung, Mao Tse-tung, Hsu Hsiang-chien, Kuan Hsiang-ying, and Wang Sheng-ying. See *HSCH*, No. 2, December 18, 1931, p. 4.

[16] For this information on the military commission, see *HSCH*, No. 78, May 11, 1933.

Problems of Policy Perspective

The issues raised and debated in the policy conflicts between Mao and Chou were less concerned with any particular policies of the central soviet government than with the question of the way in which the Red Army should be deployed to meet the forthcoming encirclement campaign of the KMT forces. Issues of military strategy — such as the choice between guerrilla warfare and positional warfare — were hotly debated. Mao, as a member of the Central Revolutionary Military Commission, participated in the determination of military policy.

A difference over strategy had already developed between Mao Tse-tung and Chou En-lai in the summer of 1932 (in all probability at the Ningtu Conference of August 1932) centering on the methods of dealing with the fourth KMT encirclement campaign. However, Chou did not press hard enough to change the military strategy, because he was stricken with illness in the summer of 1932. Meanwhile, a series of debates over the issues of "guerrilla warfare" and "positional warfare" reportedly took place in the Party's military-affairs committee, which was headed by Chou En-lai. In this dissension over strategic policy, Chou and Otto Braun, the Comintern's military advisor to the CCP, reportedly proposed the strategy of a direct confrontation between the Red Army and the KMT forces by establishing a front line, whereas Mao advocated the continuation of the strategy of guerrilla warfare by luring the enemy forces deep into the soviet areas.[17]

Mao was reported to have advanced two convincing arguments for continuing guerrilla warfare. First, it would test the will and determination of the people living in the soviet area, that is, whether they were firmly convinced of the superiority of the soviet system of government. (Mao had no doubt whatsoever about the commitment of the peasant masses to his soviet government.) Second, the will and determination of the people of the soviet area would be hardened against the Nationalist Army because they would be exposed to its evil conduct and exploitative actions. Therefore, Mao argued, guerrilla warfare would accomplish two main objectives of the soviet government during the fourth KMT campaign: the creating of an environment in which the masses would participate directly in the revolutionary war,

[17] Although this part was written earlier and my conclusion was reached independently, more recent studies of the military aspect of the Kiangsi soviet period basically support my general views. An excellent translation of and commentary on "Resolutions of the Tsunyi Conference" by Jerome Ch'en is now available. See *The China Quarterly*, No. 4 (October–December 1969), pp. 1–38. See also Chi-hsi Hu, "Hua Fu, the Fifth Encirclement Campaign and the Tsunyi Conference," *The China Quarterly*, No. 43 (July–September 1970), pp. 31–46; Dieter Heinzig, "The Otto Braun Memoirs and Mao's Rise to Power," *The China Quarterly*, No. 46 (April–June 1971), pp. 274–288.

and the winning of a victory over the Nationalist forces by cutting off
their communication lines and supply routes after luring them deep
into the soviet areas.[18]

Mao's view of guerrilla tactics was consistent with his earlier belief
that "when the Red Army fights, it fights not merely for the sake of
fighting but *exclusively* to agitate among the masses, to organize them,
to arm them, and to help them establish political power; apart from
such objectives, fighting loses its meaning, and the Red Army the reason for its existence." [19] Mao's concept of linking war and politics during the KMT campaigns meant that the revolutionary war should involve the mobilization of the masses by providing them with economic
incentives such as land redistribution.

Mao's strategic thinking, however, did not prevail among the members of the joint military-affairs council of the Party and government.
Nevertheless, they reportedly debated his plan, and this caused them
to split into two groups: those who supported Chou's and Braun's
strategy of a direct confrontation by establishing a battlefront and
those who supported Mao's strategy of guerrilla warfare. The balance
of power between the supporters of the two leaders being equal, Liu
Po-ch'eng, the chief of staff of the Red Army headquarters, gave his
support to Chou's military strategy.[20] It was probably at this time
that Mao's power and influence began to decline in the sphere of military policy. Chou's influence and power in the policy-making process
of the Party's military-affairs committee had obviously increased, because he was appointed general political commissar of the Red Army
in May 1933, succeeding Mao in that position. Mao consequently was
removed from participation in the sphere of military policy but continued to exercise his power and influence in the policy-making of
the central soviet government. Guerrilla tactics were by no means
abandoned by the military strategists. The tactics of positional warfare
and guerrilla warfare coexisted throughout the military campaign,
though greater emphasis was placed on the former, which Mao later
charged was a mistake of the military leadership.

If Mao had been removed from his position of power and influence
in the sphere of military strategy, and had withdrawn to concern himself only with government and economic policy, which was reported to
have happened sometime in the spring of 1933, how can one account
for his prominent role in the Second Congress of the Soviets and his
election as chairman of the presidium of the CEC in February 1934? As

[18] Yang Yüeh-pin, *The CCP History*, collected in Hatano, *Chūkyō-shi*, V, pp. 576–
577.

[19] A resolution drafted by Mao Tse-tung in December 1929 for the Ninth Conference of the Communist Party Organization of the Fourth Army of the Red Army.
This quotation is from Schram, *The Political Thought of Mao Tse-tung*, p. 199.

[20] Yang Yüen-pin, *CCP History*, collected in Hatano, *Chūkyō-shi*, V, p. 576.

indicated earlier, the structure of power and institutional arrangement in the Kiangsi soviet base was by no means cohesive and monolithic; it was rather diffuse, and was shared among the key members of the three elements of power. It was entirely plausible that Mao should gradually build up his power base, winning the support of such leaders as Liu Shao-ch'i, Wang Chia-hsiang, and Nieh Jung-chen in the government bureaucracy, along with some disillusioned members of the returned-student group — including Chang Wen-t'ien and Wu Liang-p'ing — in the Central Executive Council, the CRMC, and the People's Commission for National Economy. Between the spring and fall of 1933, Mao was actively engaged in the formulation of mobilization policies within the general framework of the central soviet government's policy, and gradually won over some of the powerful military leaders, notably Wang Chia-hsiang and Yang Shan-k'un, to support his policy of economic mobilization, leaving the strategic aspect of military policy to Chou En-lai and Otto Braun.

There is no exact means of identifying the positions of the key policy-makers, because the policy statements of the Kiangsi soviet government did not include the voting records of the policy-makers, if indeed they ever voted on policy decisions. Certain inferences, however, may be drawn from the published documents and policy statements of the top leaders, and some generalizations may be made about their policy perspectives. There were a dozen or so top leaders in the policy-making machinery of the Party, the government, and the military establishment. They were instrumental in formulating and implementing the policies, and they expressed their views in various official publications.[21] By examining the signed editorials, signed articles, and policy statements of various policy-makers, one can ascertain their positions. Among these policy-makers, Ch'in Pang-hsien, Chang Wen-t'ien, and Wang Chia-hsiang represented the views of the returned-student leaders, whereas Mao Tse-tung and Wu Liang-p'ing, respectively chairman of the central soviet government and deputy commissioner of national economy, represented the position of the government agencies. Chou En-lai, Hsiang Ying, and Yang Shan-k'un were spokesmen for the views held by the military and veteran leaders.

Among the policy-makers, Ch'in Pang-hsien, the Party's general secretary, and Chang Wen-t'ien, the Party's propaganda chief, were the most prolific writers; each produced more than two dozen articles on policy (probably many more if one could find the missing numbers of the party and government journals). Whereas Ch'in concentrated on

[21] Since more than fifty articles were signed and published by the key policy-makers I shall not even attempt to list all of them here. I shall cite only the specific articles that I consider relevant to the content of my discussion. To discover the policy positions of the policy-makers, I read, of course, many more articles than I mention here.

such theoretical issues as the strategy of revolutionary war, the method of using the issue of "antiimperialism," and the party's ideological stance, Chang Wen-t'ien devoted his writings to such procedural issues as the methods of collective leadership, the techniques of institution building, and the procedures of policy implementation. Mao Tse-tung, like Chang Wen-t'ien, wrote at least a hundred pieces, including the central soviet government's directives and policy proclamations with his signature. Mao continued to devote himself, as indicated earlier, to such matters as the procedural method of building organizations, operational techniques for the local-level organizations, and organizational techniques of mass mobilization. Wu Liang-p'ing, however, was more specifically concerned with the problems of economic reconstruction and the cooperative movement.

It is therefore interesting to note here that Chang Wen-t'ien agreed with Mao on a number of policy issues, such as the implementation of organizational techniques of mass line, the organizational principles of the soviet system of government, and the urgency of initiating economic reconstruction by putting the land-investigation movement and the cooperative movement into effect. As a staunch supporter of Mao's policy positions, Wu Liang-p'ing maintained a close functional link between the returned-student element and the leaders of the central soviet government; hence the policy was usually a compromise between the two conflicting viewpoints. In the spring of 1933 the policy-makers of the Chinese Communist movement reached an important decision — to divide the policy-making function of the central soviet government into two spheres, that of economic mobilization and that of military and strategic policy. The returned-student leaders were also divided into two functional groups: Ch'in Pang-hsien and Yang Shan-k'un were to devote themselves to the military aspect of policy-making under the direction of Chou En-lai, and Chang Wen-t'ien and Wang Chia-hsiang, using the principle of the division of labor, concentrated their work on the formulation of government and economic policies under Mao's leadership.

Faced with the problems posed by the KMT's massive military build-up and a severe economic blockade of the soviet areas, which caused a shortage of rice, other food grains, and salt, the policy-makers engaged in long and heated debates and deliberations. An analysis of the speeches and other statements of such key policy-makers as Mao Tse-tung, Chang Wen-t'ien, Ch'in Pang-hsien, Chou En-lai, and Wu Liang-p'ing indicates that two fundamental policy issues became the center of the deliberations [22] which created divisions within the re-

[22] The speeches and policy statements relevant to this discussion are:
(a) Mao Tse-tung, "Fen sui wu-tz'u wei-chiao yü Su-wei ai ching-chi chien-she jen-wu" ("The Annihilation of the Fifth Encirclement Campaign and the Task of

turned-student group as well as at the level of the policy-making machinery. The split among the policy-makers in the Kiangsi soviet base was caused by disagreement concerning two important issues. Whether "economic appeal" or the use of "antiimperialism" as a rallying cry should be adopted as the tactic of their war effort had become the central issue of the entire debate. However, every individual serving in the policy-making organ seemed to agree on one fundamental issue, the necessity of total mobilization of all societal resources in order to win victory in the revolution. Some people, however, disagreed on the organizational techniques by which this total mobilization was to be carried out both in the soviet base areas and in the nonsoviet areas.

Those who favored the policy of total mobilization by means of economic construction in the soviet areas argued that the most essential aspect of war mobilization is to improve the economic welfare and living conditions of the workers and peasants. "The soviet government must legislate and implement the labor-protection law in order to prevent capitalist exploitation," Chang Wen-t'ien insisted, "and improve the living conditions of the working class in order to arouse their

Soviet Economic Construction"), *HSCH*, No. 102, August 16, 1933, *SSCM*, Reel 17; "Ch'a-t'ien yün-tung shih kuang-ta ch'ü-yü nei ti chung-hsin chung-ta jen-wu" ("The Land Investigation Movement is the Central and Most Important Task in Vast Areas"), *HSCH*, No. 86 (June 17, 1933), *SSCM*, Reel No. 17; "Mu-chien shih-chü yü hung-chün k'ang-jih hsien-ch'ien tui" ("The Current Situation and the Red Army's Anti-Japanese Vanguards"), *HSCH*, No. 221 (August 1, 1934), *SSCM*, Reel No. 17.

(b) Chang Wen-t'ien, "The Prospects for Economic Development in the Soviet Area," *Tou-cheng*, No. 11 (August 14, 1933, collected in Hatano, *Chūkyō shi*, III, 601–609; "The Work of the Soviet Government," a report given at the Fifth Plenum of the CCP's Central Committee in January 1934, *Tou-cheng*, No. 47 (February 16, 1934), *SSCM*, Reel No. 18.

(c) Wu Liang-p'ing, "The Preliminary Summary of Economic Construction in the Soviet Area" (November 1933), in Hatano, *Chūkyō shi*, III, 585–601; "Let's Oppose Right Opportunism" in Hatano, IV, 814–824; "Mu-ch'ien Su-ch'ü ti hsien-chin wen-t'i" ("The Current Cash Problem in the Soviet Area"), *Tou-cheng*, No. 20 (August 5, 1933); "Political Report on the Soviet Work," *HSCH* (January 1, 1934), *SSCM* Reel 17; "Mu-ch'ien Su-wei-ai ho-tso yün-tung ti chuang-k'uang yü wo-men ti jen-wu" ("Current Conditions of the Soviet Cooperative Movement and Our Task"), *Tou-cheng*, No. 56 (April 21, 1934), *SSCM*, Reel No. 18.

(d) Chou En-lai, "Fen-shui ti-jen wu-tz'u wei-chiao chung chung-yang hung-chün ti chin-chi jen-wu" ("The Urgent Tasks of the Central Red Army in Destroying the Fifth Encirclement Campaign"), *Tou-cheng*, No. 24 (August 29, 1933), *SSCM*, Reel No. 18.

(e) Po Ku, "Wei fen-sui ti-jen ti wu-tz'u wei-chiao yü cheng-ch'ü tu-li tzu-yu ti Su-wei-ai Chung-kuo erh tou-cheng" ("Struggle to Destroy the Enemy's Fifth Encirclement Campaign and to Maintain the Independence and Liberty of Soviet China"), a speech originally delivered at the conference of high-level Party cadres on July 24, 1933, was later published in *HSCH*, No. 99 (August 4, 1933), *SSCM*, Reel No. 17; "Wo ti wei-chih tsai na pien, tsai ch'ien-hsien shang, chan tsai chan-shien ti tsui ch'ien-mien!" ("My Position is Over There, on the Front, Standing in the Fore-front of the Battle Line!"), *HSCH*, No. 189 (May 16, 1934), *SSCM*, Reel No. 17.

consciousness and spirit of unity, as well as to persuade the workers that
they themselves ought to participate in the management of their own
government." [23] The gist of this argument was that the peasant masses
would not respond solely to a patriotic slogan such as "antiimperialism"
unless their economic condition was improved.

The convening of an economic conference of seventeen *hsien* in
southern Kiangsi as well as a similar conference in northeast Kiangsi,
at which Mao Tse-tung, Chang Wen-t'ien, and Wu Liang-p'ing were
key participants, was a clear indication that those who were pushing
for the policy of economic appeal were winning over those who argued
for the formulation of a policy based on the "antiimperialism" issue.
"We must develop the economic-construction movement positively,"
Mao asserted, "and make the task of economic construction one of the
most essential conditions for the defeat of the fifth encirclement campaign." From Mao's point of view, the "violent development of the
revolutionary war required the soviet government to mobilize the
broad masses, to begin the mobilization campaign on the economic
front immediately, and to proceed with various aspects of economic
construction." [24]

It is therefore quite understandable that Mao's policy position of
economic mobilization should have been vigorously supported by
Chang Wen-t'ien, Wang Chia-hsiang, and other members of the returned-student group who were allied with such supporters of the
student leaders as Wu Liang-p'ing and Kao Tzu-li. They supported
Mao's policy of economic mobilization and also participated in specific
programs of the land-investigation movement, the election campaign
for the Second Soviet Congress, and the cooperative movement in
order to implement the policy of economic mobilization. However,
Mao's policy of economic mobilization for the war and revolution
encountered strong opposition from so-called "leftist comrades" within
the policy-making circles, who attacked Mao and his policy line as
being too "rightist"-oriented.

Mao himself asserted that "some comrades in the past [at the time
of policy making] argued that we simply don't have time, that we are
too busy with the revolutionary war to carry out the work of economic
construction. Therefore, those who assert the policy of economic construction are the rightists." They continued to insist that "during the
period of the revolutionary war it will be impossible to construct the
economy. Economic construction must be initiated only after we
achieve victory in the war, and therefore the implementation of the
programs of economic construction can only be carried out in an en-

[23] Chang Wen-t'ien, "Prospects for Economic Development in the Soviet Area."
[24] Mao Tse-tung, "The Annihilation of the Fifth Encirclement Campaign and the
Task of Soviet Economic Construction," HSCH, No. 102 (August 16, 1933).

vironment where peace and quietness prevail. It is not even the time to begin the discussion of the policy of economic construction." Countering such an argument, Mao charged that "It is a totally mistaken viewpoint that the soviet government should not proceed on programs of economic construction. . . . Those who take such a viewpoint always insist that we should be obedient to the requirements of war. To abandon economic construction is not actually to obey the demands of war. In order to meet the needs of the war we must actually proceed with the implementation of economic construction." [25] Mao was beginning to gain support from some of the returned students, and Chang Wen-t'ien and Wang Chia-hsiang were more in agreement with his policy position than they were with that of the key leaders of the returned students.

Even Pavel Mif, the former Comintern representative to China and the mentor of the returned-student leaders, approved and supported the policies that Mao was carrying out in the Kiangsi soviet base. As late as June 1934, Mif contributed an article to the *Communist International*, a fortnightly journal of the ECCI, in which he stressed that "although the [Chinese] Soviet government has for five years been engaged in a continuous war against the Kuomintang militarists, it cannot at the same time ignore the problems of improving the economic construction." [26] Citing Mao's political report to the Economic Construction Conference, Pavel Mif seems to have swung his support to Mao's policy as opposed to the returned-student leadership, headed by Ch'in Pang-hsien at that time.

Those who were pressing the issue of "antiimperialism" as an appeal for mass mobilization, on the other hand, insisted that the Party and the central soviet government must extend the war effort to the non-soviet areas, i.e., the areas under KMT rule, in order to mobilize the support of more people in overthrowing the imperialist power and its agent, the KMT. From their point of view, the issue of "antiimperialism" should be fully utilized as an appeal to the masses, and the policy of a united front should be implemented from below through various mass organizations. These organizations should be directed to conduct the strike campaigns and the resistance movement in order to weaken the KMT's power and in this way lessen the military and economic pressures of the KMT upon the soviet base areas. As they analyzed the objective conditions, a much better situation was created for the use of an "antiimperialism" appeal when the Japanese imperialists stirred up the Manchurian crisis and the Japanese army attacked Shanghai on February 18, 1932. Therefore, they asked, why

[25] *Ibid.*
[26] Pavel Mif, "Only the Soviets Can Save China," *The Communist International*, No. 11 (June 5, 1934), p. 373.

should it be necessary to initiate the economic-construction program in the soviet base? They were thus arguing for the adoption of a policy based on the concept of all-out war for final victory.

The policy-making elites who pressed for complete military victory were later labeled as "leftist" deviationists because they perceived that the situation in China had already reached the stage of revolutionary high tide. Thus they contended that the tide of "antiimperialism" in the period of 1931–1933 was even stronger and higher than that of the 1925–1927 period, and that the Party therefore ought to create a nationwide "antiimperialist" camp for a decisive victory over the KMT. Ch'in Pang-hsien, Chou En-lai, Hsiang Ying, and some members of the Party's military-affairs committee, which was under the direction of Chou En-lai, had taken this position during the policy debate.

Heated debates and discussions must have gone on for a considerable time before a final decision on the policy was reached. We have no way of knowing whether any vote was taken, but the policy outcome of these debates clearly indicates that the solution to the unresolved problems of "economic construction" and all-out effort to achieve the victory over the KMT's fifth encirclement campaign was a compromise. Judging from the rather long speech Ch'in Pang-hsien (Po Ku) delivered to the high-level Party cadres on the question of the "fifth encirclement campaign and the struggle for the victory of the Chinese soviet," the policy outcome was clearly an incorporation of both the issue of antiimperialism and the issue of economic construction.[27] However, Po Ku continued to place greater emphasis on the military aspect of the policy in his speech, thus leaving himself vulnerable to Mao's charge that he was nothing but a "leftist."

Mao's Leadership and the Returned Students

The formulation of new policies and the revision of old ones during the Kiangsi soviet period were thus neither dramatic nor sudden. They were rather the outcome of a series of steps in which a number of modifications in existing policy were made, and it was inevitable that the leadership of the returned-student group should pursue a zigzag course. Mao's perspectives and attitudes toward the development of the CCP's agrarian policy may serve here as an interesting case study of how his policy views and positions vacillated from the radically oriented "leftist" position of his days in the Chingkang mountain regions to a more moderate "right" position in the Kiangsi soviet base area. His behavior

[27] Po Ku, "Struggle to Destroy the Enemy's Fifth Encirclement Campaign and to Maintain the Independence and Liberty of Soviet China," *HSCH*, No. 99 (August 4, 1933).

can be explained in terms of his own policy zigzags. Mao was in neither a "radical" faction nor an "ultra moderate" group, if we assess his views and positions in relation to the formulation of the CCP's agrarian programs, but he had frequently shifted his ideological ground. Mao's agrarian policy, therefore, like all other economic and social policies of the Kiangsi soviet period, was somewhat inconsistent, and his policy position wavered between "left" and "right" during the period 1928–1934. Being a pragmatic politician, Mao frequently shifted from "left" to "right" and vice versa in order to cope with the needs and demands of the peasant masses, and also to react quickly to local circumstances.

What then are the "left" and "right" positions in the development of the agrarian policy in the Chinese Communist movement? It is necessary from the outset to establish a generally accepted definition of what we mean by "left" and "right" in our analysis of Mao's policy orientations. Such vague terms as "left" and "right" opportunists or "left" and "right" deviationists were commonly used in the annals of the Chinese Communist Party, and the creation of such labels depended on who held power and how they evaluated the preceding policy position. The leadership of Ch'ü Ch'iu-pai, who succeeded Ch'en at the August 7 (1927) Emergency Conference, was stigmatized as being "left" adventurist when its policy of military insurrection failed in 1927. Li Li-san, who actually controlled the policy-making machinery from 1928 to 1930, was again condemned as a "left" deviationist simply because he was alleged to have failed to execute the policy line laid down at the Sixth Party Congress of 1928. From Mao's point of view the leadership of the returned-student group that was in charge of the CCP from 1931 to 1934 was "the third leftist" line because it failed to execute the Party's orthodox line laid down at the Fourth Plenum of the CCP in January 1931.

The "left" and the "right" deviations in agrarian policies, however, had been centered on the question of whether the rich peasant class of the rural population was to be allied with or alienated from the process of executing the programs of the agrarian revolution. In formulating and implementing their agrarian policy in the late 1920s and early 1930s the Chinese Communist leaders commonly used the term "left deviationist" when and if the land policy was intended solely to emphasize the role of the farm laborers and poor peasants, like the industrial proletariat in urban areas, and deemphasized the role of the rich peasants and the "well-to-do middle peasants," even alienating them while pursuing the programs of land confiscation and distribution. For example, Mao's views on agrarian policy in the Chingkang mountain regions have been considered radical and hence "leftist" in contrast to the moderate policy line of the CCP's central leadership, because he carried out certain radical measures and was, moreover, opposed to the lenient rich-peasant policy adopted by the Party's Sixth Congress in 1928.[28]

Therefore, Mao's shifting policy of "left" or "right" in the Kiangsi soviet base must be analyzed and evaluated in terms of his attitudes toward the two policy issues of the Kiangsi political system: a more ideologically oriented issue of "class struggle" which tended to alienate the rich peasants, and a more pragmatically oriented issue of "mass line" which emphasized alliance with the middle peasants and even occasionally the rich peasants in the course of carrying out the Chinese revolution in general and the agrarian revolution in particular. In establishing the substantive issue of "class line" and also translating it into practical programs such as classification and differentiation of the peasant classes, the Chinese Communist leaders were never consistent. As a result, they encountered enormous problems, especially when they had to distinguish between the "rich peasants" and the "well-to-do middle peasants," as well as the "middle peasants" in the rural population, and when they attempted to establish guidelines for deciding which of these three groups was to be considered an ally and which was to be attacked in order to carry out successfully the agrarian revolution. In the course of their disputes, the Chinese Communist leaders often aligned themselves in two factional groups: whereas the "moderate" to "right" faction stressed the policy issue of "mass line," the radically oriented "leftist" faction argued for a strong emphasis on the issue of "class struggle." Mao was strongly oriented toward the issue of "mass line," though even he vacillated between it and the issue of "class line"; but Mao was more inclined to take the "mass line" approach because of his practical experience in organizing the peasant masses, whereas some of the returned-student leaders such as Ch'in Pang-hsien took the "class line" approach because of their theoretical education and ideological training in orthodox Marxism in the Soviet Union. When his techniques of "mass line" were further conceptualized and triumphed in the Yenan period, Mao labeled the leadership of the returned-student group as "third leftist deviationist."

To analyze Mao's views on the development of agrarian policy and his attitudes toward it, one must go back to the early days of his agrarian policy in the Chingkang mountains. There has been much controversy over the question whether Mao carried out a radical and "leftist" agrarian policy in the Chingkang mountain region. This controversy was caused by the ambiguity of the agrarian programs adopted by the CCP's Sixth Congress in Moscow in July 1928. In addition to a section of the political resolution on the peasant movement, the Sixth

[28] Rue, *Mao Tse-tung in Opposition, 1927–1935*, p. 110. See also Shanti Swarup, *A Study of the Chinese Communist Movement, 1927–1934*, p. 123.

Congress passed two important resolutions specifically dealing with agrarian problems — one on the peasant movement and the other on land problems.[29] These resolutions offered a long and detailed analysis of agrarian problems and the importance of their solution to the Chinese revolution. However, in accordance with the policy pattern adopted by the November 1927 Plenum, these resolutions stressed that, as the cities were to be the revolutionary centers, the CCP organizations were to direct their revolutionary efforts in the urban centers. On the same basis, Li Li-san had also carried out his insurrectionary activity in the cities. The political resolution emphasized the establishment of a "Democratic Dictatorship of Workers and Peasants under the leadership of the working class," and these phrases seem to have meant, in the view of Benjamin Schwartz, "that only the proletariat is to be allowed a separate political voice within the alliance of peasantry and proletariat. . . . No political groups claiming to represent the peasantry are to be allowed any voice in the new soviet government.[30] Even the resolution on the peasant movement continued to stress the proletariat's leadership, hence it was envisaged that the working class, especially the industrial proletariat, was to take ideological and organizational leadership in the peasant movement.

In the resolutions adopted by the Sixth CCP Congress, a certain ambiguity also existed in regard to rich peasants — a subject which later became the focus of an academic debate among the China scholars. The Chinese Communist leaders at the Congress having perceived that the revolutionary struggle at this particular juncture was that between the poor and middle peasants, on the one hand, and the big, middle, and small landlords, on the other, they failed to discuss and define the precise role of the rich peasants in the Chinese revolution. The resolution on the peasant movement and land problems simply concluded that the basic revolutionary forces were the poor and middle peasants and the aim of the agrarian revolution was to eliminate the landlord class. As a result, the substantive issue of the role of the rich peasants as well as that of the well-to-do middle peasants had not been dealt with. This was a striking example of the ambiguity manifested in the resolution adopted by the Sixth CCP Congress, the proceedings of which were under the direct influence of the Comintern in Moscow. The basic policy line of the agrarian revolution reached by the Sixth CCP Congress, therefore, was to carry out the struggle between the two elements: the poor and middle peasant class, on the one hand, and the landlord class, including the big, middle, and small landlords, on the other.

[29] The original text of these documents may be found in *Kuo-chi lu-hsien (International Line)*, published by the CCP Bureau of the Soviet Area in 1932. *SSCM*, Reel 4.
[30] Schwartz, *Chinese Communism*, p. 66.

It must be noted, however, that the political resolution contained a special warning that "it is wrong to step up the struggle against the *rich peasants* intensely, because that would confuse the major conflict between the peasants and the landlord class." [31] At the same time, the radical faction at the Congress was pushing for the adoption of an anti-rich-peasant policy, and the resolution also warned that "this [resolution not to intensify the struggle against the rich peasants], however, does not mean that the class struggle against the rich peasants and the semilandlords is to be abandoned." [32] Consequently, the issue of rich peasants became extremely ambiguous, at best. The resolution stressed, furthermore, that an alliance with the rich peasants was necessary and important in the struggle against the reactionary forces; yet it was also necessary to fight against all exploiters. The rich peasants were therefore classified into two types: the exploitative and the nonexploitative. The exploitative rich peasants were to be strongly opposed and eliminated, as Mao was doing in the Chingkang mountains, but the nonexploitative rich peasants were to be considered allies.

Although the principle of shifting the revolutionary center from the villages to the urban areas had already been confirmed by the Enlarged Politburo Meeting of November 1927, the implementation of that principle did not occur until Li Li-san took full control of the Party's machinery at the Second Plenum of the CCP Central Committee in Shanghai in June 1929. One of the main features of Li Li-san's agrarian policy between 1928 and 1930 was the idea that the villages must serve the cities, which was also the basic position of the Comintern at that time. In a personal letter to Mao in early 1929, Li Li-san expressed his fear that the development of the peasants' power in the Party might threaten the leadership of the workers and thus become detrimental to the revolution.[33] Li Li-san was quite convinced that the agrarian revolution could never be successful until the victory of the general political revolution had been achieved. Inasmuch as the victory of the general political revolution had to be brought about by a total national armed uprising of workers and peasants, Li called on the leaders of the peasant movement to direct their efforts first of all toward assuring the victory of the political revolution in the urban centers. The formulation of Li Li-san's policy of urban insurrection was thus by no means a sudden and dramatic decision on his part, but rather the result of a gradual process of modification of existing policies which the CCP had developed between the Enlarged Politburo Meeting of November 1927 and the Second Plenum of the CCP in June 1929.

[31] Brandt, et al., *A Documentary History*, p. 150.
[32] *Ibid.*
[33] Mao, *SW*, I, 121–122.

Although Mao himself asserted to Edgar Snow that he was in full agreement with the agrarian policy adopted by the Sixth Congress and that "the differences between the leaders of the Party and the leaders of the Soviet movement in the agrarian districts have disappeared," [34] the policies he developed at his soviet base in the Chingkang mountain region were quite confusing and inconsistent. The ambiguous resolutions adopted by the Sixth Congress, coupled with the policy shift of the Comintern, especially toward the rich peasants, caused many problems in Mao's agrarian policy. The Sixth Congress, under the direct supervision of the Comintern, had already adopted a dual policy of alliance with the nonexploitative rich peasants and elimination of the exploitative ones, and Li Li-san faithfully executed this Comintern line. Nevertheless, Li was later accused of having incorrectly interpreted the same Comintern policy by practicing the rich-peasant line. Why did Li have to be condemned for his pro-rich-peasant policy even though he had carried out the Comintern line faithfully?

A year after the conclusion of the Sixth Congress of the CCP, the Comintern authority mysteriously reversed its earlier policy of leniency toward the rich peasants and proclaimed that the revolutionary situation in China had entered an advanced stage in which the class struggle had to be intensified not only against the landlord and gentry class, but against the rich peasants as well. Because of the suddenness of this move, the CCP under the leadership of Li Li-san failed to respond to the Comintern's policy shift, with the result that the Comintern later criticized the CCP's "rightist" attitudes toward the rich peasants in "Letter from the ECCI to the CC of the CCP on the Peasant Question." [35] On the basis of this Comintern letter, Hsiao Tso-liang argued in his study of documents, *The Land Revolution in China, 1930–1934*, that Mao was actually following the Comintern line more faithfully than was Li Li-san. The implication of this argument is, of course, that the policy Mao was pursuing in the Kiangsi soviet base had already been laid down by the Comintern authority.[36]

An analysis of both the Comintern letter and the actual implementation of Mao's anti-rich-peasant policy, which had already been initiated before the arrival of the Comintern letter, provides an entirely different picture of Mao's agrarian policy. The Comintern letter, dated June 1929, criticized the CCP for its emphasis on the importance of a correct analysis of the different classes in the villages, and pointed out that the Chinese Communists had made serious mistakes

---

[34] Snow, *Red Star*, p. 171.

[35] For the Chinese text of this letter, see *Kuo-chi lu-hsien*, pp. 44–57, collected in SSCM, Reel 14. See also Rue, *Mao in Opposition*, p. 156.

[36] Tso-liang Hsiao, *The Land Revolution in China, 1930-1934* (Seattle, University of Washington Press, 1969), p. 37.

concerning the rich peasants. The Comintern argued that Lenin had never proposed an alliance with the rich peasants. They therefore charged that the Chinese Communists were "mechanically taking over the Leninist formulation of the attitude of the working class to the peasantry in the bourgeois-democratic stage of the revolution" and were thus making an opportunistic interpretation of Lenin's formula.[37] What the Comintern was actually saying was that although Lenin had proposed an alliance between the working class and the peasantry, the peasantry should not by any means be considered just one class. The Comintern letter argued, therefore, that the alliance with the rich peasants was wrong, the revolutionary movement in China having already passed from one stage to another, in which the rich peasants had turned against the revolution because they perceived that it had been defeated.

The shift in Comintern policy with regard to the rich peasants, however, was not necessarily based on changes in the objective conditions of the Chinese revolution, but was rather determined by changes in Stalin's attitudes toward the Russian *kulaks* (rich peasants). When the Sixth Congress of the CCP was held in Moscow in 1928, Stalin's domestic policies were severely challenged by his leftist opposition. Under such circumstances Stalin had to ally himself with Bukharin and other rightists, who advocated, on the basis of Lenin's concept of the bourgeois-democratic stage of the revolution, that the Chinese Communist leaders try "dual tactics" of an alliance with the bourgeois class, of which the rich peasants formed a major part, since China was still in the stage of bourgeois-democratic revolution. The CCP leadership under Li Li-san therefore pursued the dual tactics of carrying out the revolution in the urban centers as well as in the rural area, where they allied themselves with the rich-peasant class. By June 1929, however, the challenge of the left opposition had been defeated, and Stalin was beginning to turn against his former allies, the rightist group. To justify such tactics, the Comintern authority had to end the alliance with the rich peasants as well.[38]

At any rate, the zigzag line of the Comintern policy, together with the highly ambiguous resolutions adopted by the CCP's Sixth Congress, could hardly help Mao to determine which policy he ought to follow. Moreover, he never believed that the CCP leadership or the Comintern authority could correctly understand and analyze the peasant problems of China better than he did himself. Mao had already shifted on

[37] J. Degras, *The Comintern Documents*, pp. 33–34.

[38] For a detailed analysis of this aspect of the Comintern's policy shift, see Richard C. Thornton, *The Comintern and the Chinese Communists, 1928–1931* (Seattle, University of Washington Press, 1969), pp. 3–29.

his own initiative from a rich-peasant policy to an anti-rich-peasant policy even before the arrival of the Comintern directive. An important document supports this hypothesis. A resolution on "The Rich Peasant Problem" adopted by a Joint Meeting of the Front Committee and Western Fukien (*Min-hsi*) Special Committee, printed and distributed by the Mao-controlled machinery of the general political department of the First Front Army, clearly indicates that Mao had already begun to shift his policy position with regard to the rich peasants.[39]

This resolution, as Hsiao Tso-liang pointed out, naturally contained such important features of Mao's previous agrarian policy as the use of a criterion of per capita, instead of working ability, in determining land distribution, and the principle of "draw on the plentiful to make up for the scarce, draw on the fat to make up for the lean."[40] It might be concluded, therefore, that Mao was faithfully following the Comintern directive of dual tactics. Yet one must also analyze the other aspect of this resolution. For the first time, this resolution made the well-to-do middle peasants the target of attack: all of their land was to be confiscated and all of their credit was to be canceled because, like the rich peasants, they were now perceived to have collected excessive interest on loans and made profits from the sale of farm products. Why, then, did Mao shift his policy position from a pro- to an anti-rich-peasant line? To answer this question Hsiao Tso-liang argues quite unconvincingly that it was a direct result of the Comintern directive of June 7, 1929. Yet if the Comintern directive had any impact on Mao's shift in agrarian policy, it should also have affected the formulation of Mao's 1930 land law, which was adopted six months after the receipt of the Comintern directive. Moreover, by the spring of 1930 Mao reverted to his earlier position of leniency toward the rich peasants. Why, then, did he have such a harsh attitude toward the rich peasants between June 1929 and February 1930?

One plausible explanation of the reason for the change in Mao's policy position at that particular time may lie in the ambiguity and inconsistencies of the policy line adopted by the Sixth CCP Congress, as well as in Mao's direct response to the course of current political events in China. As mentioned earlier, the confusing agrarian program adopted by the Sixth Congress was misinterpreted by Li Li-san and other leaders of the CCP. Furthermore, the KMT forces in Kwangtung, Fukien, and Kiangsi provinces announced publicly that they were preparing themselves for an extermination campaign against the Com-

[39] The original Chinese text of this resolution is available in *SSCM*, Reel 17. The English translation may be found in Hsiao, *The Land Revolution*, pp. 152–170.

[40] Hsiao, *The Land Revolution*, pp. 34–35.

munists and would soon launch a military attack on the soviet base. Faced with such a threat from a formidable enemy, Mao seems to have perceived that the rich peasants would inevitably turn against the revolution and defect to the enemy. He felt, too, that in order to win the loyalty and support of the majority of the intermediate class, including the middle peasants, he had to meet the needs and aspirations of the poor and middle peasants, who demanded the confiscation of all land and the cancellation of all debts. In these circumstances, Mao developed a harsh attitude toward the rich peasants and was even willing to sacrifice their interests to the larger interests of the poor and landless peasantry. The same perception and attitude of Mao also influenced the policy formulation of the CCP leaders in 1933 when they were debating how to cope with the KMT's forthcoming fifth encirclement campaign. However, his policy shift toward the anti-rich-peasant line was by no means a dramatic one; it was a gradual process, because the confiscation of all land, including that of the rich peasants, and the cancellation of all debts, including those owed to the rich peasants, had been incorporated into his new land law when it was adopted in early 1930.

Mao always favored a per capita criterion, rather than working ability, to determine the amount of land to be distributed. The adoption of the per capita criterion for redistribution of land was based on Mao's conviction that an agrarian program must satisfy the needs of the great majority of the peasant population if it was ever to be successful in winning the support of the masses. Thus Mao's pragmatic approach to his agrarian policy based on his concept of mass line was reflected in the new land law adopted on February 7, 1930, and promulgated by the Chinese Revolutionary Military Council.[41] According to the principle of per capita distribution, almost everyone was entitled to receive land, including the dependents of village bosses, the gentry, and even reactionaries if they had no other means of support (article II). Because of this moderation, Mao was later criticized as having followed a pro-rich-peasant policy. The principle of "draw on the plentiful to make up for the scarce, draw on the fat to make up for the lean" was a new and distinctive feature of the law and certainly reflected Mao's own ideas which had originally been introduced at the conference of February 7, 1930.

From Mao's own point of view, therefore, these principles were not necessarily characteristic of a pro-rich-peasant policy. They were rather the best practical measures available to him to win the support of the

[41] The original Chinese text may be found in *Chih-fei fan-tung wen-chien hui-pien* (*A Collection of Red Bandit Documents*), vol. 5, *Land Problems*; SSCM, Reel 20. See also Wang, *Chung-kung shih-kao*, II, 356; and Hsiao, *The Land Revolution*, p. 17.

majority of the peasant population, including the middle and rich peasants. Mao always held the conviction that the choice between alliance with them or alienation from them might determine the outcome of the revolution. He would rather ally himself with the rich and middle peasants and win the revolution than lose it by alienating them. The Communists should do everything possible, Mao believed, to win over the middle and rich peasant classes in order to consolidate the victory of the Chinese revolution. Thus Mao's land policy or agrarian program was more a reflection of the reality of actual practice in the rural hinterland than the mechanical application of an abstract theory or complicated ideology.

An explanation is in order as to why the Chinese Soviet Republic adopted a more radical land law in November 1931. There has been some controversy over the question of whether the land law was directly influenced by the Comintern's anti-rich-peasant policy. To answer this question one must analyze the process by which the land law of the Chinese Soviet Republic was formulated and adopted. If one scrutinizes the steps by which the CCP leadership revised the radical Draft Law outlined by the CCP Central Committee in March 1931 and brought out as the Land Law of the Republic in November 1931, one cannot help concluding that that program was the outcome of a compromise between two conflicting perspectives: the concept of "class line" reflected in the argument of the returned student group and Mao's concept of "mass line" based on his practical approach to the solution of agrarian problems. Because of Mao's special concern with protecting the interests of the middle and nonexploitative rich peasants, the provisions in the new law to protect the interests of the middle peasants, including the rich peasants, were reflections of Mao's moderate policy positions. On the other hand, such distinctive features as other discriminatory measures against the rich peasants reflected the returned students' class-line approach. Consequently, the dual characteristics of the agrarian program were stipulated in the new law. For example, middle peasants, poor peasants, and farm laborers had the advantage of using the number of persons (i.e., the per capita criterion) as the only criterion for receiving the redistributed land, which meant that they were entitled to receive a full share of land regardless of their working ability. This was, of course, Mao's original idea and had even been applied to the rich peasants at one time. But under the new law, working ability was the main criterion for the rich peasants, and the number of persons was the supplementary one, which meant that they were entitled to full shares of land if they had the required working ability, but otherwise were entitled only to half shares. Another example of compromise was that the definition of rich-peasants' property

subject to confiscation was enlarged to include not only farm implements and livestock but also houses, water mills, and oil-pressing
mills. In this way the distinctive features outlined in the letter of the
ECCI Presidium sent to the CCP in July 1931 [42] and the practice of
Mao's moderate approach to the rich peasants were carefully and unmistakably compromised and juxtaposed in the adoption of the new
Land Law of November 1931.

The returned-student leaders were faced with pressure from three
different directions from the Comintern to correct the rest of Li Li-san's
tactical mistakes; from Hsiang Chung-fa, Chang Kuo-t'ao, and other
veteran leaders who continued to wield considerable power within the
CCP's policy-making machinery; and from such leaders of the soviet
base as Mao Tse-tung and Chu Te. Consequently, it was inevitable
that the returned-student leaders should zigzag in their formulation of
new agrarian policy between the Comintern's "class-line" and Mao's
"mass-line" approach. In view of these facts, if we compare the draft
law of March 1931 and the land law of November 1931 we find some
modifications.

Under the new law, the category of people entitled to receive land
was expanded somewhat to include independent laborers who were not
entitled to it under the draft law. The final version also extended more
protection to the middle peasants than did the draft law, The middle
peasants, for example, did not need to participate in land redistribution if the majority of them did not wish to do so (article V). These
modifications were, of course, closely connected with Mao's practice in
the Kiangsi base, and because of his special concern for the interests of
the middle peasants the returned students accepted Mao's proposals
to modify the original draft. Contrary to Rue's argument that the
land law of the Soviet Republic reflected Mao's lenient rich-peasant
policy,[43] the new law contained harsher and more discriminatory
measures against the rich peasants than had the draft law, so Mao's
policy of favoring the rich peasants was not incorporated into the new
measure. The new leadership of the returned students attempted, in
the formulation of a new agrarian policy, to reach a compromise solution to the peasant problems rather than attacking Mao's practice in
the base areas of the Kiangsi soviet.

Although the confiscation and redistribution of land were essential
features of the agrarian policy, there emerged no systematic and uni-

[42] The Chinese text of the letter of the Presidium of the ECCI may be found in
Hung-se wen-hsien (Red Documents) (Chieh-fang chu'-pan-she, 1938), pp. 376–404,
SSCM, Reel 15. The English translation, entitled "Resolution of the ECCI Presidium
on the Tasks of the Chinese Communist Party," issued on August 26, 1931, may be
found in Jane Degras, *The Comintern Documents*, III, 167–176.

[43] Rue, *Mao in Opposition*, pp. 249–250.

form pattern of classification and redistribution of land during the period between November 1931, when the Republic was established, and June 1933, when Mao wrote and published the most comprehensive and systematic guidelines on "How to Analyze the Classes" and "Decisions Concerning Some Problems Arising from the Agrarian Struggle." [44] Therefore, it is evident that the actual processes of implementing the agrarian policies varied from region to region, and a great deal of flexibility existed in the soviet area. As mentioned in chapter 2, administrative practices varied greatly from the southwest Kiangsi soviet to the northeast Kiangsi soviet. Such flexibility permitted administrators in certain regions to follow the same old policy of favoring the rich peasants, while the administrators of other regions were allowed to use much harsher measures in dealing with them. Thus the stepped-up campaign of the "anti-rich-peasant struggle" in 1932 was still in line with what Mao had developed earlier in the 1930 land law, although the campaign was gradually moving toward a more radically oriented policy of "class line."

From Mao's viewpoint the agrarian revolution in China involved three important steps: land confiscation and distribution, land investigation, and land reconstruction. [45] These three steps, however, were not necessarily taken in this sequence. In some soviet areas, the three stages had occurred simultaneously; in others, a combination of them had been carried out. [46] The process of implementing agrarian policy varied from region to region, and there was no uniform pattern in the execution of agrarian programs in the Kiangsi soviet from 1931 to 1933. Therefore, in 1933, the central soviet government under the leadership of Mao decided to launch two important political campaigns in preparation for the convocation of the Second Soviet Congress: the land-investigation movement, which was carried out from June to

[44] Mao Tse-tung, "Tsen-yang fen-hsi chieh-chi" ("How to Analyze the Classes"), *HSCH*, No. 89 (June 29, 1933), *SSCM*, Reel 17. A revised version dated October 1933 is in Mao, *SW*, I, 137–139, under the title "How to Differentiate the Classes in the Rural Areas." This document was originally adopted by the Eight-hsien Conference on the Land Investigation Movement on June 17–21, 1933, and was proclaimed by the Central Soviet Government on October 10, 1933.

"Kuan-yü t'u-ti tou-cheng chung i-hsieh wen-t'i ti chüeh-ting" ("Decisions Concerning Some Problems Arising from the Agrarian Struggle"), published by the People's Commissariats of the Central Soviet Government on October 10, 1933. Collected in *Chih-fei fan-tung wen-chien hui-pien*, III, 989–1010, *SSCM*, Reel 17. The English translation may be found in Hsiao, *The Land Revolution*, pp. 257–282.

[45] Mao Tse-tung, "Ch'a-t'ien yün-tung shih kuang-ta ch'ü-yu ti chung-hsin chung-ta jen-wu" ("The Land Investigation Movement is the Central Task of Great Magnitude in Vast Areas"), *HSCH*, No. 86 (June 17, 1933).

[46] Mao Tse-tung, "I-chu nung-ts'un chung chieh-chi tou-cheng ti fa-chuang-t'ai ti ch'a-pieh ch'ü k'ai-chan ch'a-t'ien yün-tung" ("Open the Land Investigation Drive According to the Disparity of the Conditions of the Development of the Class Struggle in the Rural Districts"), *HSCH*, No. 866 (June 23, 1933).

August 1933, and the reapportionment of the administrative districts to conduct the general election for the soviets at each level, from September to November 1933.

The sphere of military policy-making was under the direction of the Central Revolutionary Military Commission after May 1933, but Mao had taken full responsibility for formulating policies and directing programs in the sphere of economic reconstruction. Mao consequently still had power, however limited, and was able to influence policy-making in the central soviet government. Between June and October 1933 he was beginning to win over certain key leaders of the returned student group, including Chang Wen-t'ien and Wang Chia-hsiang, and finally lined up their support behind his policy positions. Three important political campaigns — the land-investigation movement, the economic-reconstruction movement, and the mobilization campaigns of economic resources, all of which were launched in the latter part of 1933 and in all of which Mao took an important role — seem to suggest that Mao had not been completely ousted from his leadership position, at least in the sphere of government policy. He was still in control of the government bureaucracy, and the returned-student leadership could not oust him completely, if they ever tried. Therefore, Mao's role in such campaigns must be analyzed in terms of his expressed policy position.

Various political campaigns and movements (yün-tung) in the latter part of 1933 must also be analyzed and understood in the general context of the political and social forces that existed in China at that time. Although a power struggle and various policy disputes reportedly went on between Mao and his supporters on the one hand and the so-called returned-student group on the other, during the period immediately following the completion of the move of the CCP Central Committee from Shanghai to Juichin in early 1933, the Kiangsi political system did not in any way break down, because the CCP leaders of both factions had to take into account the simple fact that their survival, in the face of the strong offensive by the KMT Army, was much more important than their adoption of either the "class-line" or the "mass-line" policy. Therefore, the primary concern of the policy-makers when they gathered to discuss the issues of political survival was how to gain the support of the people as a whole in order to win the revolutionary war and to defeat the KMT's campaigns. To this end they began to pay more attention to Mao's concept of "mass line" by which the majority of the peasant population was to be mobilized and involved in the military effort. However, the concept of "class line" put forward by Ch'in Pang-hsien and other returned-student leaders was by no means ignored or abandoned. Mao himself did not ignore completely the issue of "class struggle," as is shown by his article "How to Analyze the Classes," but his own speeches and writings between June and October 1933 appear to indicate that he was more in favor of adopting economic and agrarian policies based on the concept of "mass line." The two concepts of "class line" and "mass line" thus interacted with each other and reinforced one another in the policy process, but Mao's concept of "mass line" played the key role in mobilization campaigns whereas the Comintern's concept of "class line," reflected in the policies of the returned-student leadership, was applied to such economic ends as grain collection, taxation, and bond sales.

What emerges from the massive collection of policy statements and documents concerning organizational development reproduced in the *Ch'en Ch'eng Collection* is that the policy-making and implementation processes of the period were shared by the three elements of power. Mao and his associates, including Chang Wen-t'ien and Wu Liang-p'ing, were able to make a significant contribution to the formulation and implementation of various mobilization policies. Thanks to Mao's capacity to develop new organizations and to manipulate certain key forces in the policy-making machinery, such as the People's Commissariat and the Presidium of the Central Executive Committee, he rose to unchallenged leadership in Yenan as well as in the People's Republic.

V

MASS MOBILIZATION POLICIES AND ORGANIZATIONAL TECHNIQUES*

One of the most challenging organizational goals of the Chinese Communist movement during the Kiangsi soviet period (1931–1934) was to mobilize the broadest possible mass participation in the revolutionary processes of the Chinese Soviet Republic. The principal economic and social policies of the central soviet government, as described in the preceding chapter, were formulated with the aim of preserving the Kiangsi political system, expanding the revolutionary base to other areas of China, and strengthening the Red Army to guard against external attacks. Mass mobilization was considered to be essential to this end.

By emphasizing the central concept of "mass participation," the soviet government had considerable success in mobilizing the population while implementing its newly formulated social and economic policies in the soviet area. One can discover in Chinese Communist concepts and practices during the Kiangsi period, therefore, the roots of "mass-line" politics that have been so important in China since 1949. The first moves toward evolving the "mass line" can be seen in the political style and organizational techniques by which the Chinese Soviet Republic was able to implement its policy of mass mobilization in the early 1930s. One can trace the origins of the "mass line" to that period, even though the concepts involved were not fully developed and refined until the Yenan period and even later.

The Kiangsi soviet system can be viewed, in one sense, as consisting of three major groups: the militant vanguard made up of leading Party and soviet-government personnel; auxiliaries, consisting of the mass organizations that paralleled the soviet government at all levels; and administrative cadres who worked in the subordinate units of the soviet

*An earlier version of this chapter was published in A. Doak Barnett, ed., *Chinese Communist Politics in Action* (Seattle, University of Washington Press, 1969), under the title "Mass Mobilization Policies and Techniques Developed in the Period of the Chinese Soviet Republic," pp. 78–98. It has been considerably revised, however, on the basis of further research on the poor-peasant corps, the farm-labor unions, and the land-investigation movements.

system of government. To understand fully the mobilization policy and organizational techniques characteristic of the Kiangsi political system, due attention must be given to the structure and operations of mass organizations that served as administrative auxiliaries, including the poor-peasant corps and the farm-labor union, which were developed within the general framework of the Party's overall mobilization policy.

The Kiangsi soviet period is particularly important in the history of the Chinese Communist movement, because it was then that the Chinese Communist leaders, for the first time in their struggle for power, acquired control over a definite geographic area comprising approximately 150 *hsien* and a population of twelve to fifteen million people.[1] The central soviet government in Juichin experimented with various economic and social programs, and, as already stated, the institutional theories and administrative practices that have since developed in China are deeply rooted in the programs evolved in the Kiangsi period. Mao's concept of mass mobilization was first developed during the Kiangsi experiment in the "class struggle" and "mass campaigns" of that period.

In sum, there are identifiable, important parallels between many of the patterns of mobilization practiced in the Kiangsi period and the methods later utilized by Mao in the Yenan period and after he achieved power on the China mainland, and even after he launched the Great Proletarian Cultural Revolution.

Mao clearly had already begun to formulate and articulate the concepts underlying his distinctive style and techniques of mass mobilization when he was head of the central soviet government, and he emphasized the need to arouse and organize the masses. For example, in 1934, he declared:

> The central task of [the soviet government] is to mobilize the broad masses to take part in the revolutionary war, overthrow imperialism and the Kuomintang by means of such war, spread the revolution throughout the country, and drive imperialism out of China. Anyone who does not attach enough importance to this central task is not a good revolutionary cadre. If our comrades really comprehend this task and understand that the revolution must at all costs be spread throughout the country, then they

[1] The geographic limits and population of the soviet area during the Kiangsi soviet period varied from time to time, and no two writers agreed on the extent and population of the Chinese Soviet Republic. For example, in an interview with Edgar Snow in 1936, Mao estimated that the maximum population of the central Soviet area in 1934 was nine million. However, Hatano Ken'ichi argued that the area and population of the entire soviet area (including the central Soviet area), at its peak, were 300 *hsien* and 30 million respectively; see *Chūkyō-shi*, I, 635. Many of the 300 *hsien* claimed may have had only small pockets of guerrillas in them.

should in no way neglect or underestimate the question of the immediate interests, the well-being, of the broad masses. For revolutionary war is a war of masses; it can be waged only by mobilizing the masses and relying on them.[2]

It was on the basis of this concept that Mao adopted various social and economic policies — in close collaboration, it should be noted, with a segment of the returned-student group, which then controlled the central organs of the CCP. Even though the student group based their views on the Russian model as they had observed it, whereas Mao Tse-tung had developed his theories from personal experiences in Kiangsi, the evidence suggests that the Russian-trained Party leaders, who were in control of the central party operations, and Mao Tse-tung, who led the central soviet government, were in essential agreement as to basic organizational approaches and compromised in the process of implementing their policies.

It is true, of course, that there were ideological debates and policy conflicts between factions in the Chinese Communist movement, and within the central leadership itself, following the debacle of 1927. They centered on two major policy issues: the relation of guerrilla tactics to the revolution in the urban centers and the question of what agrarian policy to follow. These two issues were utilized interchangeably by factions competing against each other. It is also true that Mao and the Party's Central Committee were at times in disagreement concerning these two issues during the period between 1927 and 1933. The discussion that follows will focus on aspects of the evolution of organizational strategy during the Kiangsi period, inasmuch as the question of the relation between guerrilla tactics and revolutionary strategy in the urban areas has already been explored in some detail by other scholars, and it will attempt to relate this to the development of the Party's mass-mobilization concepts.

Organizational Techniques of Land Distribution

To understand the issues involved in the development of organizational strategy during the Kiangsi period, one must begin by analyzing the content of more than a dozen resolutions adopted by the CCP on the organizational question, as well as the official documents published by the central soviet government for the period 1930–1935.[3] These

[2] Mao, *SW*, I, 147. The words in parentheses were altered by the Peking authorities. When Mao actually spoke at the Second Soviet Congress in January 1934, he used the term "the soviet government." For the original text of his speech, see *Hung-se Chung-hua*, No. 148 (February 12, 1934).

[3] Many of these documents are collected and analyzed by Tso-liang Hsiao in his

documents indicate that one of the major concepts underlying the development of organizational strategy was the idea of "mass mobilization." The policy aimed to create a psychological atmosphere and conditions under which the peasants would feel, for the first time in their lives, that they were actually involved not only in the process of land confiscation and distribution, but also in the political processes of managing local affairs.

It is difficult in some respects to generalize about Mao's agrarian policy inasmuch as he was neither wholly consistent nor comprehensive, as pointed out earlier, in stating his views about the various issues raised. In fact, at first he oscillated between "left" and "right" positions before finally deciding to base his agrarian policy firmly on the concept of "mass line."

When Mao was in the Chingkang mountains, his agrarian policy was at first radical and "leftist," and he believed at that time that all *"tzu-keng-nung"* (peasant proprietors) should be viewed as potential enemies; in fact, he advocated execution of peasant proprietors.[4] However, his position had shifted greatly by February 1930, when he drafted the so-called 1930 land law, which stressed the goal of obtaining broad mass support. Under that law, the principle underlying land distribution was to be that only the land and capital owned by landlords, plus the land that rich peasants rented to tenants, was to be confiscated, and this land was to be distributed to farm laborers and poor and middle peasants, under the slogan, "Distribute All Land Equally to the Peasants."[5] Considering that the farm laborers and the poor and middle peasants constituted more than 85 percent of the rural population of China in the 1930s,[6] and that even rich peasants were allowed to keep land that they themselves tilled, Mao's organizational strategy at this time clearly aimed at creating a very broad base of mass support.

Both Mao's 1930 law and the revised May program stipulated that "only the land rented from the rich peasants by the tenant farmers was to be confiscated";[7] consequently, both Mao and the central leadership now advocated similar land policies — even though Mao had previously disagreed with the CCP Central Committee on the question of land confiscation.[8] Both now stressed mass mobilization on a broad base. (As mentioned in the preceding chapter, the regime started in

study of documents, *Power Relations within the Chinese Communist Movement,
1930–1934,* and in *The Land Revolution in China, 1930–1934.*
[4] For this interpretation, see Rue, *Mao in Opposition,* pp. 194–196.
[5] *Ibid.,* pp. 196–202.
[6] Wang, *Chung-kung shih-kao,* I, 187–190.
[7] For the Chinese text of this law, see *ibid.,* II, 357–362.
[8] See Rue, *Mao in Opposition,* pp. 195–203.

1932 an anti-rich-peasant struggle that tended to narrow the base of mass mobilization somewhat, but this campaign itself provided the basis for continuing efforts to mobilize the majority of ordinary peasants.)

The main objective of land distribution during the Kiangsi period, as specified in the resolutions adopted by the CCP as well as documents published by the central soviet government, was to obtain as broad support as possible from the peasant masses by giving them a sense of participation not only in the revolutionary cause but also in direct management of the land confiscation and distribution. The available evidence indicates that it was because the leaders of both the Party and government were concerned with obtaining the broadest possible mass support in this period that they included the rich peasants in the land-distribution program, in order not to antagonize or alienate them. (By 1932, when an anti-rich-peasant struggle was begun, this attitude had obviously undergone some change, although even then the aim was stated to be to "transform" the rich peasants rather than to suppress them.)

This relatively moderate policy clearly had an effect on the rich peasants, and one report submitted by a CCP agent in the northeast Kiangsi soviet area to the CCP Central Committee in Shanghai [9] claims that some of the rich peasants even sought refuge in the soviet border areas after escaping from the white (noncommunist) areas. Methods of dealing with the rich peasants continued to be a focus of discussions and a source of tension among Communist policy makers, but the policy implemented at the time was the moderate one specified in Mao's land law of 1930.

What were the organizational techniques by which the program of land confiscation and distribution was carried out at the grass-roots level? A review of the administrative process of agrarian policy at the local level would provide a better picture of the way in which organizational techniques were developed in the course of implementing agrarian policies. According to Mao, the implementation was actually carried out in three stages — land confiscation and distribution, land classification, and land improvement (or construction). Whenever a Red Army unit first occupied a rural region, it immediately established three new bodies to carry out the land policy — a land committee, a confiscation committee, and a workers' and peasants' inspection team

[9] Ma Lo, "Report to the CCP Central Committee on the Situation of the Northeast Kiangsi Soviet Area." Collected in Torao Himori, "Shina sekigun oyobi sovietō kuiki no hatsuten chōkyo" ("The Chinese Red Army and the Development of the Soviet Area"), *Mantetsu Chōsa Geppō (Monthly Research Report of the South Manchurian Railway Company)* (September, 1932), pp. 57–66.

(*Kung-nung chien-ch'a tui*) with the active participation of the local peasants.[10]

The confiscation committee first conducted a general census covering all households, and classified the population of the occupied region into five major groups: the landlords; the rich, middle, and poor peasants; and the farm laborers. This preliminary survey included information on the number of individuals in each household, indicating the sex, age, occupation, and class status of each person, and data on the quantity and quality of each land holding. The results of this survey were announced on a large wall poster displayed in a public place so that everyone in the community would be able to see it.

The posting of the survey results was intended to convince the peasant population that there was to be no secrecy in the administration of local affairs and, furthermore, to give them the impression that they had the power to make final decisions on important matters. They were invited to contribute suggestions for improvement and to make criticisms. The decision to follow these "democratic" processes meant that more than two months usually elapsed between the general survey and the actual implementation of land distribution. (The confiscation committee also stressed the concept of mass participation and tried to obtain popular support when it carried out the complicated processes of conducting land surveys and distributing the land.)

Subsequent to the preliminary survey of land and population carried out by the confiscation committee, the task of distributing land was usually turned over to the land committee. As mentioned earlier, such committees were organized in every village and *hsiang* in a newly occupied region. Each committee included the chairman of the local soviet government, the leaders of the poor-peasant corps and the farm-labor unions, and family representatives of the Red Army. This emphasis on representation involving many people in a local mass organization aimed to create a sense of popular participation. The actual management of the land distribution was the responsibility of professional cadres assigned this task by the land departments of the village and *hsiang* soviet governments. All of these cadres received professional training in party schools on how to handle the administration of the land-reform program.

The size of the land committees varied from region to region and depended largely on the extent of the occupied area and its population. A land committee in a *hsiang* was reported to have averaged thirteen to seventeen members, and each village land committee generally had five to seven members. In general, these committees had the same structure

[10] Mao Tse-tung, "Ch'a-t'ien yün-tung ch'u-pao tsung-chieh" ("Preliminary Summary of the Land Investigation Movement"), *Tou-cheng*, No. 24 (August 29, 1933).

as the committees formed by soviet governments at all levels. Each committee elected a chairman to convene the committee's meetings and supervise the committee's work. Besides the chairman, each *hsiang* land committee maintained two clerical staff members, two research and statistical cadres, and an executive secretary. The members of a village committee performed all functions of administration without the aid of any standing committees.

The central task of a land committee was to supervise and manage all aspects of distribution in the land-reform program. It also was responsible for land improvement. The land committees at the grass-roots level reportedly continued in existence even after the completion of their initial functions, and served as the administrative bodies of local governments to handle the second and third stages of the land-reform program.[11]

The workers' and peasants' inspection teams investigated complaints made by peasants, especially claims that mistakes had been made concerning their class status. They also evaluated general peasant opinions and attitudes toward land distribution. Each of these committees included almost every key member in a village. In many respects, the committees served as the eyes and ears of the local soviet government and helped it to determine whether economic equality and social justice had resulted from land confiscation and distribution.

The methods of land distribution varied. One of the simplest procedures was that established by the O-yü-wan (Honan-Hupeh-Anhwei) soviet government, which is described in a booklet entitled "How to Distribute Land." According to this booklet, land distribution in the soviet area at that time followed the principle of "all land to the peasants based on the number of individuals (per capita) and the strength of the labor force (working ability) of each household."[12] In describing how land distribution was actually carried out, the booklet stated that each land committee began its work by apportioning twenty to thirty *mou*[13] of good land in each *hsiang* to support the Red Army. Such land was usually called public land (*kung-t'ien*) and was directly managed by the *hsiang* soviet government with the help of the village soviet governments, which contributed the necessary labor and implements to cultivate it. The produce from the public land was used to support the Red Army; approximately 70 percent was for direct use by the army units, and the other 30 percent was deposited in a retire-

[11] Ch'i Ch'i-sheng, "Chih-ch'ü ti nung-yüeh cheng-chih" ("Agrarian Policy of the Red Area"). Originally published in *Kuo-wen chou-pao*, and collected in Hatano, *Chūkyō-shi*, V, 169–195.

[12] *Ibid.*, p. 186.

[13] A Chinese land measure that varied in different provinces, but 6.6 *mou* equal approximately 1 acre.

ment fund. The profits from this retirement fund served to support retired Red Army personnel. (A detailed report on the work of the West Hunan and Hupeh soviet government, which was made to the CCP Central Committee in Shanghai, states that the *hsiang* soviet governments were responsible for managing public land and keeping a record of annual production and the status of the retirement fund.) [14]

Each land committee, after collecting statistical data on all land in its jurisdiction, classified it into three categories, the "best" (*shang*), "good" (*chung*), and "poor" (*hsia*) land, and then divided it for distribution to farm laborers and poor and middle peasants. The fertility of land, which was taken into account in the distribution, was determined on the basis of the annual yield as well as of location and of soil quality. The location factor was determined by accessibility to transportation facilities and also the topography.

Part of the land in each of the above three categories was assigned to each household, in accordance with the number of individuals it comprised. One report made by the Anhwei soviet government stated that the amount of land actually distributed was allocated on the following basis: five *mou* to each adult, three *mou* to each child between the ages of nine and fifteen, and two and a half *mou* to each child under the age of nine.

In some areas, however, the division was based on the amount of harvested rice produced by the land. Under this system, each adult received land yielding five piculs of rice per year; [15] each child in the age group between nine and fifteen received land yielding three piculs of rice per year; and each child under nine received land yielding two and a half piculs. [16]

In either case, the rich peasants received land at this time on the same basis as the others, if they expressed the intention to cultivate it with their own labor. The middle peasants kept the land they already owned and cultivated.

After completing the plan for allocating land to the peasant families, the land committee would announce it on a wall poster in a public place so that the peasants in the community had an opportunity to make suggestions and present complaints if they felt that the plan contained any injustices. During this period of adjustment, not only could

[14] "Hupeh Hunan nan-hsi pu su-wei-ai kung-tso" ("The Soviet Work in the Hupeh and South-West Hunan Areas"). Collected in Torao Himori, "Shina sekigun oyobi sovieto kuiki no hatsten" ("The Chinese Red Army and the Development of the Soviet Area"), *Mantetsu Chōsa Geppō*, pp. 111–123.

[15] A *picul* is approximately equivalent to 133 pounds.

[16] *Ta Wan Pao* (*The Evening News*), "Chih-se ch'ü ti tsu-chih yü chien-she" ("The Organization and Construction of the Red Areas"), published in Shanghai on May 15, 1932; collected in *Mantetsu Chōsa Geppō*, pp. 140–149.

the peasants air their grievances, but the government could observe the general attitudes and behavior of the peasants toward the land-distribution program. If no one objected to the proposed plan of land distribution, or if there were no complaints, the land committee proceeded to register the land and issue land-ownership certificates after necessary adjustments had been made.

The poor peasants and farm laborers who acquired new land, as well as the middle peasants or rich peasants who kept the land they had previously cultivated, were required to register their land formally with the land committee and to obtain land-ownership certificates that contained information on the size, boundaries, and yield of the allocated land. These certificates constituted legal evidence that the peasants actually owned the land,[17] and because this was the first time that many of them had ever owned any, the certificates were psychologically important to them.

The *hsiang* soviet district generally functioned as the basic unit in the process of land confiscation and distribution, but a village could serve as the basic administrative unit if the peasants in that village decided at a mass rally to carry out the land-reform program.

The Poor-Peasant Corps and the Farm-Labor Union

The peasants were actively involved in the processes of land confiscation and distribution partly as a result of the creation of two auxiliary organizations under the *hsiang* soviet government's jurisdiction: the poor-peasant corps and the farm-labor union. These mass organizations had considerable success in arousing class consciousness and a sense of participation on the part of the masses of ordinary peasants.[18] This was the first time in Chinese history that any serious attempt had been made to involve the ignorant mass of ordinary peasants in meaningful activities aimed at social change and modernization.

A brief analysis of the development and structure of the poor-peasant organizations in the Kiangsi soviet base should help to clarify some of the issues raised in the discussion of organizational techniques and of the leadership in the Land Investigation Movement. Poor-peasant corps and farm-labor unions did not exist when the Chinese Soviet Republic

[17] The form of the land-ownership certificates varied from province to province. I saw several types of these certificates collected in the display room of the Bureau of Investigation of the Ministry of Justice in Ch'ing-tan, Taiwan. An interesting aspect of the certificates was the fact that the Kiangsi Provincial Soviet Government issued three sets of them — one for the rich peasants, one for the middle peasants, and still another for the poor peasants.

[18] For a discussion of the participation of the masses in the administrative process of the society, see James R. Townsend, *Political Participation in Communist China* (Berkeley and Los Angeles, University of California Press, 1967), p. 46.

was created in November 1931. This was another indication that the organizational process in the Kiangsi soviet base was not necessarily a direct imitation of the model that the returned-student leadership had acquired in Moscow. It is also true that the establishment of both the poor-peasant corps and the farm-labor unions was called for in a resolution adopted by the political secretariat of the ECCI on July 23, 1930,[19] but its impact on the actual development of such organizations in China was minimal because neither organization was fully established until the Land Investigation Movement was launched in June 1933. However, it might be useful to survey briefly the contents of the Comintern resolutions and the way in which the functions of these two organizations were changed when they came to be established in the Kiangsi base.

The Comintern resolution stipulated that the aim of poor-peasant corps and farm-labor unions was to establish a link between the task of the land revolution and the revolutionary efforts of the poor peasants and farm laborers. Therefore, the function of the poor-peasant corps was to unite middle peasants and poor peasants and to promote and execute policies designed to protect the interests of both the poor and middle peasants. The poor-peasant corps were conceived of as the organizational foundation on which the rural soviet was to be constructed. However, even before the Comintern call, Mao had already converted his peasant associations into the soviet government and had formed the soviets on the basis of existing peasant associations as early as 1927. The organizational goals of the poor-peasant corps and the farm-labor unions were to assume some of the functions of the peasant association after it was transformed into the soviet government. The poor peasants were to be organized into a corps with the leadership provided by the soviet government. Moreover, farm laborers and coolies, according to the "Draft Resolution on the Land and Peasant Problems in the Soviet Areas," [20] adopted by the Far Eastern Department of the Comintern on November 15, 1930, were to be recruited into the organizations of the labor unions over which the Party had special jurisdiction. Within the poor-peasant corps, however, there were established two special small teams (hsiao-tzu), one of which was later to become an independent farm-labor union within the organizational framework of the poor-peasant corps. In the areas where the peasant associations had not yet been transformed into the soviet administra-

[19] ECCI Political Secretariat, "Chung-kuo wen-t'i chüeh-i" ("Resolutions on the Chinese Question"), July 23, 1930, collected in Hung-se wen-hsien (Red Documents) (Chieh-fang she, 1938), pp. 349–350, SSCM, Reel 15.

[20] Eastern Department of the Comintern, "Su-wei-ai chü-yu t'u-ti nung-min wen-t'i i-chüeh-an" ("Draft Resolution on the Land and Peasant Problems in Soviet Areas") in Chih-fei chi-mi wen-hsien, III, 40, collected in SSCM, Reel. 20.

tion, the resolution stressed, small teams of poor peasants were to be established under the direct jurisdiction of the peasant association. The poor-peasant corps would not be organized unless the peasant association had been converted into the soviet government.

Another important document of the Comintern, which also referred to the organizations of the poor peasants and of farm labor, was the "Resolution on the Chinese Peasant Problem,"[21] circulated in the soviet area on February 18, 1933. The primary task of the CCP in the soviet area, as outlined in this document, was to establish farm-labor unions parallel to the ordinary labor unions composed of the industrial proletariat, and the poor-peasant corps, like the existing peasant associations, were to be under the leadership of the labor unions. At the same time, it stressed that the poor peasants and rural workers were to be recruited into the poor-peasant corps on a voluntary basis rather than by coercion. In this way the poor-peasant corps recruited not only poor peasants and rural workers but also the women and youth of the villages.

What, then, was the relationship between the peasant associations previously organized under Mao's leadership and the proposed organizations of new peasant corps and farm-labor unions? Once the peasant association had been converted into the soviet government, as mentioned earlier, there was no need to reestablish it. The leaders of the soviet government who were formerly leaders of the peasant association would take full responsibility for organizing the poor-peasant corps and farm-labor unions and share with the new leadership some of the organizational responsibility that had not yet been taken over by the soviet government. However, the peasant associations that were not in the soviet areas and hence were under the influence of the rich peasants or the KMT agents were to be abolished rather than converted into the soviet governments. In many respects this was a continuing process of separating friends (Communists) from enemies (the KMT), which had begun with the CCP-KMT split in 1927. As they went about abolishing the KMT-influenced peasant associations, the CCP leaders developed new techniques of winning over the support of the poor and middle peasants to the Communist side by organizing and consolidating such peasants within the associations and by helping them take responsibility for guiding and directing the associations. Many of these people later became leaders of the soviet government or the poor-peasant corps. By parliamentary procedure, as the poor and middle peasants definitely formed the majority in the peasant associa-

[21] "(Kuo-chi) tui-yü chung-kuo nung-min wen-t'i chüeh-i-an" ("Comintern Resolution on the Chinese Peasant Problem"), *Chih-fei chi-mi wen-hsien*, III, 33–38, *SSCM*, Reel 20.

tions, the rich peasants and class heretics were gradually eliminated from leadership positions in the process of transforming the peasant associations into the soviet governments.

After establishing organizational principles and structures, the poor-peasant corps and farm-labor unions took over some of the functions theretofore performed by the peasant associations. They acquired these new functions during the implementation of the anti-rich-peasant policy beginning in 1932.[22] The two organizations were designed to function as the most effective instruments in carrying out the policy of opposing the rich peasants by separating them from the poor and middle peasants, who were also being separated from the class heretics. Although an organic law — regulations governing the poor-peasant corps and a provisional regulation for farm-labor unions — were adopted as early as 1931, the emergence of these two organizations as dynamic political forces at the grass-roots level did not come about until June 1933 at the time of the Land Investigation Movement.

The organizational principles of the two mass organizations — poor-peasant corps and farm-labor union — were in many respects similar. Their functions at the grass-roots level therefore overlapped and were almost identical. The poor-peasant corps, according to the "Regulations for the Poor Peasant Association," [23] was divided into five categories which were basically similar to those of the farm-labor union. However, the poor-peasant corps placed more emphasis on allying itself with the middle peasants and on supporting the middle peasants' opposition to oppression and exploitation by the landlords and rich peasants. Whereas the keynote of the farm-labor union was the concept of class struggle, the poor-peasant corps placed greater emphasis on the alliance of the poor and middle peasants based on Mao's concept of "mass line." The two conflicting concepts — the "class line" of the returned-student leaders, and the "mass line" of Mao — were also reflected in the organizational forms of "farm-labor unions" and "poor-peasant corps."

The organizational activities of the poor-peasant corps, like those of the farm-labor unions, were divided into several areas in accordance with functional specialization. In addition to its primary functions with regard to organization, propaganda, and finance, the poor-peasant corps was responsible for youth and women's activities at the grass-roots level. The basic difference between the poor-peasant corps and the farm-labor union was in the variety and extent of their functions

[22] Mao Tse-tung, "Mao Tse-tung kei Yuan Kuo-p'ing ti hsin — Kuan-yü ch'ün-chung kung-tso ti chih-shih" ("A Letter from Mao Tse-tung to Yuan Kuo-p'ing Concerning the Directive of Mass Work"), *SSCM*, Reel 14.

[23] "P'in-nung-hui chang-ch'eng" ("Regulations for the Poor Peasant Association"), by the General Political Department, Central Revolutionary Military Council. Collected in *Chih-fei chi-mi wen-hsien*, vol II, *SSCM*, Reel 20.

at the grass-roots level. The poor-peasant corps absorbed all the organizational functions of the farm-labor unions at the *hsiang* and village level, and the farm-labor unions, if they were organized, were gradually incorporated into the poor-peasant corps and were completely under their jurisdiction. However, the activities of the poor-peasant corps above the district level, if they were organized, seem to have been included in the organizational responsibilities of the farm-labor unions, because there was no separate structure of the poor-peasant corps at the level above the *ch'ü* (district) soviet government.[24] Consequently, the only important mass organization functioning as the auxiliary of the soviet government at the grass-roots level (*hsiang* and village level) was the poor-peasant corps.

Poor-peasant corps were thus important auxiliary organizations of the soviet government at the basic level, and their organizational techniques were closely linked with those of the local soviet government. The organizational principles and regulations governing the poor-peasant corps stressed the idea that an extremely close, even indisoluble relationship had to be maintained between them and the soviet government.[25] The soviet government performed the function of providing leadership over the structure of the poor-peasant corps; the poor-peasant corps, on the other hand, supervised and checked the work of the soviet-government personnel at the grass-roots level. A check and balance was attempted, therefore, at least in principle, by the organizational theorists in the Kiangsi soviet base.

The recruitment of membership in the poor-peasant corps extended to a much broader group of people than the category on which the farm-labor unions were based. The farm-labor unions recruited only farm laborers, but the poor-peasant corps took in, besides the poor peasants, hired farm hands, manual workers, coolies, and handicraft workers. Evidently, the most important function of the poor-peasant corps seems to have been to reach as broad and varied a range of the poor and miserable masses as possible in the rural areas. The corps served as channels through which the masses of poor people could register their grievances and express their sufferings and also as instruments for articulating their interests to the local soviet government. In his speech inaugurating the Land Investigation Movement in June 1933, Mao dwelt upon the function of the poor-peasant corps in carrying out the central task of surveying the current status of land distribution and

[24] "P'in-nung-t'uan tsu-chih yü kung-tso ta-kang" ("General Principles of Organization and Functions of the Poor-Peasant Corps"), issued by the Central Soviet Government on July 15, 1933, collected in *SSCM*, Reel 11.

[25] "P'in-nung-hui tsu-chih-fa chi ch'i jen-wu" ("Organic Law of the Poor-Peasant Association and Its Tasks"), Circular No. 20 of the CCP Southwest Kiangsi Special Area Committee, in *Chih-fei chi-mi wen-hsien*, II, 35–38, *SSCM*, Reel 20.

determining who had the greatest grievances after the first stage of land distribution.[26]

The poor-peasant corps were restructured in June 1933 to mobilize poor peasants fully for the execution of the Land Investigation Movement. However, the reorganization of poor-peasant corps had already taken place during the period of anti-rich-peasant policy in 1932, in order to implement that policy at the local level. The prime purpose of the reorganization was to arouse the peasant masses' revolutionary consciousness based on the "mass line" approach and to stimulate class struggle based on the concept of "class line." The poor-peasant corps were organizations through which the peasant masses could express their views, find outlets for their psychological frustrations, and to some extent participate directly in the decision-making processes of the local soviet government and administration.

Each corps was organized at the *hsiang* level according to the following procedure. A mass meeting elected an executive body of seven to nine members, which in turn elected a four-member standing committee consisting of the chairman, an organization director, a propaganda director, and a secretary. The members of both the executive committee and the standing committee were elected at three-month intervals to allow as many peasants as possible to acquire administrative and managerial experience.

Wherever the *hsiang* executive committee of a poor-peasant corps was established, it sent cadres to organize mass meetings in all the villages of the area and to establish a poor-peasant corps in each village. The leadership of each village peasant corps was chosen in a way similar to that of the *hsiang* and consisted of a three- to five-member executive committee. Each village-level poor-peasant corps was further divided into smaller teams (*hsiao-tzu*), based on occupations; these could include a farm-laborers' team, a handicraft-workers' team, and a coolies' team. The organizational structure of the poor-peasant corps was hierarchical, but unlike that of the farm-labor unions, it comprised only three levels: *ch'u* (district), *hsiang* (township), and *ts'ün* (village).

The poor-peasant corps at the three levels functioned as the primary organization since none was established above the *hsien* level (articles VII and VIII). In some cases, the district-level corps was not set up because it was genuinely intended that the poor-peasant corps should be a grass-roots-level organization, hence the two-tier structure (the village and *hsiang*) of the corps became the common practice. The farm-labor unions being organized at the district level and exercising their juris-

<hr />

[26] Mao Tse-tung, "Ch'a-t'ien yün-tung shih kuang-ta ch'ü ti chung-hsin chung-ta jen-wu" ("The Land Investigation Movement Is the Central Task of Great Magnitude in Vast Areas"), *HSCH*, No. 86 (June 17, 1933).

diction over the farm workers in general, there was no need for the functions of the poor-peasant corps and the farm-labor unions to over-lap at the district level. If two centers of leadership had been created — the farm-labor unions for the leadership of the working class and the poor-peasant corps for the leadership of the peasant class at the district or *hsien* level — the two centers would have weakened the leadership of the working class, obscured the revolutionary consciousness, and mini-mized the class struggle.[28] At the same time, farm-labor unions were not independently organized at the village and *hsiang* levels, hence the leadership structure of mass organization at the level above the district and *hsien* was greatly unified under the leadership of the soviet government.

One of the important functions of the poor-peasant corps in general was to serve as an administrative auxiliary of the local soviet govern-ment, and it performed various administrative tasks for the government in the course of implementing the land-reform programs. Conversely, it was the local soviet government at the district level that sent the cadres who initially helped to establish the poor-peasant corps. The local *hsiang* soviet government led all of the poor-peasant corps in its area, and the leaders of the poor-peasant corps often formed a reservoir from which personnel were drawn for the administrative committees of the *hsiang* soviet government.

Whenever a *hsiang* or village soviet government initiated a new pro-gram, it usually invited one leader from each of the village peasant corps to participate in the discussions of the council meeting. Upon his return to his own village after participating in the council meeting of the soviet government, this village representative was charged with the responsibility of organizing mass meetings to discuss the implemen-tion of the policy. These discussion sessions generally resulted in adop-tion by the entire membership of the poor-peasant corps of a resolution supporting the policy.

Each *ch'ü* (district) soviet government called a meeting at least once a week for the leaders of the peasant corps at the *hsiang* and village level. The purpose of these meetings was to explain the administrative directives of the central soviet government, to solicit the views and opinions of the poor-peasant-corps leaders, and to ascertain peasant attitudes toward government policy and the land-reform program. They provided an opportunity for the leaders of all the poor-peasant corps to visit and attend meetings at the capital of the *ch'ü* soviet

---

[27] For general principles of organization and functions of the poor-peasant corps, see note 24.

[28] See "Organic Law of the Poor-Peasant Associations," in *Chih-fei chi-mi wen-hsien*, II, 35–38, *SSCM*, Reel 20.

government and to make suggestions as to ways of implementing policy.

Each *hsien* soviet government also maintained a close link with the poor-peasant corps by sending its representatives to attend the meetings of the poor-peasant corps' leadership at the *hsiang* and village level. The leaders of the poor-peasant corps functioned, in this respect, as an important transmission belt for the diffusion of the central government's policy at the grass-roots level, and to some extent they also served as a channel for "feedback" from the peasants.

In theory at least, the poor-peasant corps operated on a strictly voluntary basis and were not to use coercion in dealing with the mass of peasants.[29] They were sometimes tightly controlled, however, and the majority of peasants and workers in the villages were obliged to participate in their operations. They attempted to function as fairly spontaneous organizations and did not meet regularly, because it was said that regular meetings would be too mechanical. There were no membership dues. They did not maintain any organizational structure at the provincial, *hsien*, and *ch'ü* levels, such as those maintained by the farm-labor unions, which will be described below. They existed only at the level of the lowest, "basic" governmental units, such as the *hsiang* and the village, where they could best mobilize the peasant masses, and they exemplified the idea of mass participation at the basic governmental level. Then, too, they provided a channel through which the peasants could express their opinions or grievances to the proper authorities.[30]

The farm-labor union (or the tenant-farmers' union) was different in one basic way. It exhibited a hierarchical structure of organization at all levels of the governmental system from the district to the province. At the bottom of the hierarchy, each farm-labor team was usually made up of three or four farm laborers (tenant farmers). "Sub-units" of the village farm-labor union consisted of approximately three teams, and three or four "sub-units" together usually formed one village union. Each *hsien* farm-labor union then was constituted by grouping together three or four district farm-labor unions. The hierarchical structure directly paralleled the various levels of the soviet governments, from the

[29] Chung-hua su-wei-ai kung-he-kuo lin-shih chung-yang cheng-fu jen-min wei-yüan-hui hsün-ling, ti shih-i hao — shih-hsing kuang-fan shen-ju ti ch'a t'ien yün-tung (Directive No. 11 of the Council of People's Commissars of the Provisional Central Government of the Chinese Soviet Republic — Launching an Extensive and Intensive Land Investigation Movement), issued on June 1, 1933, printed in *HSCH*, No. 87 (June 20, 1933). Hereafter cited as *Directive No. 11 of the Central Soviet Government*.

[30] Hara Masaru, "Chūgoku sovetō ni okeru hinnō oyobi kōno no soshiki tō sono tōsō kōryo" ("Organizations and Programs of the Poor Peasants and Farm Laborers in the Chinese Soviet Areas"), *Mantetsu Chōsa Geppō*, 15, No. 5 (May 1935), 137–248.

district to the province. Mass meetings of the farm-labor union were normally convened at three-month intervals, at which time the leaders of the executive committee and its standing committees were chosen.[31] Otherwise the farm-labor union was very similar to the poor-peasant corps. The main organizational difference was that the former maintained a vertically hierarchical structure whereas the latter had a looser horizontal structure.

The primary goals of the farm-labor unions, according to the "Provisional Regulations for the Farm Labor Unions," were to consolidate the strength of the farm laborers, to carry out the class struggle by resisting oppression and exploitation and fighting for the liberation of the working masses, and to strengthen the leadership of the labor masses in their struggle for land revolution and the consolidation and expansion of the soviet government in rural areas (article II). In order to attain such broad goals, farm-labor unions were assigned more specific and concrete functions: the organizational work of establishing and leading subordinate labor unions at all levels and training cadres for union activities; the issuing of oral and written propaganda such as leaflets, pamphlets, and pictorials, and of providing guidance for propaganda activities at all levels of the union; and the educational work of raising the political and cultural standards of the workers and of administering educational institutions such as workers' schools, labor clubs, physical-education associations, book- and newspaper-reading clubs, and lecture series. However, the most important function of the farm-labor unions was to pursue all of the kinds of class struggle outlined in article II.

Membership in the farm-labor unions was limited to farm laborers whose labor was their only source of income. Farm laborers were defined as those workers who sold their labor in the activities of rural production. As a rule, they owned no land. Even those who had been allotted land in the first stage of land redistribution, if they still worked on a long-term basis, were also considered farm laborers and were allowed to join the farm-labor unions (article III). Every member of the union had the right to vote, to seek election to various offices, and to express his own opinions and propose policy recommendations concerning the union's welfare. The members also had the right to benefit from the educational, cultural, and mutual-aid programs sponsored by the union (article V). In return they were obliged to pay membership dues and other cash contributions whenever they could. They were also required to attend all union meetings and strictly observe and abide

<hr>

[31] "Ku-nung kung-hui chan-hsing chang-ch'eng" ("Provisional Regulations for the Farm-Labor Union"), *Chih-fei chi-mi wen-hsien*, II, 31–35, SSCM, Reel 20. For the English translation, see Hsiao, *The Land Revolution*, pp. 170–275.

by all union rules and decisions (article IV). Each member's right to discuss, recommend, and vote, as well as his duty to observe and abide by the decisions reached at the union meetings, was based, of course, on the principle of democratic centralism.

The structure of the farm-labor unions, as mentioned earlier, was hierarchical. Three or four farm laborers formed a small team (*hsiao-tzu*); three or more small teams formed a farm-labor branch; and three or more branches formed a *ch'ü* (district) union. Three or more district unions were grouped together to form a *hsien* (county) union, and the provincial or special soviet union was composed of three or more *hsien* unions (article VI). As already mentioned, there were no farm-labor unions at the village or *hsiang* level. The small teams and branches of the farm-labor unions at the village or *hsiang* level, however, were set up to correspond to village and *hsiang* soviet governments. It is interesting to note here that the small teams and branches of the farm-labor unions at the grass-roots level frequently assumed leadership of the poor-peasant corps when its leaders moved up to take the responsibilities of leadership in the village and *hsiang* soviet governments.

Because of the small size of the branch or team, the frequent election of officers at these levels seems to have caused no difficulties. Frequent elections in the mass organizations at the grass-roots level made it possible for many people to participate in administrative and management training. One of the most important reasons for the creation of mass organizations having been to provide the peasant masses at the basic level with a genuine sense of participation in the political process, the frequent elections and the large number of people to be elected to office in the various organizations (poor-peasant corps, farm-labor unions, the soviet government) fulfilled this requirement. The frequent meetings of committees or councils at the local level were also attempts to create a sense of participation in the local decision-making process. Executive committees and delegate councils at the basic level met more frequently than at the level above the *ch'ü* (district) or *hsien* (county) .

Organizational Techniques of the Land Investigation Movement

Once such mass organizations as the poor-peasant corps and the farm-labor unions were established, they were used to mobilize the majority of the peasant masses to participate in the class struggle as well as in the administrative process at the local level. In fact, the Kiangsi provincial soviet government stated in 1932 that the primary purpose of the poor-peasant corps was "to oppose the rich peasants and suppress their reactionary attitudes by establishing the closest possible alliance between the poor peasants and the middle peasants."[32] In some respects, however, policy toward the rich peasants continued to be restrained. They were not to be executed but rather transformed into "revolutionary" peasants through education and the use of the "class struggle." In carrying out this newly defined anti-rich-peasant policy, the poor-peasant corps emerged in mid-1932 as the most powerful organization at the local political level.

The development of the anti-rich-peasant policy is a complex story. All available documents and official pronouncements lead one to believe that the launching of the policy was neither economically motivated nor the result of factional struggles within the Party and the government.[33] The available evidence indicates that the policy was a logical development and an extension of the policy of mass mobilization. In short, this new form of class struggle was adopted as a compromise in the policy conflicts between the CCP leadership and Mao Tse-tung, and it served as a new means of mobilizing mass support among the majority of the peasantry during the Kiangsi period.

At that period the Japanese army was extending its control not only over the coastal areas of China but also to the important cities of the interior of the country, and the central soviet government declared war on Japan (April 15, 1932) in order to profit by the growing force of Chinese nationalism to promote its mass-mobilization program.[34] At that time, also, the fourth encirclement campaign was launched by the KMT army against the Kiangsi soviet area. Because of these circumstances, the Chinese Communist leadership (including the central Party leaders as well as the leaders of the central soviet government) launched an all-out campaign to mobilize the population of the soviet areas. The establishment of the poor-peasant corps and the initiation of the Land Investigation Movement were the main instruments in the peasant-mobilization program, and these were linked to a new anti-rich-peasant policy designed to arouse the consciousness of the masses.

The situation within the Kiangsi soviet area was somewhat different in 1932 from what it had been in 1930–1931, because of the results of the land-distribution campaign that had been started in 1930. The

---

[32] "Resolution on the Work of the Poor-Peasant Corps," adopted by the Kiangsi provincial soviet government on July 14, 1932, cited in Hara Masaru, *Chūgoku sovetō ni okeru.*

[33] Some scholars contend that the initiation of the anti-rich-peasant policy was closely associated with the 28 Bolsheviks' consolidation of their position as the most powerful leadership of the CCP. For this interpretation, see Rue, *Mao in Oppostion;* Hsiao, *Power Relations;* Swarup, *A Study of the Chinese Communist Movement.*

[34] The evidence now available on the Kiangsi soviet period indicates that Chalmers A. Johnson's thesis may not be applicable to the Kiangsi soviet period. See his *Peasant Nationalism and Communist Power: The Emergence of Revolutionary China 1937–1945.*

first stage of land confiscation and distribution had improved the economic position of the lower-middle-peasant class in the area and resulted in some increased socioeconomic mobility. Some former poor peasants had moved toward the status of middle peasant, and some members of the former middle-peasant class had moved toward rich-peasant-class status. As a result, a new policy issue was posed: how to treat the newly created rich-peasant class. Should the central soviet government treat them as it had previously treated rich peasants during the first stage of land distribution, or should it try to devise new approaches by which not only middle peasants but also new rich peasants who did not exploit others (i.e., who cultivated all their own land) could be mobilized to meet the external pressures of the time? The leadership of the CCP and the central soviet government seems to have decided on the latter course, as was evidenced by both the newly emerging poor-peasant corps and the Land Investigation Movement (ch'a-t'ien yün-tung) initiated at this time.

The organizational techniques developed to implement the Land Investigation Movement were a combination of ruthless class struggle with a mass political movement requiring large-scale mobilization of the masses. The intensification of class struggle was a means of implementing the agrarian programs, and the mobilization of the masses during the Land Investigation Movement was the most effective method of organizing to achieve the goals of the revolution. In an article emphasizing the importance of organizational mobilization, Mao stressed that only when concrete action was taken simultaneously by the Party, the soviet government, and mass organizations would the task of the Land Investigation Movement be fulfilled. Therefore, as the head of the central soviet government, he outlined several mobilizational tasks of the soviet government at all levels.[35]

The number-one task was to correct the mistaken view that the Land Investigation Movement was the concern of the land department alone. It should be realized, Mao stressed, that not a single unit of the soviet-government organizations could dissociate itself from the campaign and that each department must carry out the specific work of the movement assigned to it. However, the executive committees of the soviet government at each level must take the leadership of the movement as a whole. The Party organization, according to Mao, was not assigned to take any important responsibility in this movement. The land departments, judicial departments, workers' and peasants' inspection departments, and offices of the state political security bureau of the soviet government at each level, along with the special com-

[35] Mao Tse-tung, "The Land Investigation Movement is the Central Task of Great Magnitude in Vast Areas," HSCH, No. 86 (June 17, 1933).

missioners, were to perform the tasks of thoroughly solving the problem of agrarian revolution. In order that the government bureaucracy might carry out such important functions, Mao called on it to restructure and reform the organization of the soviet government at each level. In the course of the reorganization of the governmental structure, the counter-revolutionaries were to be found and suppressed. The military-affairs departments of the soviet government at each level were also instructed to reorganize themselves and to recruit as many people as possible to serve in the Red Army units. The departments of the Commission for National Economy at each level of government were assigned the responsibilities of restoring and increasing agricultural and handicraft productions, and of establishing and expanding the cooperatives. The educational departments were assigned the tasks of supplying propaganda materials to the cadres and the masses and of assisting in raising cultural and educational standards. Finally, the trade unions of every occupation were called on to mobilize their own cadres and their staff personnel to participate in the movement, and were to play an active role within the organization of the poor-peasant corps.[36] The objective of the Land Investigation Movement was thus to resolve agrarian problems and at the same time to reorganize and reform the structures of the government and mass organizations in order to mobilize the masses and to involve them in the organizational processes of the movement.

Mass mobilization was accomplished in two stages — first the mobilization of personnel working in the soviet government and its departments at each level, and then the mobilization of the people in various mass organizations. The *hsiang* (township) served as the basic unit of mobilization effort and its soviet government usually initiated mobilization activities in the area. In addition to the formal convocation of the delegate assembly (legislature) of the *hsiang* soviet government, such mass organizations as labor unions, poor-peasant corps, women's associations, Red Guard units, and Youth Vanguard groups called their own meetings as frequently as possible in order to study and discuss the issues of the Land Investigation Movement. The *ch'ü* and *hsien* soviet governments called their own mass meetings as often as they could and the key members of the mass organizations in the areas were also invited to participate in the planning and reviewing of the work being carried out in the Land Investigation Movement. The entire network of organizational activities during the Land Investigation Movement was directed and coordinated by the land-classification committees of the

[36] Mao Tse-tung, "Ch'a-t'ien yün-tung ti ti-i pu-tsu-chih shang ti ta-kuei-mu tung yuan" ("The First Step of the Land Investigation Movement — A Large Scale Mobilization of the Organization"), *HSCH*, No. 87 (June 20, 1933), p. 3.

hsien and *ch'ü* soviet government in the region. Those committees bore the basic responsibility of planning and implementing the movement in the area. They also planned various programs connected with the movement, educated cadres with deep understanding of the goals and tasks of the movement, established the criteria by which the class status of the population was to be evaluated, and frequently reviewed the current status of the work of the movement. The Land Committees, although a department of the soviet government at each level, usually consisted not only of government personnel but also of key leaders of the mass organizations in the region, thus imparting a sense of broad participation in the movement.

In the process of implementing the Land Investigation Movement, with the aim of improving mass mobilization, some of the returned-student leaders, including Chang Wen-t'ien and Wang Chia-hsiang, began to collaborate closely with Mao Tse-Tung and other leaders of the central soviet government in devising new organizational techniques. They reached an agreement that the poor-peasant corps should be fully developed to function as the vanguard of the poor-peasant masses, to establish a powerful alliance between the poor and the middle peasants, and to carry out the broadest possible mass mobilization, based on Mao's concept of "mass line." However, the class struggle based on the concept of "class line" advocated by the other group of returned-student leaders, such as Ch'in Pang-hsien (Po Ku), was not ignored or abandoned. The cadres at all levels of the soviet government were also directed "to take seriously the anti-rich-peasant policy as the form of class struggle and as the means to generate the latent power of peasant masses in the struggle to carry out the Chinese revolution."[37]

The organizational activities of the poor-peasant corps were thus closely related to the Land Investigation Movement that the central soviet government launched in 1933. In fact, the poor-peasant corps were the main instrument for implementing the Land Investigation Movement and carrying out land reclassification and redistribution at that period, and they performed many of the functions that had previously been part of the task of the land committees of the local soviet government.

In his analysis of the current status of land distribution in the central soviet area, Mao said that approximately 80 percent of the area had not yet completely solved the problems presented by the land distribution. He therefore called on the leaders of the local soviet

[37] "Chung-yang-chü kuan-yü ch'a-t'ien yün-tung ti chüeh-i" ("Resolution of the Central Bureau on the Land Investigation Movement"), in *HSCH*, No. 87 (June 20, 1933).

governments, the poor-peasant corps, and the farm-labor unions to launch the "land-classification campaign" as soon as possible throughout the region. "The Land Investigation Movement should be able to light the flames of class struggle among the two million peasants in the area," Mao asserted, "and eliminate completely the remainder of the feudal elements." [38]

The important questions to answer in this drive, Mao said, were whether the land had been equally distributed, whether the first stage of confiscation had attained the objectives of the land law of the Chinese Soviet Republic, and whether the former landlords and rich peasants had been able to continue in existence and had continued to accumulate wealth after the first stage of land confiscation had been carried out.

After Mao's speech concerning the Land Investigation Movement, the central soviet government called a conference of the leaders of the eight *hsien* governments, which convened from June 17 to 21, 1933, to discuss the new policy. This conference adopted a resolution stating that "the purpose of launching the Land Investigation Movement is to eliminate the landlord and feudal forces, and to further strengthen and improve the work of soviet governments through the mobilization of the peasant masses in the soviet areas." [39] It was followed by another conference, which brought together the poor-peasant corps' leadership from June 25 to July 1, to discuss the reasons for instituting the land-classification campaign and to establish procedures for carrying out the campaign in the soviet areas. At this meeting it was argued that certain landlords had disguised themselves as rich or middle peasants during the first stages of land distribution and had infiltrated the local soviet governments in order to receive a better portion of land, and that the new campaign was necessary to eliminate these elements through intensified class struggle. [40]

At the last-mentioned conference, Mao declared that "The Land Investigation Movement is unquestionably one of the most extraor-

[38] Mao Tse-tung, "Ch'a-t'ien yün-tung ti ch'u-pu tsung-chieh" ("Preliminary Conclusions Drawn from the Land Investigation Movement"), *Tou-cheng*, No. 24 (August 29, 1933), pp. 4–12.

[39] "Chung-yang cheng-fu t'ung-kao — Chao-chi pa-hsien ch'ü i-shang su-wei-ai fu-tse jen-yüan hui-i chi pa-hsien p'in-nung t'uan tai-piao ta-hui" ("Circular of the Central Government: Calling a Conference of Responsible Soviet Authorities of Eight Counties on or above the District Level and a Conference of Delegates of the Poor-Peasant Corps of Eight Counties"), *HSCH*, No. 85 (June 14, 1933). The eight *hsien* which sent delegates to this conference were Juichin, Hui-ch'ang, Yü-tu, Sheng-li, Po-sheng, Shih-ch'eng, Ning-hua, and Ch'ang-t'ing.

[40] "Conclusions Reached by the Conference of Responsible Soviet Authorities of Eight Counties on or above the District Level on the Land Investigation Movement," in *HSCH*, No. 89 (June 29, 1933), pp. 5–7.

dinary and severest forms of class struggle," and went on to say that "we must mobilize the broadest possible mass support from the poor peasants and farm laborers, and make them our foundation and vanguard." Mao urged the leaders of the local soviet governments to strengthen their alliance with the poor and middle peasants and the farm laborers, and to mobilize them in order to utilize their power. He also proposed that new cadres be recruited for the local soviet governments from the most ardent revolutionary cadres in the poor-peasant corps.

The Land Investigation Movement was not the responsibility of the poor-peasant corps alone; in fact, an effort was made to involve the entire bureaucracy of the soviet governments in it. The leaders of the various soviet governments were charged with the responsibility of serving as the organizers of the campaign. At the *hsien, ch'ü,* and *hsiang* levels, the local soviet governments were directed to establish land-classification committees, in cooperation with the poor-peasant corps, and these included the department heads of the soviet governments along with the leaders of the nongovernmental mass organizations.

The *hsien* soviet governments were instructed to establish plans for carrying out land classification within the month, and each plan was to be reviewed each month to determine whether the campaign within the *hsien* soviet area had been accomplished according to the original concept. The *ch'ü* and *hsiang* soviet governments were instructed to call meetings of the chairmen of the local soviet governments and the leaders of the poor-peasant corps at least once a week, to draft concrete schedules and establish inspection systems to check on the progress of the campaign. At the level of the *hsiang* soviet governments, efforts were made to generate maximum support from all the members of the *hsiang* delegate council, the poor-peasant corps, the labor unions, and the other mass organizations, in order to induce the broadest possible participation in the campaign.

The *hsien* soviet governments were also charged with the responsibility of organizing training programs for the cadres who would bear the major burden of implementing the campaign. These training programs, during the months of July, August, and September, usually consisted of ten days of specialized training for the leaders recruited from each *hsiang* within the *hsien* district, and the most revolutionary members of the poor-peasant corps, the farm-labor union, and the *hsiang* delegate council (the soviet) were also given specialized training at the *hsien* soviet government headquarters. After completion of the training, they returned to their villages to serve as the organizers and leaders of the land-classification campaign.

The *hsiang* soviet governments revived their confiscation and distribution committees, which now usually included the leaders of the local poor-peasant corps in the area. These committees, under the supervision and direction of the *hsiang* soviet government, performed the actual tasks of confiscating and redistributing the land owned and cultivated by the landlords and rich peasants. Directives from the CCP Central Bureau urged these land-classification committees to pay special attention to strengthening the alliance with the middle peasants, for the reason that "the middle peasants are the vanguard of the revolutionary masses, and the administration and success of our policies depends greatly on the support and participation of the middle peasants." [41]

All the decisions made by the poor-peasant corps and the *hsiang* soviet governments were carefully explained to the middle peasants in an effort to gain their support. The poor-peasant corps and the soviet governments "must listen to the voice of the middle peasant," it was said. Moreover, "any attempt to exterminate the rich peasants should be stopped," because they, unlike the members of the landlord class, possessed a revolutionary potential.[42] Nevertheless, in the actual distribution of land, the rich peasants (defined, as indicated earlier, as all those who exploited others) were no longer allowed to keep any land that they tilled themselves. In effect, the pre-1930 policy was revived; as a consequence, part of the rich-peasants' land was confiscated and replaced with less fertile land.

Reading through the Party directives, the resolutions of the various conferences, and the speeches delivered by Mao Tse-tung about the mobilization campaigns in the Kiangsi period, it seems clear that the aim of the campaigns was not simply to classify and distribute land and to differentiate the various peasant classes. Underlying these objectives was the broader basic goal of developing an effective mass-mobilization strategy.

"The great achievements of the Land Investigation Movement sufficiently prove that it is still necessary to pay attention to the class struggle in the rural areas of the local soviet government," Mao declared at the Second National Soviet Congress in January 1934, "and the Land Investigation Movement is our most important technique for conducting the continuous class struggle in the rural areas, and our best method of completely exterminating the remainder of the feudal forces." [43] Thus Mao did not ignore completely the programs of class

[41] "Resolution of the Central Bureau on the Land Investigation Movement," *Toucheng*, No. 24 (August 29, 1933).

[42] *Ibid.*

[43] Mao Tse-tung, "Chung-hua su-wei-ai kung-ho-kuo chung-yang chih-hsing wei-yuan hui yü jen-min wei-yuan hui tui ti earh-tz'u ch'üan-kuo su-wei-ai tai-piao ta-hui ti pao-kao" ("Report of the Central Executive Council and People's Commissariats

struggle based on the "class line" concept put forward by the returned-student leaders.

Organizational Techniques of the Cooperative Movement

The cooperative movement in the Kiangsi soviet base, like the land-investigation movement, was an essential part of Mao's strategy for mass mobilization. His organizational concepts and techniques for the mass-line approach were fully reflected in it. Wu Liang-p'ing, Mao's ardent supporter and deputy commissioner for national economy, initiated it in connection with the land-investigation movement directed by Mao himself. Calling for an immediate implementation of the principles and methods of the cooperative movement, Wu Liang-p'ing established specific methods of operation.[44]

All the factories, industrial plants, labor unions, schools, and Red Army units of the soviet areas were urged to come to full understanding of the significance of the cooperative movement and immediately begin organizing mutual-aid committees with each organization. They were to vote for the members of these committees, who would in turn decide which town or district needed most assistance in organizing cooperatives. Following the selection of the specific town or village, the committee was asked to send a mutual-aid team to the selected locality to launch the cooperative movement. The primary responsibility of the team was to help the local people undertake the immediate tasks of the revolution and also to assist them in accomplishing successfully the duties assigned to them by the Party and the central soviet government.

It was the responsibility of the mutal-aid team to come to grips not only with the local situation but also with its own work so that it could explain its function to the local population and arouse interest in the cooperative movement. For better results in mutual-aid work, the committee within each organizational unit was urged to sponsor various kinds of competition between the mutual-aid teams operating under its supervision. The essential purpose of the mutual-aid program, however, was to establish a close functional relationship between the farm laborers, the poor peasants, and the working masses of the villages, and then to provide leadership and assistance to the farm-labor unions and the poor-peasant corps. Each mutual-aid team was instructed to set aside at least one working day, preferably Saturday or Sunday, to

of the Chinese Soviet Republic to the Second National Soviet Congress"), in *HSCH*, No. 148 (February 12, 1934); also in its special issue for the Second Soviet Congress, *HSCH*, No. 7 (February 3, 1934).

[44] Wu Liang-p'ing, "Ying-kai li-ke k'ai-shih shih-hsing hsieh-chu yün-tung" ("Mutual-Aid Movement Ought to Begin Immediately"), an editorial of *HSCH*, No. 55 (February 22, 1933), p. 1.

help cultivate the public land (*kung-t'ien*) of the Red Army, which was almost the only instance of collective production by the teams. Channels of communication between the mutual-aid teams and the masses were established by calling mass meetings at which the teams made reports to the people and listened to their complaints and grievances.[45]

The primary objectives of the cooperative movement were "to arouse the positive enthusiasm of the working and peasant masses," Wu Liang-p'ing asserted, "and to strengthen the leadership and supportive functions of the working class to the peasant masses." These tasks had already been outlined by the Party's Central Bureau when it adopted programs to counter the enemy's fourth encirclement campaign: (1) to recruit one million Red Army men during a month-long period (February 20–March 20, 1933); (2) to make preparations for the conversion of the volunteer army into a compulsory army of the workers and peasants; (3) to let the soviet government borrow 200,000 *tan* of food grains (one *tan* equals 400 pounds) from the people to support the revolutionary war; (4) to increase land productivity by early spring cultivation; and (5) to mobilize the masses of people in order to oppose not only Japanese militarism but also all imperialist plots to divide the effort of Chinese revolution.

Faced with the fourth encirclement campaign of the KMT forces and alarmed by the recent Shanghai incident created by the Japanese military, the Party's Central Bureau and the central soviet government jointly formulated policies, as discussed earlier, to mobilize societal resources to counter the external threats as well as to cope with the problems of economic reconstruction. The mutual-aid program was, of course, an essential part of economic reconstruction, for its goal was to increase land productivity, raise the people's standard of living, and increase state revenues. Although the central soviet government had already initiated the organizational work of the cooperative movement as early as the spring of 1932, the drive for mass mobilization did not gain momentum until the land-investigation movement was launched in early 1933.

Mao had experimented with cooperatives (*ho-tso-she*), a traditional form of mutual aid, as early as 1929 in the Kiangsi soviet base. In November 1929, a consumer cooperative was organized in Ts'ai-chi *ch'ü* of Shang-hang *hsien*, which had 80 members and 40 *yüan* worth of capital. By the end of 1931, the capital had increased to 300 *yüan*. The cooperative's membership rose spectacularly to 1,040 and its capital more than doubled (741 *yüan*) by August 1933, after the Economic Construction Conference. This cooperative exemplified the way in which

45 *Ibid.*

the mobilization campaign of 1933 changed the structure of rural social organization.[46]

"The most important task in the cooperative movement," Wu Liang-p'ing asserted, "is to generate the creative potential of the masses and then transform our method of work and techniques of leadership" to make them functional within the cooperative movement.[47] This was the main thrust of the cooperative movement as perceived by the supporters of Mao. It is also interesting to note here that the central soviet government under Mao's careful leadership did not anticipate the collectivization of agriculture nor a quick transition to socialism. Wu Liang-p'ing, therefore, urged that the Chinese cooperative movement learn from the Russian experience, because the Russian workers and the Red Army units had helped develop the cooperatives in the Soviet Union. "Tens of thousands of urban workers were sent to the villages to help the peasants improve their material, cultural, and working conditions as well as increase land productivity," Wu pointed out. This finally led "the peasants to launch the collectivization of agriculture." This great Russian achievement during the 1928–1933 period was one of the most significant in world history, but "the collectivization of agriculture is not our primary task at the current stage of bourgeois-democratic revolution in China," Wu Liang-p'ing stressed. "The cooperative movement therefore should serve as one of the essential techniques of creating unity and solidarity between the workers and peasants." [48]

Under this principle, mutual-aid teams, like the mutual-labor-aid teams, were organized in early 1933 when the first spring planting drive was launched by the central soviet government.[49] The peasants' participation in the mutual-aid teams, according to the official line, was strictly on a voluntary basis, but some pressure was exerted by the establishment of a quota system in an attempt to organize the mutual-labor-aid teams as widely as possible. For example, in a *hsiang* with a population of more than one thousand, according to one source, 300 people (30 percent) were supposed to become members of the mutual-aid teams, but in a *hsiang* with fewer than one thousand inhabitants, a quota of 200 was to be recruited into the mutual-aid organizations.[50]

[46] See "I-ko mu-fan ti shao-fei ho-tso she" ("One of the Model Consumer Cooperatives"), *HSCH*, No. 139 (January 1, 1934), p. 3.

[47] Wu Liang-p'ing, *op. cit.*, p. 1.

[48] *Ibid.*

[49] The call for the development of a mutual-aid program was issued by the Central Executive Council in its Directive No. 18, "On Carrying Out Spring Planting Early and Concentrating Every Strength to Destroy the Massive Invasion of the Enemy," sent out on December 28, 1932. See *HSCH*, No. 46 (January 17, 1933), p. 1.

[50] "Ch'ün-keng yün-tung ying-kai chün-pei le" ("It is Time to Prepare for the Spring Planting Drive"), *HSCH*, No. 144 (January 16, 1934), p. 3.

Thus at least one mutual-aid team was organized in each village, whether small or large.

The persistent drive to develop the mutual-aid organization began in early 1933 and reached its highest point during the following year. In Hsing-kuo *hsien*, for example, 318 teams were organized by February 1934, with a total membership of 15,615 (6,757 male and 8,858 female). After two months of organizational drive, however, there were 1,206 teams, with 22,118 members.[51] It was reported that in May the total membership had reached 51,715, or an increase of 133 percent over the April figure. In Juichin *hsien*, the total membership of the mutual-aid teams in April was only 4,429, but within a month the membership jumped to 8,978, a 100-percent increase.[52]

In the drive to increase the membership of the mutual-aid teams, the soviet government at each level usually encouraged the establishment of a model team for other localities to emulate. This model team — such as a planting team or a harvest team — was composed of those peasants who demonstrated the greatest enthusiasm and possessed extraordinary productive skill. It was naturally a great honor to be chosen for a model team because its members not only were enthusiastically received by the peasant masses but also received prizes and the title of "labor hero" at the mass meetings.[53] The concept of mutual aid was applied to almost every aspect of social organization, and various teams, such as ploughing or temporary harvesting teams, were also organized. The ploughing team, for example, was assembled to help cultivate public land reserved for the Red Army personnel and also to render assistance to soviet-government workers and families of Red Army men.

A typical ploughing team, to use the example of Shih-shui *hsiang* of Juichin *hsien*, consisted of four brigades with a total of 520 members. One division of two brigades was formed in village "number one" and village "number three," which had populations of 800 and 700 respectively. The other two brigades were organized in village "number two" because it had a population of more than 1,200. A female ploughing team, similar to the male ploughing team, was organized in the same *hsiang*, with a total membership of about 400.[54] Smaller teams were formed in the smaller villages.

[51] See "Ho Hsing-kuo pi-i-pi" ("Compete with Hsing-kuo"), *HSCH*, No. 182 (April 20, 1934), p. 5.

[52] Ting I, "Ch'ün-keng yün-tung tsai jui-chin" ("Spring Planting Drive in Juichin"), *Tou-cheng*, No. 54 (April 7, 1934), p. 11.

[53] Wang Kuan-lan, "Jui-chin yun-chi ch'ü ch'ün-keng ch'in-pao" ("Information on the Spring Planting Drive in the Yun-chi *ch'ü* of Juichin *hsien*"), *HSCH*, No. 165 (March 22, 1934), p. 3.

[54] See "Tsen-yang ling-tao hsia-keng yün-tung" ("How to Lead the Summer Planting Drive"), issued by the Land Commissariat of the Central Soviet Government on April 22, 1933, *HSCH*, No. 73 (April 26, 1933), p. 506.

The function of temporary harvesting teams, like the ploughing teams, was to help the peasants during the busiest season, thus applying the principle of mutual aid to the harvesting of the crops. These teams were usually composed of the following categories of people: (1) government staff personnel and servicemen, (2) refugees, and (3) prisoners in the labor correction camps. The team members except the refugees, provided their own meals and did not receive compensation for their work.

There was a much higher percentage of women than of men on the mutual-aid teams because a large part of the male population was serving in the Red Army or in governmental organizations. The female membership (8,858) in Hsing-kuo *hsien* in April 1934, for instance, was greater than the male membership (6,757). Each *hsiang* soviet government established a labor-education committee to train the women to perform the work of the mutual-aid team. Peasants experienced in mutual-aid work or in the cooperatives were appointed by the *hsiang* soviet government to serve as the instructional staff of the women's labor-education committee. This training program was pursued in the field rather than the classroom and its philosophy was to learn by doing.

The organizational principles of the cooperative movement were, of course, closely linked with the concept of mutual aid to increase agricultural productivity and to deal with the problems of the labor shortage.[55] The mutual-aid teams served as the organizational foundation on which the cooperatives were later expanded. "We must use all our strength to organize the consumer cooperatives of workers and peasants and expand the organization of the cooperatives to each village and *hsiang*," Chang Wen-t'ien asserted. "Then we must build up the *hsien*, provincial, and finally the central organization of the cooperatives in order to strengthen the leadership of the Party and government within them."[56] A movement to unify the existing cooperatives at the provincial level began in the fall of 1933 and a provincial congress of representatives of the cooperatives in Kiangsi and Fukien was convened in November 1933 to unify the cooperatives.[57]

The organizational drive for expansion and unification of the cooperatives started in August 1933, following the Economic Construction

[55] Pao Cheng, "Jui-chin tsai ch'u-shou chung tsen-yang chieh-chüeh lao-tung-li ti wen-t'i" ("How Juichin Solved Its Labor Power Problems during the Autumn Harvest"), *HSCH*, No. 216 (July 19, 1934), p. 5.

[56] Chang Wen-t'ien's statements is quoted in "Po-sheng An-fu *ch'ü* ho-tso-she chuang-hsiang t'iao-sha" ("The Status Survey of the Cooperatives in An-fu *ch'ü* of Po-sheng *hsien*"), *Ch'ing-nien Shih-hua* (*The True Story of Youth*), No. 15, May 14, 1933, p. 32. Collected in *SSCM*, Reel 19.

[57] Cho Fu, "Chiang-hsi chi-chi t'ung-i ho-tso-she yün-tung" ("The Positive Movement of Unifying the Cooperatives in Kiangsi"), *HSCH*, No. 125 (November 14, 1933).

Conference, and was beginning to yield some positive results by the end of the year. However, the cooperatives had already begun to spread in the early spring of 1933, when the central soviet government had instructed the department of national economy to expand them, and various kinds of cooperatives had been established throughout the base area. A good description of the expansion of the cooperatives in Kiangsi province can be found in an article entitled "The Recent Situation of the Cooperative Movement in Each *Hsien* of Kiangsi," which appeared in a weekly youth magazine, *Ch'ing-nien Shih-hua (The True Story of Youth)*.[58]

During June and July 1933, consumers' and producers' cooperatives in Wan-t'ai, Hsing-kuo, Po-sheng, An-yuan, Yung-feng, and Yü-tu *hsien* had been suddenly and dramatically extended, according to the report. The breakdown by *hsien* was as follows: Hsing-kuo *hsien* had 118 consumer cooperatives with 16,613 members; Sheng-li *hsien*, 30 cooperatives with 1,628 members; Po-sheng *hsien*, 15 cooperatives with 3,131 members; Wan-t'ai *hsien*, 33 cooperatives with 3,600 members; and Yü-tu *hsien*, 15 cooperatives, although their membership was not reported. The producers' cooperatives, such as textile mills, steel mills, tobacco manufacture, and various handicrafts, also proliferated throughout the Kiangsi base, and the breakdown of these cooperatives by *hsien* was as follows: Sheng-li *hsien*, 7 producers' cooperatives, with 26 members; An-yuan *hsien*, 2 cooperatives, with 58 members; Yung-feng *hsien*, 6 cooperatives, with 2,741 members; and Po-sheng *hsien*, 12 cooperatives, with 1,848 members. The figures for the producers' cooperatives in Hsing-kuo *hsien* were not reported in this article. In what might be characterized as a mass political movement in the expansion of the cooperative organizations, a total of more than 29,350 persons joined the cooperatives as new members in June and July 1933 in Kiangsi province.

Statistics for Hsing-kuo and Juichin *hsien*, the two model *hsien*, illustrate how one aspect of the cooperative movement reached its peak in the spring of 1934. For example, more than 66 draft-animal cooperatives had been organized in Hsing-kuo *hsien* alone, with a total of 102 draft cattle, 28 of which were purchased by a fund borrowed from cooperative capital. By April, however, the number of cooperatives increased to 72 with a total of 121 cattle, 5,168 *yüan* of capital, and a membership of 5,552 persons.[59] Under a program adopted by Juichin

[58] Liu Yü-tang, "Chiang-hsi ko-hsien ho-tso-she yün-tung chin-hsiang" ("The Recent Situation of the Cooperative Movement in Each Hsien of Kiangsi"), *Ch'ing-nien Shih-hua*, No. 26, August 27, 1933, pp. 21–23.

[59] Hsieh Shao-wu, "Hsing-kuo je-lieh chun-pei ch'ün-keng kung-tso" ("Hsing-kuo has Vigorously Prepared for the Work of Spring Planting"), *HSCH*, No. 151 (February 18, 1934), p. 1.

hsien in February 1934, 95 cattle cooperatives, one in each *hsiang*, were planned, and 95 head of cattle, one ox for each *hsiang*, were to be purchased. Although by April 1934 only 37 cooperatives existed, with a membership of 3,638 and a capital of 1,539 *yüan* in cash and 815 piculs of grain,[60] the following September a total of 284 draft-cattle cooperatives with a membership of 15,075 and a capital of 11,719 *yüan* were reported to have been organized in Kiangsi province.[61]

These statistics do not provide a complete picture of the organizational development of the mutual-aid teams or the cooperative movement in the base areas of the Kiangsi soviet; the figures are given simply to illustrate the intensity of the organizational drive generated by the central soviet government at the height of the economic-construction campaigns. Even at the peak of the organizational drive, the cadres encountered enormous problems in educating the impoverished peasants to see the benefits of the cooperative movement. The rural population remained passive, if not openly hostile, toward the mobilization effort of the central soviet government. In several *hsien* of Kiangsi province, where the central government was located, the peasant masses had not even heard of mutual-aid teams or the cooperative movement after the organizational drive had been in progress for more than a month.[62] The organizational principles and operational procedures established by the central soviet government met with lack of enthusiasm among the cadres and suffered from insufficient propaganda and education while they were being implemented in the rural hinterland. There was perhaps too much fighting on the battlefield and too little time to mobilize the peasant masses when the fifth encirclement campaign was in full swing.

Information regarding the actual management and administration of the cooperatives is scanty at best in the *Ch'en Ch'eng* collection. The management committee (*Chih-tao wei-yüan hui*) of the cooperatives was created in the People's Commission for National Economy when the latter was established in early 1933, according to the "Provisional Summary of the Organization of the National Economy at Each Level."[63] This committee had sweeping jurisdiction over the cooperatives in the Kiangsi base and possessed wide authority and supervisory power, which included the power to create new types of cooperatives,

---

[60] Ting I, "Ch'ün-keng yün-tung tsai jui-chin" ("Spring Planting Drive in Jui-chin"), *Tou-cheng*, No. 54, April 7, 1934, p. 10.

[61] Ting I, "Liang-ke cheng-ch'üan liang-ke shou-ch'eng" ("Two Kinds of Regimes and Two Kinds of Harvest"), *Tou-cheng*, No. 72, September 23, 1934, p. 17.

[62] Kao Tzu-li, "Ch'ün-keng yün-tung chung t'u-ti-pu tsen-yang kung-tso" ("How Should the Land Department Function in the Spring Planting Drive)", *HSCH*, No 162 (March 15, 1934), p. 1.

[63] See the summary in *HSCH*, No. 77 (May 8, 1933), p. 5.

supervise the management system of various cooperatives, regulate the supply and demand of material goods, issue a price index on consumer goods, control speculation, and educate the working masses in preparation for the eventual transition to the path of socialism, if and when the cooperative movement was fully developed. The management committee of the cooperatives therefore was installed at each level of soviet government within the department of national economy, from the central soviet government down to the *ch'ü*. In addition, the cooperatives elected their own management committees at the general membership meetings.

The report on a model cooperative in Ts'ai-chi *ch'ü* of Shang-hang *hsien* provides an interesting example of the way in which the management committee of an individual cooperative was organized and of the kinds of administrative duties it performed. The entire membership was urged to take part in the election of their management committee as well as in its decision-making processes. The manager and five auditors, who were elected by the members at a general meeting, constituted the management committee, and they then recruited staff members to take charge of bookkeeping, sales, purchasing, and the protection of property. The model cooperative in Ts'ai-chi district being a consumer co-op, most of the purchasing activity went on in the nearby cities of Shang-hang and Fukien. To buy salt and consumer goods, the sales department usually exported such produce as rice, beans, tobacco, and occasionally paper pulp. Salt, however, accounted for 70 percent of the total imports whereas other consumer goods amounted to only 30 percent. Because the Red Guard unit in the region helped to transport the goods, the management committee did not have to pay for transportation. The local people were quite satisfied with the whole operation of the cooperative, the report said, because the consumer goods that the cooperative sold to them cost them only about one-half the market price. The cooperative also maintained two army doctors in order to provide free medical service to its members as well as to the dependents of Red Army men, and these doctors gave free medical treatment to the local people as well whenever they needed it, thus earning their good will. The model cooperative was said to have won the full confidence of the local population, and this enabled it to recruit new members.

Certain problems arose, however, in the course of operating the cooperative as the organization and its membership grew. The management committee was not organized according to the principles established by the central soviet government, and this was reflected in inefficiency. Moreover, the model cooperative failed to set aside a certain amount of money for cultural and educational activities for the members and for the masses. Though the central soviet government stressed cultural and educational activities on the part of the cooperatives in order to improve the cultural level of the peasant masses, the cooperatives had neither the time nor the money to spend on such activities.

Another management problem in this model cooperative was that of coordination. It had not yet established a good working relationship with other cooperatives in the district, such as the food-grain and drug cooperatives. Nor had it developed good coordination with the trade bureau or the food-grain-circulation office of the department of national economy in the *ch'ü* soviet government. These problems were said to have been minor management errors that could be easily corrected. But the management of cooperatives in other regions also faced problems, involving "bureaucratic commandism," passive attitudes, and corruption among the managerial staff — problems that were obviously widespread and serious, for Wu Liang-p'ing and Kao Tzu-li paid special attention to them in their writings. Consequently, the central management committee called on each *hsien* management committee of the cooperatives to select and send 300 cadres before January 15, 1934, to go through a special cadre-training program.[64]

The land-investigation campaigns, the cooperative movement, and the establishment of the poor-peasant corps and the farm-labor unions were expressions of the determination to carry out widespread mass mobilization during the Kiangsi soviet period, a determination shared by Mao and some of the returned students, such as Chang Wen-t'ien. The concepts and techniques of mass revolutionary struggle developed at that time determined the means subsequently used to mobilize the masses in China both in the Yenan period and after the Communists achieved nationwide power in 1949. Mao's concept of mass mobilization, which in time was codified as the so-called "mass line," continues to be important in China today.

[64] "Mu-chien shao-fei ho-tso-she ti chung-hsin jen-wu" ("The Central Task of the Consumer Cooperatives at Present"), *HSCH*, No. 135 (December 17, 1933), p. 2.

VI

LOCAL GOVERNMENT AND
ADMINISTRATIVE PROCESSES

The local soviet governments, as described by official publications of the Chinese soviet government issued during the Kiangsi period, comprised several administrative levels, from the province to the *hsiang*.[1] This chapter will attempt to survey the organizational patterns of each level (province, *hsien*, *ch'ü*, and *hsiang*), their functions within the general framework of the soviet system of government, and some of the problems incident to the operation of the local soviet governments.

Analysts of the Chinese Communist political system have often found it difficult to differentiate clearly between the functions of the government and those of the Party organization, because they frequently overlapped. However, the official Communist documents contained in *Ch'en Ch'eng Microfilms* (and a series of interviews accorded me by Chang Kuo-t'ao, who served as one of the two vice-chairmen of the central soviet government as well as chairman of the Hupeh-Honan-Anhwei — O-yü-wan for short — soviet government) cast light on the various problems of the government and the Party organization and provide insights into the administrative processes of the local soviets during the Kiangsi period.

As a basis for some generalizations about the operation of the soviets at three levels of local government (province, *hsien*, and *hsiang*), this chapter will present case studies of the provincial soviet government of the O-yü-wan soviet area, the Hsingkuo *hsien* soviet government, and the Changkang *hsiang* soviet government, the latter two belonging to the Kiangsi soviet area. Because both the Hsingkuo *hsien* and the Changkang *hsiang* soviet governments were considered to be "model soviet governments" in the Chinese Soviet Republic, other regions were expected to follow their example in establishing and operating

[1] *Chung-hua Su-wei-ai Kung-huo-kuo ti-fang su-wei-ai chan-hsing tsu-chih-fa (Provisional Organizational Law of the Local Soviet Government of the Chinese Soviet Republic)*, drafted by the Central Executive Council of the Chinese Soviet Republic, December 12, 1933; reproduced in *Ch'en Ch'eng Microfilms*, Reel No. 16. Hereafter cited as "Organizational Law of the Local Soviet Government."

soviet governments. Abundant materials therefore are available for research on them.

Chairman Mao Tse-tung, who headed the People's Commissariat of the Central Executive Council of the Chinese Soviet Republic, himself wrote a comprehensive and important report on the operation of the Changkang *hsiang* soviet government from the Communist viewpoint.[2] Lu Wei, the governor of the civil administration in Kiangsi province immediately after the KMT occupation of the Kiangsi soviet area, wrote a revealing report on how to rehabilitate the soviet areas, from the anti-Communist viewpoint.[3] I am not concerned with the political views presented in these two reports, but they both contain much information about the way in which the local soviet governments were organized and the methods by which they were administered at the grass-roots level.

The origin and development of soviet governments in the O-yü-wan soviet area can be traced back to 1927, when the Communists in the Wuhan government were expelled and took refuge in rural areas, where they began to transform into soviet governments the organizations that had emerged in the peasant movement. By late 1928, strong soviet bases had been established in several regions: Hung-hu in central Hupeh, Huang-an in northeast Hupeh, Shang-ch'eng in southern Honan, and Chinchia-chai in western Anhwei (where the headquarters of the O-yü-wan soviet government was later established).[4]

The Provincial-Level Government

Each of the soviet governments was headed by a council. The councils of the provincial soviet governments usually were composed of delegates elected by the councils of the *hsien, ch'ü,* and *hsiang* soviet governments of the province, as well as delegates who were directly elected by the people in a general election. The members of a provincial council therefore could be classified in two categories: those who were elected by the people of the province at large, and those who were in-

[2] Mao Tse-tung, "Hsingkuo Changkang Hsiang ti Su-wei-ai Kung-tso" ("The Soviet Work of the Changkang Hsiang in Hsing-kuo Hsien"), *Tou-cheng,* No. 42 (January 12, 1934); reproduced in SSCM, Reel No. 18.

[3] Lu Wei, "Hsingkuo shan-huo kung-tso yü fei-ch'ü chuang-k'uang" ("Hsingkuo Rehabilitation and the State of Affairs in the Bandit Area"), dated November 4, 1934. Collected in Hatano, *Chūkyō-shi,* IV, 719–738.

[4] Jao Yung-chün, "Kuan-yü O-yü-wan san-sheng ti chao-fei chün-shih yü cheng-chich" ("Extermination Campaign and Politics in Three Provinces of Hupeh-Honan-Anhwei"), reproduced in Hatano, *Chūkyō-shi,* I, 227–237. I have also carefully checked the information obtained in my interview with Chang Kuo-t'ao against such official documents as Party directives, resolutions of the O-yü-wan soviet government, and published Communist materials captured by the KMT Army during its campaign against the soviet area in the summer of 1932.

directly elected by the members of the councils at each level of soviet government. In many respects, the election system to choose the council members at each level was designed to create an atmosphere in which the broadest possible electorate might participate in the election of the local administrators, so as to give people the feeling that they managed their own political affairs.

The people in all *hsiang* elected delegates to the *ch'ü* councils, which in turn elected delegates to the *hsien* councils; the latter then chose delegates to the provincial councils. At all levels, the delegates elected by the lower-level councils accounted for only 30 percent of the provincial councils; the other 70 percent were directly elected by the people in a general election. The number of delegates chosen in the direct election was based on the size of the population in each *hsien*.

Each provincial council elected from among its own members a provincial executive committee, the size of which varied from province to province, depending on the population. This committee performed the legislative function of the provincial council when the latter was not in session. Yet even this committee was considered too large to function continuously, so it established from among its own members a standing committee, which in practice served as the top administrative body of the provincial soviet government.

Considerable information on the organizational principles and operations of the O-yü-wan soviet government was made available to me by Chang Kuo-t'ao, who served as chairman of that government, and additional information is available from other sources, such as documents captured by the KMT Army.[5] The following description of the operation of regional and provincial soviet governments will focus on the O-yü-wan soviet government.

The O-yü-wan soviet area, which included ten *hsien*-sized soviet areas in Hupeh province, four *hsien*-sized soviet areas in Anhwei province, and five *hsien*-sized soviet areas in Honan province, was organized under the O-yü-wan regional soviet government, which in turn had under it three provincial soviet governments located in southeast Honan province, northwest Anhwei province, and northeast Hupeh province. Under each of the provincial soviet governments, *hsien, ch'ü,* and *hsiang* soviet governments were established on the pattern prescribed in the organizational law of the soviet government.[6]

The O-yü-wan regional soviet government's standing committee had under it ten committees, organized on functional lines, which dealt with foreign affairs, military affairs, communications, finance, economics, internal affairs, land problems, culture and education, labor

[5] *Ibid.*
[6] See note 1.

problems, and the judiciary. Each member of the standing committee was assigned either to head or to serve on one of these ten functional committees, and these committees carried out the day-to-day administrative tasks of the O-yü-wan soviet government.

That government, like some of the constituent republics of the U.S.S.R. subsequent to the Bolshevik Revolution, established its own foreign-affairs commissariat to handle the foreign relations of the region; however, no information on the activities of this committee is available at present.[7]

The military-affairs commissariat was charged with the responsibility of commanding and directing the work of the Red Army units stationed in the provinces of Honan, Hupeh, and Anhwei, and it supervised the Army headquarters, general political departments, chiefs of staff, military-training centers, logistic offices, and military hospitals under its jurisdiction. Military committees were also created in each *hsien* soviet government, and each was directed by a full-time military commander and vice-commander. These *hsien* organs were directly responsible to the military-affairs commissariat of the O-yü-wan soviet government, and under it they directed the military activities in each *hsien*.

The communications commissariat supervised the post offices, telephone and telegraph services, bus depots, railway stations, maritime-transport offices, and other transport offices.

The finance and economic-affairs commissariat had jurisdiction over the departments of accounting, construction and planning, and taxation. It also established a workers' and peasants' banking system, and organized various economic cooperatives.

The internal-affairs commissariat had under it the marriage-record office, census bureau, social-welfare office, Red Guard bureau, and public-health department.

The land commissariat had jurisdiction over the irrigation and fertilizer departments and the department of land confiscation and distribution. The latter department handled the work of land investigation and registration, issuance of certificates authorizing use of land, and other matters concerned with the confiscation and distribution of land in the O-yü-wan soviet area. The land commissariat was also responsible for the office of grain investigation and statistics.

The culture and education commissariat was composed of the following departments: education, social culture (*she-hui wen-hua*), and the state publishing house.

The labor commissariat supervised unemployment insurance, employment offices, and the labor-protection and inspection bureaus.

[7] For mention of this committee, see Hatano, *Chūkyō-shi*, I, 626.

The judicial commissariat, which consisted of twenty-five to thirty-nine workers and peasants directly elected by the people at a general election, had jurisdiction over the revolutionary court of the O-yü-wan soviet area, which was headed by a chairman, two vice-chairmen, and two lay assessors. The judicial commissariat also supervised the work of the prosecutor's office, which initiated suits, and the judicial administration bureau, which supervised the prisons and labor-correction camps.[8]

The security bureau of the O-yü-wan soviet government, which was directly responsible to the state-security bureau of the central soviet government in Juichin, Kiangsi, controlled the secret police of the region and handled security clearances for government employees and workers in other administrative agencies.

The three provincial soviet governments under the jurisdiction of the O-yü-wan soviet government were structured in a way that may be considered typical of provincial soviet-government organizations during the Kiangsi era. The composition of one of these will illustrate the pattern. At the top of this provincial soviet government was the provincial executive committee (PEC), elected once every year by the provincial council; it was the policy-making organ of the government. The standing committee, elected by the PEC, consisted of nine to thirteen members and was the administrative organ of the provincial soviet government. It was headed by the chairman and two vice-chairmen. Although the number of committees and bureaus under the standing committee varied slightly from province to province, normally there were about ten functional committees and two bureaus. The committees included those for economics, land, finance, administration, labor, culture and education, social welfare, workers' and peasants' inspection (*Kung-nung chien-ch'a wei-yüan-hui*), the military, and the judiciary. The security bureau and the internal bureau were also under the standing committee. However, the security bureau was a more or less independent body, because it was responsible directly to the state-security bureau of the central soviet government.[9]

The function of the economic-affairs committee at the provincial level was to supervise the management of industry and commerce, to assist the consumers' and producers' cooperatives, and to guide the

[8] For a detailed description of the governmental structure and functions of the O-yü-wan soviet government, see the following Chinese source: T'ien Chih, "Ch'ih-fei ti sheng-yin, tsu-chih, shan-huo" ("The Origin, Organization, and Reconstruction of the Red Bandit"). The article originally appeared in *Tientsin Ta Kung Pao* and was reproduced in Hatano, *Chūkyō-shi*, I, 313–348. This report was based on documents captured on the spot and direct interviews with the people who were under the soviet system of government after O-yü-wan soviet area was captured by the KMT Army.

[9] T'ien Chih, "Ch'ih-fei," pp. 327–328.

trade and exchange of agricultural produce. The land committee was in charge of distribution of land, improvement of agriculture, and management of irrigation works. The finance committee collected taxes, checked on the budgets at local-government levels, promoted credit organizations, and managed confiscated properties. The administrative committee (called the general-affairs committee in some provinces) was responsible for the welfare of government employees at the provincial-government headquarters, and the labor committee operated unemployment-aid centers and employment agencies.

The culture and education committee supervised the school system and the work of socialist education, and the social-welfare committee aided aged or disabled Red Army personnel and their families, and helped orphans and lost children to find homes. The function of the workers' and peasants' inspection committee, which was a special organ of the provincial soviet government, was to supervise administration and recommend policies to improve all administrative work in the general fields of politics, economics, finance, land, taxation, culture, and education. Party and military affairs were not within its jurisdiction, however; the military-affairs committee had jurisdiction over all policies relating to military strategy and tactics and supervised the establishment and management of all military facilities, including ordnance depots and army hospitals.

The function of the judicial committee was to supervise all civil and criminal courts and their administration. The internal-affairs bureau exercised jurisdiction over municipal administration, the civilian police force, and the bureau of criminal administration. However, the security bureau, whose members were appointed by the central executive council of the central soviet government and were responsible to it, was responsible for clearing government employees and for dealing with all subversive activities in the province.

"The successful development of the soviet movements in this region cannot be attributed only to the success of Communist agents," said one reporter for the *Tientsin Ta Kung Pao*, who investigated the situation immediately after the Communist evacuation of the area, "but the growth of the soviet movement should be understood in the context of the deteriorating social and economic conditions of recent years. The economic and social conditions of the region were becoming so deplorable that any organization could move in and achieve considerable success by taking advantage of these explosive conditions."[10] This reporter asserted that worsening economic and social conditions in the region, together with the prevailing discontent among young students who were unable to find work after graduating from school, provided

[10] *Ibid.*, p. 313.

opportunities for the organizers of the peasant movement and soviet governments to create institutions through which the discontented young people could participate in the administration of local affairs and find outlets for their frustrations.

Shang-ch'eng *hsien* of southern Honan, for example, was a rich county — in fact, the richest in the entire province — but virtually all its land was owned by a few rich landlords, and the majority of the population in the region consisted of tenant farmers. Almost no ordinary farmers owned land, and few could rent enough to feed their own families. When the *Ta Kung Pao* reporter who wrote the above-mentioned article interviewed peasants in the region immediately after the Communist forces were evacuated in the summer of 1932, he reported that "no peasant denied the fact that malicious oppression and exploitation by the landlord class had existed there before the soviet system of government was instituted. The landlord class required that the tenant farmers pay much higher rent and also demanded that they make a deposit of a year's rent in advance. The deposit was to pay the rent in the event that the tenant farmers were unable to produce enough to pay it." [11] Apparently the amount of the rent was set at a figure much higher than the amount of grain the land could yield each year, so that the tenant farmers were not able to meet the requirement that they pay advance rent. The tenant farmers, wrote the *Ta Kung Pao* reporter, were consequently always in debt. Moreover, usury and bribery were prevalent among the local officials and village bosses, and the situation was ripe for revolutionary change.

When Communist agents came into the area, they promoted such slogans as "Down with the Landlord and Gentry Class!" and "Confiscate all Land and Distribute it to the Peasants!" According to the *Ta Kung Pao* reporter, they presented a challenge and an opportunity for the unemployed and discontented young people of the area to join the soviet movement in order to help eliminate oppression and exploitation by the landlord class and to aid in creating social justice and economic equity in the region. "The soviet movements in south Honan and central Hupeh undoubtedly gained the support of the peasants and youth of the region as the direct result of deteriorating economic and social conditions. This situation, moreover, provided the impetus to overthrow the rule of the gentry class and establish a new system of government, whatever it might be." [12]

The soviet movement in this region slowly gained momentum and eventually expanded to link all the scattered soviet areas together. A

[11] *Ibid.*
[12] *Ibid.*, p. 314.

consolidated soviet base, and the O-yü-wan soviet government, were finally created in January 1931. By that time, soviet organizations were already in operation in forty-four of the sixty-nine *hsien* in Hupeh province.

Under these circumstances the newly established central Party leadership, consisting of Russian-returned students, decided to establish a CCP subbureau in the O-yü-wan soviet area to coordinate the work of the soviet governments in the region.[13] Chang Kuo-t'ao, one of the founders of the CCP who had just returned from Moscow, where he had served as a Chinese representative to the Comintern, was sent by the Russian-trained Party leaders to head the CCP bureau of the O-yü-wan soviet area. Chang stated that after he had received an order from the CCP Politburo to establish the CCP subbureau (*Chung-yang fen-chü*), he left Shanghai in late March 1931 and arrived in the O-yü-wan area in the middle of that year.

The O-yü-wan soviet area, second only to the central soviet area in size, was not at that time under the direct jurisdiction of the central soviet area in Juichin, Kiangsi, and Chang Kuo-t'ao not only became head of the CCP subbureau but also served as chairman of the O-yü-wan soviet government. When Chang went to the O-yü-wan area, he was accompanied by two of the Party's Russian-returned student leaders: Shen Tse-min and Ch'en Ch'ang-hao. Shen became head of the coordinating committee for Party work under Chang's jurisdiction and concurrently served on the military-affairs committee of the O-yü-wan soviet area, and Ch'en headed the Communist Youth League of the O-yü-wan soviet area and also was a member of the CCP subbureau under Chang.[14] Chang asserts that he controlled the entire region of the O-yü-wan soviet area and was free from interference by the central soviet government. "My government was quite free from direct control by the central soviet government, and those of us who were involved in the operation of the O-yü-wan soviet government were able to formulate our own policies and implement them according to our own wishes," Chang claims. "However, the formulation of policies and the administration of political programs was carried out within the general framework of the policy line established by the Party's Central Committee in Shanghai."

[13] *Ibid.*

[14] According to one KMT intelligence report, Chang Kuo-t'ao was originally a member of the Li Li-san faction, but was attracted to the Pavel Mif–Wang Ming faction while Chang was serving as a Chinese representative in Moscow in 1930. This was prior to his return to Shanghai to be appointed head of the CCP subbureau of the O-yü-wan soviet area. See *Tzu 1931 nien chih 1933 nien liang-nien lai chih Chung-kuo Kung-ch'an tang (The CCP from 1931 to 1933)*, in the Bureau of Investigation, Ministry of Judicial Administration, Taiwan. Document No. 291.2/811/9748.

Political Control and the Hsien Soviet Government

Concerning the effectiveness of his control over the *hsien, ch'ü,* and *hsiang* soviet governments, Chang Kuo-t'ao asserts that the O-yü-wan soviet government effectively controlled the entire soviet area under its jurisdiction and established close communication with the soviet governments at each lower level. He admits, however, that the O-yü-wan soviet government faced enormous problems in implementing central decisions at the *hsien, ch'ü,* and *hsiang* levels. Because of this, he says, the O-yü-wan soviet government decided to decentralize much of its policy-making power and delegate it to the local soviet governments. Many policies relating to nonmilitary matters — such as education, public health, labor problems, and peasant questions — were formulated by the *hsien*-level soviet governments, but they had to be consistent with the general framework of policy goals outlined by the overall O-yü-wan soviet government. Policy decisions of a military nature — relating to strategy and tactics and problems of logistical support of the Red Army — were kept in the hands of the standing committee of the O-yü-wan soviet government.

Party organizations were formed to parallel the soviet governments at each level, from the provinces to the village. They supervised the work of the soviet governments but did not take over the direct operation of the soviet institutions. In many respects the Party organizations served as watchdogs over the soviet governments. They supervised local soviet work through the "Party fractions" (*Tang-t'uan*) that were created within the government organs of the soviet governments at each level. The Party fractions, organized at each level, were directly responsible to the Party committees operating parallel to the governmental structure.

According to Chang Kuo-t'ao, a great deal of power was delegated to the *hsien*-level Party and government organs as well as to those at lower levels. "Even the Party organizations operating at levels below the *hsien* committees had considerable freedom to make their own decisions so far as local problems were concerned," Chang says. The reason for this practice, he states, was that the Party was short of well-trained Party cadres to direct soviet work at levels below the *hsien*. When decisions were reached by organizations under the *hsien* Party committee, however, these decisions were reported immediately to it for approval. Then the *hsien* Party secretary would usually consult with the Party's O-yü-wan subbureau about such decisions. "The subbureau would usually approve them, if they were formulated within the general framework of Party policy," Chang claimed. "Most of the time the CCP bureau would also approve policy recommendations from the *hsien* Party committee,"

Chang says. "We never rejected, so far as I can remember, any policy recommendations from the *hsien* Party committees in the O-yü-wan soviet area."

The military-affairs committee of the O-yü-wan soviet area, consisting of about a dozen individuals, was composed only in part of military men; it also included other influential persons in the region, including key members of the provincial Party committees and the chairmen of the provincial soviet governments. It met quite frequently and made decisions relating to strategic problems affecting the soviet area. All decisions reached by this committee were then immediately reported to the CCP subbureau. If the chairman of the military-affairs committee disagreed with the majority opinion of other committee members on any strategic question, he referred the matter directly to the CCP subbureau for decision. Other decisions on problems not relating to strategy — for example, those of logistical support and recruitment for the Red Army — could be reached by the military-affairs committee itself, so long as they were within the general framework of Party policy.

Chang Kuo-t'ao strongly emphasizes the important role that the *hsien* Party committee played in formulating policies in regard to local problems, but he also says that in practice the question of who controlled and operated the *hsien* and *ch'ü* soviet governments depended greatly on the personalities of the *hsien* Party secretary, the chairman of the *hsien* soviet government, and the chairman of the military-affairs committee of the *hsien* soviet government. "If one of these three leaders possessed a more domineering personality than the other two men," Chang states, "he could certainly exercise his control over the operation of all three organizations, regardless of which of these three positions he held in the administrative organs of the *hsien*-level government." Other things being equal, however, the Party secretary of the *hsien* usually had the greatest influence over the policy-making processes of a *hsien* soviet government.

The *hsien* soviet governments were the centers of administrative activity at the local level, but as Chang Kuo-t'ao says, the *hsien* administrators generally took orders from the central and provincial soviet governments and performed administrative duties which were delegated to them by the central authorities. In the traditional political system of China, the *hsien* governments were sometimes more than the agents of the central or the provincial governments, and on occasion the *hsien* magistrates seem to have acted as if they were independent governors of the regions rather than agents of the Imperial Government in Peking.

The Function of Hsien-Level Soviet Government

In view of the fact that the *hsien* government was so important as an administrative unit in the traditional political system,[15] it is pertinent here to analyze how the Chinese soviet government actually organized and operated the *hsien* soviet governments. Several articles written by KMT military leaders and reporters describing soviet work at the *hsien* level throw considerable light on the general organizational pattern of the *hsien* soviet governments and their operational methods.[16] These sources, which were hostile to the soviet regime, probably distort some facts about society under soviet rule, so they need to be compared with the information available from the official publications of the Chinese soviet government.[17] The following analysis is based on information from both these types of sources.

Immediately after its proclamation of November 1931, the central soviet government made an attempt to establish a uniform pattern of organization for the *hsien* soviet governments (HSG), when it drafted the "Organizational Law of the Local Soviet Government."[18] Before the adoption of that law, the organization of the *hsien* soviet governments had varied from *hsien* to *hsien*, because of differences in the backgrounds of the establishment of soviets and the economic and social conditions of different *hsien*, but despite this fact the operations of the HSG seem to have been fairly similar throughout the soviet areas.

It is possible to draw a general picture of the structure and functioning of the HSG. Each *hsien* elected a *hsien* council of workers', peasants', and soldiers' representatives, through a popular general election. All people in the *hsien*, except those who were classified as counterrevolutionary, participated in electing their own delegates to the council. Every thirteen industrial workers elected one delegate to represent them in the *hsien* council, and every fifty peasants and poor people selected one delegate. The *hsien* council in turn elected some of its members, generally one of every five (the number varied from *hsien* to *hsien*, however, and a certain *hsien* council elected one of seven delegates) to form the *hsien* executive committee, which was the most im-

[15] See, for example, T'ung-tsu Ch'u, *Local Government in China Under the Ching* (Cambridge, Harvard University Press, 1962).

[16] See, for example, Chang Shao-tan, "Hsien Su-wei-ai kung-tso" ("The Work of the *Hsien* Soviet Government"), collected in Hatano, *Chūkyō-shi*, V, 215–241; Yun Hai-sheng, "Ningtu Hsien ti-shih-ching" ("The Situation in Ningtu *Hsien*"), dated November 10, 1934; and Li Yü-sheng, "Juichin Fei-huo chi" ("Report on the Bandit Trouble in Juichin"), dated November 20, 1934; reproduced in Hatano, *Chūkyō-shi*, IV, 754-773.

[17] Various reports and resolutions of the *hsien* soviet government, contained in *Ch'en Ch'eng Microfilms (SSCM)*.

[18] See "The Organizational Law of the Local Soviet Government," cited in note 1.

portant policy-making organ of the HSG.[19] The *hsien* executive committee then elected, and delegated its power to, a standing committee, consisting of seven to nine council members, which functioned as the actual administrative body of the *hsien* soviet government. The standing committee was headed by a chairman and two vice-chairmen, and the other members of the committee were assigned to direct the work of each committee (sometimes called departments) established under the direct jurisdiction of the standing committee. These committees often included ones dealing with general affairs, land, finance, economy, social welfare, culture and education, and the military. Each committee, headed by a chairman and a vice-chairman (both of whom were members of the standing committee), consisted of four or five members who carried out day-to-day administrative tasks. (The committees often had departments; for example, one general-affairs committee was divided into departments of documents, accounting, printing, and statistics.) Together they acted as the administrative arm of the soviet and constituted the *hsien* bureaucracy.

The internal-affairs committee supervised construction work, transportation, urban administration, bridges and highways, marriage licenses, and public-health work in the *hsien*. It also established under its jurisdiction a "people's police corps" to maintain public order and guard the *hsien* capital. The "people's police" reportedly settled occasional disagreements among the people, but serious disputes were usually turned over to the judiciary committee for settlement. The military committee had jurisdiction over the Red Guard units and guerrilla units and supervised the peasant volunteer corps, which was led by a military commander, a political officer, and a chief of staff, and functioned as the reserve from which the Red Army could recruit its men. Guerrilla units were reportedly organized in each *hsien* and *ch'ü* soviet district, and they too served as a reserve force from which Red Army men were recruited. The guerrilla units were financed by the *hsien* governments, but the Red Guard units received only military training from the Red Army.

The functions and duties of the land committee of the *hsien* soviet government were to survey farm land, supervise forestry, lakes, and housing, and ensure an equal distribution of farm land to the peasants. It also had the responsibility of collecting and distributing grain through its grain-coordinating bureau.

The labor committee had charge of the execution of the Labor Protection Law and the social-welfare program of the workers. It established under its jurisdiction a labor tribunal to handle disputes among

[19] Chang Shao-tan, "Hsien," p. 224.

workers and settle wage problems. It also maintained employment offices and labor-inspection stations.

The workers' and peasants' inspection committee was closely related to the labor committee, yet it functioned independently. Under its jurisdiction was an "appeals bureau" to receive the complaints and grievances of the workers and peasants. The cadres of this committee were recruited from the "most faithful and reliable peasants" in the rural area and were assigned, after special training, to work in the countryside and collect complaints and appeals from the peasants. To facilitate gathering complaints and information about inequities among the workers and peasants in a village, the cadres installed an "appeals box" in each village so that any villager might propose a new policy or suggest a new idea without identifying himself to the cadres. The workers' and peasants' inspection committee also organized a "shock-troop unit" recruited from the workers and peasants to perform surprise inspections and check on the work of local soviet governments at all levels. The main function of this committee, was to combat bureaucratic methods of administration and to discover and eliminate corrupt and inefficient bureaucrats at the local level. Such committees are said to have had considerable success (even according to an unsympathetic observer of the soviet government) in combating bureaucratic corruption.[20]

The culture and education committee was charged with raising the cultural and educational standards of the peasant masses in the *hsien* soviet district. Under its jurisdiction were established five specialized departments, dealing with culture, fine arts, physical education, dramatic arts, and wall posters.

The judicial committee supervised the administration of the civil and criminal courts. It was alleged, however, that this committee had no tasks to perform because criminal and civil cases, it was claimed, were nonexistent in the Kiangsi soviet areas.[21]

The function of the economic committee was to supervise the cooperatives and to conduct, through a trade bureau established under its jurisdiction, secret trade with business firms outside the soviet areas. In some cases, the economics committee apparently absorbed the functions of the finance committee — which levied all kinds of taxes and supervised the budgetary processes of the *hsien* soviet government — as well as the functions of the grain committee.

Besides the committees mentioned above, a "security bureau" was established at the level of the *hsien* soviet government. However, it was responsible neither to the *hsien* council nor to the *hsien* executive

[20] *Ibid.*, p. 238.
[21] Lu Wei, "Hsingkuo," p. 732.

committee, but was under the direct jurisdiction of the state-security bureau of the central soviet government. One function of the security bureau was to ascertain the reliability of government employees. The *hsien* bureau reportedly had about 120 cadres of its own, many of whom were assigned to work in village, *hsiang*, and *ch'ü* level governments. The function of these cadres was mainly to discover and investigate counterrevolutionary elements or subversive activities among government employees. When the bureau found such a case, however, it did not itself punish the offender but always turned him over to the judiciary committee for hearings and trials.[22]

Altogether, the bureaucracy within the *hsien* soviet government included approximately one hundred staff personnel (not counting the security cadres, mentioned above, who were assigned to lower levels) to operate its complex organization. (The number of staff members, however, varied slightly from *hsien* to *hsien*, depending on the size of the population and the geographic area of the *hsien*.) The *hsien* government did not pay the salary of these administrators, but it did provide them with such daily necessities as food and shelter. The administrative tasks of the *hsien* bureaucracy mainly concerned the implementation of executive orders, Party directives, and legislation adopted by the councils at the higher levels.

From the available information on the operation of the *hsien* soviet governments, it appears that a *hsien* soviet government had considerable freedom to formulate its own policies and implement its own administrative programs, so long as they conformed to the policy line of the Party and the central soviet government. A *hsien* soviet government was expected both to direct and coordinate the work of the village, *hsiang*, and *ch'ü* soviet governments under its jurisdiction and to interpret correctly and implement swiftly the policy decisions transmitted from the provincial and the central soviet governments. Each *hsien* soviet government administered various economic and social programs designed to meet the needs and demands of the people in its district.

Administrative processes in the *hsien*-level soviet government involved a number of meetings — including council meetings, committee meetings, and departmental meetings — which were aimed at making the peasant masses feel that they were participating directly in the decision-making process affecting their own affairs. Such meetings explained and discussed policy issues and also disseminated policy decisions among the population of the *hsien* through the delegates who represented the people and participated in the meetings. The *hsien* standing committee called committee meetings frequently in order to

[22] *Ibid.*

communicate its basic policy line to the council members and through them to the population in general.

To coordinate administrative work between the *hsien* government and its subordinate units, the *ch'ü, hsiang,* and village soviet governments, an inspection system was established. Inspection was usually based upon the work plans submitted by subordinate administrative units, and was carried out to see if they fulfilled their tasks according to the plan. Each village and *hsiang* soviet government was expected to submit periodic reports on its work to the *hsien* standing committee.

One key to the success of the work of the *hsien* administration was the degree to which it made each representative on the *hsien* council fully aware of and committed to the basic policy line of the *hsien* government. Unless the council members understood the policy line, ordinary people could hardly be expected to conform to it. The available evidence indicates that, in contrast to *hsien* government under the previous regimes, the soviet government was able to transmit both the policy and the administrative orders of the central soviet government directly to the peasants at the grass-roots level, through the mechanism of the soviets' representative councils and their numerous committee, whereas previous regimes were unable to reach the people at the grass-roots level because policy instructions often went no farther than the *hsien* magistrates. Administrative programs, political resolutions, or executive orders transmitted from the central soviet government reached the peasant masses at the village level in a matter of a few days or even hours.

In performing their major administrative tasks, *hsien*-level soviet governments during the Kiangsi period placed heavy emphasis on popular mobilization. The *hsien* governments made a major effort to mobilize the peasant masses to participate in its administrative organs, the councils, the standing committees, and other specialized committees. And through various reporting and inspection mechanisms, they coordinated and controlled the work of subordinate soviet governments.

One urgent and immediate task of *hsien* soviet governments throughout the Kiangsi period was to promote the extension of the soviet area by strengthening the Red Army. Whenever the enlargement of the Red Army was called for by the provincial soviet government, the *hsien* soviet governments were expected to meet the need by sending experienced Red Army troops. Persons working at the local-government level were therefore urged to induce the peasant masses to join the Peasant Volunteer Corps and prepare themselves to be transferred to the Red Army after preliminary training. Each *hsien* soviet government was authorized to build up a unit of the Red Army the size of a regiment and to pursue a training program to protect the *hsien* soviet district as well as to supply manpower for the Red Army at the front. The *ch'ü* soviet governments also maintained battalion-sized units to guard the *ch'ü* soviet district. To supply weapons, food, and shelter for a regiment-sized unit at the *hsien* level was not an easy task for any local government, and a major source of supply in the *hsien* districts had to be the confiscated lands or properties of the landlord or gentry class.

Administrative Processes at the Rice-Roots Level

An analysis of the structure and functions of the *ch'ü* and *hsiang* soviet governments during the Kiangsi period indicates that the soviet system carried out a wide range of activities at the "rice-roots" level.

In April 1934, Mao Tse-tung, then the chairman of the presidium of the central executive council of the Chinese Soviet Republic, and Chang Wen-t'ien (Lo Fu), one of the Russian-returned student leaders and the chairman of the people's commissariat (the presidium or the cabinet) of the Chinese Soviet Republic, coauthored a booklet entitled *Ch'ü Hsiang Su-wei-ai Tsen-yang Kung-tso* (*How to Conduct the Work of the Ch'ü and Hsiang Soviet Government*).[23] This important work was a clear indication of the close collaboration between Mao and some members of the returned-student group and also is essential for anyone wishing to understand the organizational principles and operations of both *hsiang* and *ch'ü* soviet governments. It included Mao Tse-tung's advice as to the performance of the work of the *hsiang* soviet government, and Chang Wen-t'ien's explanation of the procedures for carrying out the work of the *ch'ü* soviet government. (The collaboration on this work by Mao and one of the top returned-student leaders illustrates the cooperation at that period between the Russian-returned student leaders and veteran Party leaders in evolving new organizational principles and techniques.)

"The *hsiang* and city soviet governments are the basic organizations in the soviet system of government," Mao asserted, "therefore they must lead the masses and carry out the revolutionary tasks. The administrative tasks of the *hsiang* and city soviet government must be directed to reach the broadest possible masses of the region."[24] In order to mobilize the masses as fully as possible and induce them to take part in the revolutionary work, said Mao, the basic organizations of the soviet system had to be properly established and effectively operated.

[23] Chang Wen-t'ien and Mao Tse-tung, *Ch'u Hsiang Su-wei-ai Tsen-yang Kung-tso* (*How to Conduct the Work of the Ch'ü and Hsiang Soviet Government*), published by the People's Commissariat of the Chinese Soviet Republic in Juichin, Kiangsi (April 1934), p. 63; reproduced in *SSCM*, Reel No. 10.

[24] *Ibid.*

The primary function of the *hsiang* and city soviet governments was to reach the entire population of the region and involve them in its administrative processes.[25] The work of the *hsiang* soviet government was to be closely linked with the needs and wishes of the people in the region, and its task was to assist them to meet their needs. Mao stressed that by helping the people to meet their economic needs, the *hsiang* and city soviet government should be able to mobilize and organize them to participate in the administrative processes.

The work of the *hsiang* and city soviet governments was to be closely coordinated by the executive committee of the council of the *ch'ü*, of which the *hsiang* and city soviet governments were a part. The authority of the *ch'ü* soviet governments can be explained in terms of the relationship between the two functional organizations at each level of government.

The *ch'ü* executive committee, the overall policy-making body of the region, was elected by the *ch'ü* council once every six months, and the number of committee members varied from *ch'ü* to *ch'ü*, depending on the size of the population. The *ch'ü* executive committee in turn elected a standing committee, an administrative body which consisted of five members headed by the chairman and a vice-chairman. The standing committee then formed under its own jurisdiction various committees, such as those for administration, land, finance, economics, culture, and education. The chairman was responsible for directing not only the work of these committees but that of other organizations as well: the Peasant Volunteer Corps, commanded by a military officer (assisted by a political officer and a chief of staff); the security office, whose agents came from the state security bureau of the central soviet government; and the people's court, which handled all legal suits and trials in the *ch'ü* soviet district. (A general-affairs committee was responsible for all clerical work in the *ch'ü* government, such as keeping the records of government employees and supervising their pay rolls.)

At least one member of the *hsiang* executive committee served on the standing committee of the *ch'ü* soviet government, just as one member from the *ch'ü* executive committee served on the *hsien* executive committee. This arrangement was intended to maintain close coordination and effective control over the subordinate units.

The basic administrative tasks of the *hsiang* soviet governments were performed by the executive departments of the *hsiang* standing committees, which were elected every month by the *hsiang* councils. The *hsiang* and city executive committees usually had under them the departments of internal affairs, land, military affairs, labor, health, culture and education, grain, and workers' and peasants' inspection. Each

---

[25] *Ibid.*

department was headed by a chairman, called the executive officer. In some respects, the administrative functions of these departments were very similar to those of the *hsien* or *ch'ü* soviet governments, but there was an important difference: in the *hsiang* soviet government the chairman played a larger role and the executive committees were generally organized temporarily as the work required. However, the organizational pattern of the *hsiang* soviet government varied from one soviet district to another. According to one source, for example, some executive committees of the *hsiang* soviet governments in central Hupeh were elected by the *hsiang* councils once every three months. The *hsiang* council created standing committees headed by a chairman and two vice-chairmen, under which various executive departments were permanently established.[26]

The task of the *hsiang* executive committee was to supervise the routine day-to-day business of the *hsiang* administration when the *hsiang* council was not in session. The five- to seven-member standing committee was usually elected by the *hsiang* council, and was headed by a chairman, often assisted by a deputy chairman or a secretary. The organizational responsibility of the chairman was to supervise and coordinate all administrative work, and he also served as a link to the *ch'ü* soviet government. The meetings of the *hsiang* executive committee, which were convened at least once every five days, were attended by the entire standing committee as well as by all the executive officers of the village soviet administrations under their jurisdiction.

Mao Tse-tung stressed that the administrative task of the standing committee was to "comprehend local conditions and fulfill the responsibility assigned by the *hsiang* council." [27] Its members were also responsible for supervision of the village-council meetings, the mass-organization rallies, and the committee work of each executive department. It therefore coordinated all administrative activities of the *hsiang* soviet government. Besides preparing the agenda for the *hsiang* council meetings, it bore primary responsibility for drafting and approving the administrative programs of all village councils under its jurisdiction.

Mao specifically urged that the meetings of the standing committee be convened immediately after those of the *hsiang* council, so that the standing committee could assign work and supervise it effectively when tasks were still fresh in its members' minds. The chairman of the *hsiang* standing committee usually presided over the *hsiang* council meetings, transmitted policy directives to the village executive officers, and ap-

[26] T'ien Chih, "Fei-ch'ü shih-ch'a chi" ("Report on the Observation of the Soviet Area"). This article was originally published in *Tientsin Ta Kung Pao* in 1931; reproduced in Hatano, *Chūkyō-shi*, II, 277–312.

[27] Chang Wen-t'ien and Mao Tse-tung, *Ch'ü Hsiang*, pp. 1–39.

pointed secretaries in each village to write reports on the work of the soviet. Such reports usually concerned recruitment of Red Army personnel, distribution of land, collection of land taxes, progress of the agricultural cooperatives, preparation of general elections, etc.

The chairman of the *hsiang* standing committee received a salary. He was responsible for the administrative work of the village councils, and was obliged to make detailed reports to the *hsiang* council on the activities of the village executive officers after his routine inspection tours of each village under his jurisdiction. The chairman was also expected to deal with any emergency and to direct relief work whenever natural calamities, famines, or other disasters struck the *hsiang* soviet district.

The secretary of the *hsiang* standing committee was charged with entire responsibility for the clerical work of the *hsiang* soviet government. He kept the census records, statistics of land distribution, and records of marriages, births, and deaths. He also bore the responsibility of making periodic reports to the *ch'ü* soviet government on political and economic conditions in his *hsiang* district, disseminating governmental decisions to each village, issuing passes to the residents of his *hsiang* who wished to travel to other areas, and helping the families of Red Army men write letters. In the event that the chairman of the *hsiang* soviet government could not read or write, the secretary was obliged to serve as reader for him. He kept the minutes of all meetings and reminded the chairman and deputy chairman of what was to be done. He thus shared the work load of the chairman and the deputy chairman.

Apparently the CCP often had difficulty in extending its primary organizations at the grass-roots level throughout the soviet areas. Sometimes it recruited the secretaries of the *hsiang* soviet governments into the CCP organizations, but in other instances it sent its own agents to serve as Party representatives at the level of the *hsiang* governments.[28]

Broadly speaking, the standing committees of the *hsiang* soviet governments were to serve as the core of the administrative authority in rural areas. They were to disseminate policy directives from higher administrative organs, inspect the village administrators who were under their jurisdiction, and educate all members of the *hsiang* council who were sufficiently active in performing the soviet's work. The executive departments of the standing committee constituted a highly developed system of committees. An executive department either was a committee itself or organized several committees under its supervision, depending on the nature of its work. Each committee was usually

[28] Tu Chen-nung, "Kan tung-pei su-wei-ai ch'ü ti kung-tso pao-kao." In Hatano, *Chūkyō-shi*, III, 311–385.

headed by a member of the *hsiang* executive committee, and committee members were recruited from each village council so that they could carry the decisions of the committee directly to their villages. Some committees under the standing committee were permanent ones, but others were temporary. The permanent committees were concerned, for example, with strengthening the Red Army, volunteer work to support the Red Army, the Peasant Volunteer Corps, air-raid shelters, agricultural production (special committees for spring sowing and fall harvesting were temporary), education, forestry, irrigation, research and records, health, transportation, food, and inspection. Temporary committees included those dealing with the confiscation of land, the land tax, elections, etc., and were usually dissolved immediately after their functions had been fulfilled.[29]

The process of organizing the committees under the *hsiang*-level government was also an administrative one. All committees were responsible to the *hsiang* standing committee (administrative organ of the *hsiang* soviet government) and also involved each village council. A chairman of a village council, for example, was usually appointed to one of the executive committees of the *hsiang* soviet government. The members of the village committees were first screened by the *hsiang* standing committee and then appointed by the *hsiang* council. The chairman of each village council usually nominated one or more active members from his own council to serve on various committees of the *hsiang* executive committee, but the nominees had to be approved, as a rule, by the *hsiang* council. In most cases the committees were reorganized at six-month intervals, to eliminate inactive members and bring in new ones. In order to link committee work in the *hsiang* and the villages, the chairman of each executive committee (or department) under the *hsiang* soviet government was urged to attend appropriate committee meetings in each village. For example, the chairman of the education committee of the *hsiang* standing committee was to attend the meetings of each village education committee. The *hsiang* and villages were thus expected to bring in as many persons as possible to participate in the work of various committees. This was intended to give people a sense of being involved in the decision-making processes of the local administration, and in this way, it was assumed, the local administration would attain the goal of mass participation.

According to an authoritative source, the number of full-time staff members actively engaged in the management and operation of the committees of the *hsiang* soviet government was about twenty, though the number varied from *hsiang* to *hsiang*.[30] (At the *ch'ü* level of soviet

[29] Chang Wen-t'ien and Mao Tse-tung, *Ch'ü Hsiang*, pp. 1–39.
[30] Lu Wei, *Hsingkuo*, p. 733.

government, it was estimated that there were about seventy or eighty staff members.)

The council of a *hsiang* soviet government, which met approximately every ten days, was composed of one or two representatives elected from each village in the *hsiang* soviet district. It was, in principle, the highest political body of the *hsiang* soviet government, with authority to formulate and debate all regulations and policies and to direct the work of the *hsiang* executive committees. Understandably, the leadership of this body was considered to be one of the most important elements in the soviet system of government.

Mao Tse-tung emphasized in his writings on institution-building the importance of the *hsiang*-council meetings in the functioning of the soviet system of government. Because the councils consisted of delegates who knew the situation in their own villages, it was believed that they could recommend policies that were most suitable to them.[31]

Council meetings usually were divided into two periods, one for reports and the other for discussion. The chairman of a *hsiang* executive committee and the delegate members who represented the *hsiang* people at the *ch'ü* council customarily made reports on their activities since the previous meeting; no report was to exceed ten minutes. The executive officers of all villages were also called upon to report on the activities of their village committees and to discuss how the decisions of the previous meeting had been carried out. When the council dealt with specific problems of a technical nature, the village executive officers were expected to present facts and figures to make their reports more comprehensible to the members of the Council.

Council meetings were also called whenever special problems or important subjects had to be dealt with. For example, special meetings were called to discuss the procedure for the spring planting, the organizing of workers' mutual-aid teams, the managing of the labor cooperatives, and other questions closely related to the work of the *hsiang* and village soviet governments.

The sessions that followed the reports generally dealt with practical matters, and the delegate members from each village discussed the problems of their own villages. All of these sessions were expected to result in specific conclusions or policy recommendations. For example, a discussion on "how to organize the workers' mutual-aid teams" centered on the questions of how many organizers could be recruited from each village, how many workers each village could contribute to the teams, and what the role of a village executive officer should be in recruiting and utilizing this labor force. In theory, the discussion usually was fol-

[31] *Ibid.*

lowed by a specific decision, based on a majority vote, and all decisions were recorded by the secretary of the *hsiang* council.

The secretary of a *hsiang* council was expected to keep in close touch with the village executive officers in order to follow up on the execution of the council's decision, and to report on this. The standing committee had to prepare reports on its work and select important items for discussion at each council meeting. The chairman of the standing committee was responsible for planning the council meetings, with the assistance of his deputy and the secretary. As a rule, a presiding officer was elected at each meeting, but Mao suggested that a permanent chairman of the council meetings be elected so that there could be continuity. Mao also suggested that the chairman of the standing committee could best serve as the permanent chairman, because he was often the best-informed person in the *hsiang* soviet district.

Each council meeting started with a roll-call by the presiding officer. The standing committee maintained a full record of the attendance of the delegate members, and also kept information on the background of each delegate, including name, sex, age, and position in the delegate's village. This roster was frequently sent to all the villages to keep the people informed of the activities of their delegates to the *hsiang* council.

In many areas an effort was made at the *hsiang* level to establish a "model soviet government" which other *hsiang* soviet governments could emulate. Changkang *hsiang* soviet government in Hsing-kuo *hsien* of Kiangsi province and Ts'ai-ch'i *hsiang* soviet government in Fukien province were two such "model soviet governments" within the Chinese Soviet Republic. Mao himself wrote detailed reports on these two "model soviet governments," and the reports were publicized widely in the soviet area.[32] In his introduction to these reports, which were written in November 1933, Mao asserted that "everyone knows the importance of soviet work at the *hsiang* level, but few seem to know the ways and means of carrying out such work."[33] Mao charged that "the leaders in the higher echelons of the soviet government are satisfied when they have dispatched executive orders and political resolutions to the lower echelons; thus a bureaucratic tendency has developed in the soviet work."[34]

The main tasks of the soviet government at the *hsiang* level, Mao explained, were to lead the work of mass mobilization and to help the Red Army fight the war. "It is therefore very important to learn from

[32] Mao Tse-tung, "Hsingkuo Changkang Hsiang ti Su-wei-ai Kung-tso" ("The Work of the Soviet Government in Changkang *Hsiang* in Hsingkuo Hsien"), *Toucheng*, No. 42 (January 12, 1934); reproduced in *SSCM*, Reel No. 18.
[33] *Ibid.*
[34] *Ibid.*

the experience of a *hsiang* soviet government which has successfully completed its task." Several soviet governments at the *hsiang* level were charged with having committed errors in their work as a result of bureaucratic handling of affairs, and by this time Mao seems to have regained the power and influence that he had lost a year before, in October 1932. His reports on the "model soviet governments" were intended to be circulated widely among *hsiang* leaders to help them correct past mistakes. An analysis of these two reports makes clear the strong influence of Mao in the sphere of government policy-making and also throws additional light on the administrative processes at the *hsiang* level of soviet government.

Mao's report on the Changkang *hsiang* model government [35] covers a wide range of subjects, including organizational techniques applicable to *hsiang* soviet governments. It provides a good general picture of what Mao believed the soviet system at the *hsiang* level should be during the Kiangsi period.

Changkang *hsiang* was a part of Shangshe *ch'ü* in Hsing-kuo *hsien*, in Kiangsi province, and it consisted of four villages: Changkang, T'ang-pei, Hsinch'i, and Szukang. It had 437 households and a population of 1,784, of whom 320 were serving in the Red Army and 1,464 remained in the *hsiang*. A breakdown of the latter by age groups was as follows: 196 male and 185 female youths were in the age group of one to fifteen, and of these only 13 boys and 12 girls were classified as middle peasants; 111 men and 80 women were in the age group of sixteen to twenty-three, including 4 men and 3 women who were classified as middle peasants; 66 men and 146 women were in the age group of twenty-four to forty-five, and included 3 men and 7 women classified as middle peasants; and 112 men and 160 women were in the age group over forty-six, of which 11 men and 13 women were classified as middle peasants. Persons classified as belonging to the proletarian class numbered 102; these included industrial workers, farm laborers, and coolies. Seventy-six persons were classified as belonging to the land-lord and rich-peasant classes.

About 80 persons from Changkang *hsiang* had joined the Red Army during the years between 1928 and 1930; then the number increased by 139 in the year 1933 alone (not counting 7 others who volunteered to work in a guerrilla unit). A total of 94 had also volunteered to help the Red Army as civilian workers. In all, therefore, 320 persons — more

[35] It is divided into twenty-one chapters: administrative districts, census, delegate council, election procedure, committee work, local troops and air defense, livelihood of masses, problems of labor force, cooperative movement, cultural work, health work, women's work, antiimperialism, poor-peasant corps, social aid, children's work, industrial workers, propaganda units, shock troops, and revolutionary competition.

than 12 percent of the *hsiang* population — were engaged in work for the Red Army.

The Changkang *hsiang* council consisted of fifty-five representatives, about fourteen elected by each of the four constituent villages. The breakdown of the delegates was as follows: fourteen delegates represented a population of 500 in Changkang village; fourteen, a population of 490 in T'angpei village; thirteen, a population of 330 in Hsinch'i village; and fourteen, a population of 400 in Szukang village. The meetings of the Changkang council (the soviet) were also usually attended, in the pattern noted above, by one or two observers from the *ch'ü* soviet government. Discussions in the council often concentrated on such questions as these: how to mobilize people to strengthen the manpower of the Red Army; how to mobilize the economic resources of the region to support the revolutionary cause; how to organize the cooperatives and save grain, vegetables, and other staples; how to construct and repair roads; and how to mobilize the population to guard and protect the *hsiang* soviet district from outside attack. Each of the council members was expected both to represent and to supervise twenty to fifty persons in his own village. Because each council member lived in his own village, he could keep a detailed record concerning each of his constituents, and he was expected to be able to report on the background and activities of those whom he represented whenever he was called upon to do so at the *hsiang* council meeting.

(In 1932 a reapportionment of the administrative district had resulted in some changes in the composition of the *hsiang* council. Previously Changkang *hsiang* had consisted of seven villages with a population of 3,000 persons, for which eighty delegates were elected, but after the reapportionment, as discussed earlier, the number of delegates was reduced to seventy-five, when a general election was held on November 1, 1933. Of the seventy-five delegate members, twenty-nine were reported to have volunteered to serve in the Red Army by May 1, 1933. They were therefore replaced by alternate members of the council.)

The political stability of a *hsiang* soviet government was often analyzed in terms of the attitudes and behavior of the council members. Mao's report stated that about 60 percent of the *hsiang* council members were politically highly reliable, 35 percent were fairly reliable, and 5 percent were not very reliable. Four delegate members, two men and two women, classified as the least reliable ones, were portrayed as "very stupid and the most inactive."[36] For example, they had attended only four council meetings out of ten that had been called, had not even tried to listen to the reports made by other council members, and had

[36] *Ibid.*

not participated in the discussion. Their attitude toward the village people whom they represented was said to be extremely unfriendly, and it was reported that their constituents paid no attention to them. Consequently, a new election was held, and they were replaced.[37]

In Mao's report, sixteen women delegates were described as follows: eight who were the best had often volunteered to work in the administrative activities of the *hsiang* soviet government and had fulfilled their duties well; six were in the middle category and had not volunteered for duties but when assigned tasks for the soviet administration they usually fulfilled them; and two belonged in the category of the least reliable ones who did not even carry out the tasks assigned to them. (All members of the Changkang council were assigned to work on various executive committees, and were sent to their constituent villages to direct soviet work there and perform inspections for the *hsiang* soviet government.)

The electoral process for choosing *hsiang* council members, as described in this report, was interesting, because the elections obviously reflected effort on the part of the soviet organizers to create a sense of mass participation among the entire population. *Hsiang* election committees were usually formed, with nine members, including the secretary of the *hsiang* CCP committee, the women's secretary of the *hsiang* CCP committee, the head of the peasant organization, the head of the artisans' organization, the head of the poor-peasant corps, the head of the youth corps (pioneers) , and three other members of the *hsiang* council. The plan was to hold the election in September, but it was later postponed to November 1, 1933. It was held to prepare for the election of delegates to the Second Soviet Congress, which met in January 1934.

The propaganda for this election was designed to inspire the population to resist and repulse the encirclement campaign of the KMT Army, then under way, and to assist in establishing soviet administration. Each village was an election unit, and all factory workers in the *hsiang* were considered one election unit. The Changkang soviet district therefore had altogether five election units — four villages and one factory-workers' unit.

Each person who had reached the age of sixteen, except for some landlords and rich peasants, had the right to cast a vote and to be elected to any office. Landlords and rich peasants were classified into two groups: those who could vote in the election and those who could not. This classification was based on their political attitudes and behavior rather than the amount of property they had owned previously, and exemplified an administrative policy based on Mao's concept of "mass line."

[37] *Ibid.*

When the election took place on November 1, 1933, three members of the *ch'ü* soviet government were sent to the *hsiang* as observers. (They also were to observe the establishment of the *hsiang* council and the election of the *hsiang* executive committee by the newly elected council members.) More than 90 percent of the *hsiang* population was reported to have participated, and the remaining 10 percent, it was said, could not participate because of illness and for other reasons. The political attitudes of the fifty-five council members who were chosen in this election were analyzed as follows: thirty-six were highly active and nineteen were fairly active; no delegate was classified as least active. Hence the political stability of the Changkang *hsiang* was considered to be excellent.

Immediately following the general election, the first session of the *hsiang* council was convened to elect an executive committee to serve as the policy-making organ of the council. This body consisted of a chairman, a vice-chairman, a secretary, and seven representatives who served as the *hsiang's* representatives in the *ch'ü* council. The *hsiang* executive committee in turn elected its standing committee, which was the administrative organ of the *hsiang* soviet government. This body consisted of a chairman, a vice-chairman and a secretary, and under it the permanent and temporary committees were organized, on the basis of the administrative needs of the *hsiang* soviet government.

Despite its good points, however, the Changkang soviet government was said to have failed to meet standards in one respect during the election. Reportedly "the election propaganda failed to stress that the *hsiang* council was a governing body of the masses and a government by which the people could manage their own living conditions. The *hsiang* council should have been publicized as the most important political organ through which the *hsiang* people can exercise their rights and administrative duties." [38]

"The soviet system of government is an organizer and leader of the masses of people," Mao stressed, "therefore, it should concentrate its efforts on the work of improving the livelihood of the people and winning the confidence and support of the masses. It must also serve as the leader in mobilizing the masses and leading them in the work of expanding the Red Army and winning the war over the KMT campaign against the soviet area." [39] To fulfill this role, the Changkang *hsiang* soviet government organized fifteen executive committees to accomplish the urgent tasks of mass mobilization.[40] Each committee

[38] *Ibid.*
[39] *Ibid.*
[40] The committees dealt with Red Army work, land affairs, land registration, forestry, construction, irrigation, bridges, state properties, warehouse protection, confiscation, land investigation, education, health, and air defense.

consisted of five to nine members and included one or two delegate members from each village in the *hsiang* soviet district. The committee members who represented each village on each committee in turn formed similar committees in their own villages to establish functional relationships between the village soviet work and the administrative tasks of the *hsiang* soviet government. Every village committee was directly responsible to the corresponding committee of the *hsiang* soviet government.

Some of the problems of administering local soviet governments were described to me (in an interview in Hong Kong in December 1964) by Chang Kuo-t'ao, who, as mentioned earlier, had served as leader of the O-yü-wan soviet government. He stressed the importance of the problem of relations between local and outside cadres. "To maintain an effective relationship between the government administrators (who generally were recruited from the locality) and the Party leaders (who often came from outside the region)," Chang asserted, "was one of the most intricate problems of the local government during the Kiangsi period."

The problems of developing effective leadership cadres and administrative techniques at both the grass-roots and higher levels, which will be explored in the following chapter, seem to have preoccupied the thinking of the leaders of the central soviet government. Some Russian-returned student leaders, such as Chang Wen-t'ien and Wang Chia-hsiang, who controlled the central organs of the Party, and Mao and Chu Te, who had full control over the Central Soviet Government and the local government leaders, seem to have collaborated well (despite the contrary views of some analysts), and they developed highly sophisticated administrative techniques in the process of operating the complex organizations of the many soviet governments that were widely scattered throughout the soviet area.

VII

NEW CONCEPTS OF LEADERSHIP
AND CADRE EDUCATION*

Like many leaders in contemporary developing countries, Chinese Communist leaders were preoccupied, during the Kiangsi soviet period, with problems of institution-building: the creating of a new political party, the organizing of it, the establishing of governmental institutions, and the structuring of mass organizations. The recruitment, training, and promotion of prospective leaders were often the heart of the matter. As the revolutionary-base areas expanded and the population under Communist control doubled, the Chinese Communist Party became increasingly dedicated to formulating new policies that would enable it to reap maximum advantage from the changing situation. This involved, in the first place, a search for an organizational strategy that would enable it to win the support and friendship of the local population by giving heed to its interests and aspirations. The era of the Kiangsi soviet witnessed the beginning of the end of policy based purely on ideology and a change to policy based on new concepts of leadership and on new techniques of organization.

After the 1927 debacle, a series of power struggles and policy conflicts reportedly took place within the Party's central politburo while Chinese Communist revolutionary strategy was being shifted from an urban to a rural orientation. What the times required of the CCP leadership, therefore, was that it adjust its policies to meet the needs of the situation and abandon the illusion of proletarian revolution while devising a new organizational strategy that would sustain the growth of the revolution. Against a background of aggressive jockeying for supreme power in the Party in an unsettled revolutionary environment, the CCP leadership was compelled to conduct what a leading historian of Chinese Communism has called "a screening process within its leadership."[1] The so-called "Russian-returned student" leadership,

* An earlier version of this chapter was presented at the twenty-second annual meeting of the Association for Asian Studies in San Francisco, California, on April 5, 1970.
[1] C. Martin Wilbur, "The Influence of the Past: How the Early Years Helped to

which took control of the policy-making machinery at the fourth plenum of the CCP in January 1931, formulated its own policies with an eye to eliminating Li Li-san's following and bringing about decisive structural changes in the CCP by eradicating his method of organizational control over the Party structure. As a first step toward removing the harmful effects of Li Li-san's stewardship, the new leaders of the CCP called for structural reform of the Party and an immediate reorganization of revolutionary strategy.

This chapter is chiefly concerned with analyzing the emerging concepts of leadership based on the organizational techniques of the mass line which evolved during the Kiangsi soviet period (1931–1934) and with evaluating the ways in which these concepts and techniques were subsequently incorporated into policies governing the recruitment, training, and promotion of leadership cadres in the Kiangsi revolutionary base. The term cadre (kan-pu) here refers to "a leader, organizer, a person who holds command and authority in a given organizational setting."[2] The cadres in the Kiangsi soviet, unlike those of present-day China, were neither hierarchically structured nor highly stratified,[3] but they performed two important functions: as the leadership personnel in close contact with the population, they served as antennae of the Party in ascertaining the interests and aspirations of the masses; and as agents projecting the Party's policies formulated on the basis of reconnaissance among the masses, they performed the important function of implementing those policies and at the same time winning the friendship and support of the masses for the Party's goals. During the Kiangsi period, CCP leaders viewed cadres as the organizational foundation on which the techniques of the mass line were to be built. It is not really surprising, then, to find that a considerable number of resolutions and policy statements concerning cadres was issued by central organs of the CCP in Kiangsi.[4]

Shape the Future of the Chinese Communist Party," *The China Quarterly*, No. 36 (October–December, 1968), p. 26.

[2] For the cadre concept and its development, see H. Franz Schurmann, *Ideology and Organization in Communist China* (Berkeley, University of California Press, 1966), pp. 162–167; John W. Wilson, *Leadership in Communist China* (Ithaca, Cornell University Press, 1963), especially chs. 5 and 6.

[3] See A. Doak Barnett, *Cadres, Bureaucracy, and Political Power in Communist China*, p. 38. See also James MacDonald, "The Performance of the Cadres," in *Modern China's Search for a Political Form* (London, Oxford University Press, 1969), Jack Gray, ed., pp. 268–298.

[4] The resolutions of the CCP on cadre questions include *Chung-yang kuan-yü kan-pu wen-t'i ti chüeh-i* (*Central Politburo Resolution on the Question of Cadres*), dated August 27, 1931; and *Tang-ti chien-she wen-t'i chüeh-i-an* (*Resolution on the Problems of the Party's Reconstruction*), which contains the selections on creation and education of cadres and was passed by the First Congress of the Party Delegates in the Soviet area in November 1931. *Tang-ti chien-she chiang-shu t'i-kang* (*Lecture*

It is the proposition of this chapter that new concepts and methods of leadership, based on Mao's organizational concept of "mass line," had already begun to emerge during the Kiangsi soviet period — with major contributions from Mao Tse-tung if not his active support and participation. Reasonably good evidence exists to support this, in that Mao Tse-tung and such members of the Russian-returned student group as Lo Fu (Chang Wen-t'ien) and K'ang Sheng agreed on a number of policy issues in the Kiangsi soviet base and collaborated, as indicated earlier, to develop new organizational strategy of mass mobilization. Moreover, a close collaboration between Mao and Lo Fu in developing overall policy for the soviet system of government and the operational method of the local-level administration in particular was, as pointed out in the preceding chapter, an indication that a good relationship existed between Mao and certain members of the Russian-returned student group.[5] At any rate, these concepts and methods served as the foundation on which actual rule during the Kiangsi and the Yenan periods was tried and tested, culminating finally in the development of "the thought of Mao Tse-tung." It is not too difficult to prove that Mao's mass-line style of work in Yenan derived from his policies developed in the Kiangsi base, for there are certain coincidences that suggest that this was the case. It is interesting to note here that strikingly similar concepts of leadership and organizational strategy existed during two distinctive periods — Kiangsi and Yenan — in the history of the Chinese Communist movement. For example, the reform movement of 1931–1933 in the Kiangsi soviet was so like the Chengfeng rectification campaign of 1942–1944, in both goals and methods, that one is led to speculate on whether Mao Tse-tung himself contributed the basic ideas for both.[6] The large amount of instructional

Outlines for the Reconstruction of the Party) contains rich material on the cadre problems and this material seems to have served as a handbook for the leaders and organizers of the Party's branch organizations. These documents can be found in Reel 2 of the Shih Sou Collection (Microfilm made by the Hoover Institution). Some of the selected documents from the Shih Sou Collection are reprinted in Tso-liang Hsiao, Power Relations within the Chinese Communist Movement, 1930–1934, vol. II.

[5] I have tried to develop this theme, based on an analysis of Chang Wen-t'ien's policy statements as well as on my personal interviews with Chang Kuo-t'ao in Hong Kong in 1964. Some of the major works of Chang Wen-t'ien that contain the same ideas include: "On New Method of Leadership," Tou-cheng. No. 2 (February 4, 1933); "The Prospects for Economic Development in the Soviet Area," Tou-cheng, No. 11 (August 14, 1933), collected in Hatano, Chūkyō-shi, III, 601–609; "Struggle for Leading the People's Revolution for the Establishment of the People's Soviet Government," a 63-page pamphlet published by the CBSA in April 1932, collected in SSCM, Reel 16; "Oppose the Extreme Leftism of the Petty Bourgeoisie," Tou-cheng, No. 49 (March 2, 1934).

[6] For the Yenan period, I have drawn information and interpretation from Chalmers A. Johnson, Peasant Nationalism and Communist Power; Boyd Compton, Mao's

material for the training of cadres that was widely circulated in the Kiangsi soviet (most of it now available in the *Ch'en Ch'eng microfilms*) suggests that there was a systematic method of training the cadres in the soviet base of Kiangsi.

It is also interesting to note that the CCP leaders in the Kiangsi period paid as much, if not more, attention to the significance and needs of trained cadres as did the CCP leaders in Yenan. Whether by coincidence or design, the policies formulated by the Kiangsi leadership to govern the recruitment, training, and promotion of the cadres were so closely akin to those later developed by the CCP leaders of the Yenan period that one is led to conclude that the Yenan cadre policy was nothing but an extension of what had already been developed in the Kiangsi soviets.

At any rate, the formulation of policies governing the recruitment, training, and promotion of cadres during the Kiangsi soviet period seems to have taken into account some of the same factors and problems considered during the Yenan period. Common to the two periods were the problems of coordinating widely scattered base areas, winning the support and friendship of newly recruited members of the Party and government, and establishing a close relationship between the Party, the government, and the masses within the base areas.[7]

The policies controlling the recruitment, training, and mobility of cadres during the Kiangsi soviet period will be analyzed here against the background of how the new concept of collective leadership emerged, how the organizational techniques of the mass line were related to this new concept, and how this concept and these techniques influenced the CCP leaders of the period in their attempt to arrive at policies that would ensure revolutionary victory. Judging from the available documents and policy statements, the concept of leadership was based upon a "scientific division of labor" and the strengthening of the committee system, and the organizational techniques of the mass line were developed on the basis of policies governing cadre recruitment and training. The emergence and numerical growth of cadres during the period resulted directly from the newly developing concept of leadership and organizational techniques of the mass line, and the cadres were expected, in their training and education, to integrate concept as well as techniques in the development of a new organizational strategy.

China: Party Reform Documents, 1942–1944 (Seattle, University of Washington Press, 1952); and Mark Selden, *The Yenan Way in Revolutionary China* (Cambridge, Mass., Harvard University Press, 1971).

[7] For similar problems in the Yenan period, see Compton, *Mao's China*, pp. xxvi–xxviii.

The New Concept of Leadership

The picture that emerges from the available documents on the Kiangsi soviet period is one of a constant struggle by the new leadership to attain the goals of structural change within the Party and reorganization of revolutionary strategy. Changes in the leadership of the policy-making units of the CCP after the Fourth Plenum also brought about a drastic alteration in the concept and method of leadership as well as changes in the organizational techniques of formulating and implementing the Party's policies.

Three fundamental organizational principles underlay the change of Party structure and the reorganization of revolutionary strategy: the concept of "collective leadership" (*chi-t'i ling-tao*) by means of systematically dividing responsibilities; a system of inspection and coordination by strengthening the committee system; and a mass-line approach to policy formulation and implementation.[8] The principles were arrived at, according to Lo Fu (the pseudonym of Chang Wen-t'ien), after a careful analysis of the organizational status of the Party and a thorough review of the existing revolutionary environment. A system of collective leadership was urgently needed, it was argued, because Li Li-san's method of administering the Party organization had been authoritarian, bureaucratic, and formalistic. The new leadership accused Li not only of directing the Party's central organs in an authoritarian manner, but also of establishing a "family-head system" (*chia-chang chih-tu*) in Party committees at every level. The secretary of each Party committee, it was charged, exerted paternalistic control over that unit just as Li did in operating the Central Committee. In order to insure the continuity of his policy, Li installed his own friends and loyal followers to head each Party committee. A policy directive from the Party's central agencies, though it reached subordinate sections with great speed, was no more than a scrap of paper, for Party secretaries at every level were more concerned with obeying orders than with implementing policy. The accusation was therefore made that, under Li Li-san, policy directives never reached the members of the Party, nor were the directives implemented by the population because many were shelved by the secretaries of district Party committees.

Party secretaries at all levels were criticized both for such bureaucratic and authoritarian methods and for having exercised a "one-man dictatorship" (*pao-pan chu-i*) over every aspect of Party work. In many

---

[8] For these concepts, see Lo Fu (Chang Wen-t'ien), *Shin-ti ling-tao fang-shih* (*New Methods of Leadership*), a series of four articles originally printed in *Tou-cheng*, No. 2 (February 4, 1933) and then published in booklet form in April 1934. The first printing consisted of ten thousand copies. *SSCM*, Reel 14.

committees, it was alleged, the secretary alone made the important decisions, and in some instances, if the committees consisted of three or
four members, the secretary simply gave them orders and expected
obedience, thereby creating the practice of commandism (*ming-ling
chu-i*). The tradition of nepotism led the veteran leaders, it was said, to
appoint their relatives or friends to leadership positions regardless of
competence or experience. The practice was so widespread that when
the Russian-returned-student leaders took control of the Party's policy-
making organs in Shanghai, they immediately suppressed the methods
and habits of Li's organization by purging his followers.

In order to eliminate such evil methods and their influence from
every corner of the Party organization, Lo Fu explained, the new leadership proposed a new collective system based on the "scientific division
of labor." The close collaboration between the Russian-returned-
student leaders and a number of veteran leaders, notably Chou En-lai,
Hsiang Ying, Mao Tse-tung, and Chu Te, can also be interpreted as
a reflection of the new concept of collective leadership. The structural
reforms and reorganization of revolutionary strategy after the Fourth
Plenum were aimed mainly at creating a new style of leadership. In
line with the new concept of collective leadership, the Party's Central
Bureau in the Soviet Areas (CBSA) was established, immediately after
the Fourth Plenum; it consisted of Chou En-lai and Hsiang Ying (representing the views and interests of the veteran cadres in the Party's
Central Politburo) and Mao Tse-tung and Chu Te (representing the
views and interests of the soviet institutions and the Red Army in the
soviet regions), along with five other members. These included Jen
Pi-shih, Yü Fei, and Tseng Shan, and the five seem to have represented
youth, labor, and other mass organizations.[9] Although it is generally
assumed that the creation of the Party's central bureau of the soviet
area was an attempt by the returned students to exercise control over
the leaders of the soviet area, subsequent events and organizational
development within the central bureau refute this assumption. Electing
Mao and Chu Te to the Politburo of the central bureau of the soviet
area, the returned students deliberately set about winning the support
and cooperation of the leaders in the soviet areas of Kiangsi.

Confronted, on the one hand, by the challenges raised by the "right
opposition" of Lo Chang-lung and Wang K'e-ch'üan, and, on the
other, by the attack of the "left opposition" of Trotskyites, including
remnants of Li Li-san's followers, the Russian-returned-student leader-

[9] For this information, see *Chung-kung su-ch'ü chung-yang-ch'ü ti ch'eng-li chih
ch'i jen-wu* (*Circular No. 1 of the CCP Central Bureau of the Soviet Areas — Establishment of the Central Bureau of the Soviet Area and Its Tasks*), in SSCM. Also in
Hsiao, *Power Relations*, I, 150–152.

ship could hardly afford to alienate the leaders of the soviet movement in Kiangsi. Moreover, the new leadership had to cope with such external threats as the KMT police raid in 1931 on the Communist Party's underground headquarters in Shanghai, and many of its members were forced to flee to avoid persecution by the KMT police. In the light of these facts, the new Communist Party leadership of the Kiangsi soviet period appear to have been more interested in courting the support of powerful Communist guerrilla leaders in the hinterland by soliciting new ideas and policy suggestions for the Party's structural reform and reorganization of revolutionary strategy than in attempting to assert outright control over them.[10] Even the purges of the time had the primary aim of gaining the support of the masses in the soviet areas in order to implement such programs as land reform, consolidation and strengthening of the soviet base, expansion of the Red Army, and reconstruction of the shattered Party and youth-corps organizations.[11]

The structural reforms in the Party organization seem to have been designed less to achieve control over the soviet areas by the Russian-returned-student leadership than to eliminate Li Li-san's followers from the positions in which they were entrenched. Some of the cadres sent from the Party's central organs to investigate and survey Party organization in the soviet areas reported that the campaign to purge Li's adherents continued until the autumn of 1932. As an official commentator on the period asserted, "Reforming and strengthening the organization of the Party [in the soviet area] is to penetrate deeply into the Party organs, to fight the remainder of the Li Li-san line, and to struggle against rightist tendencies; it is to oppose corruption and bureaucratic methods, and to purge thoroughly the rich-peasant elements." [12] It seemed that the goal of the Party's structural reform was to extend the authority of the new leadership by winning over Party leaders and members in the soviet areas, providing them with opportunities to serve in the positions from which the followers of Li Li-san were gradually being removed.

The policy of inspection and coordination based on the emerging concept of collective leadership was formulated by the Russian-returned-student leadership in order to improve the channels of communication between upper- and lower-level Party committees and to

[10] For Tso-liang Hsiao's thesis that the Russian-returned students sought to control the soviet area, see his *Power Relations*, vol. I, ch. 13.

[11] See, for example, *Kuan-yü su-ch'ü su-fan kung-tso chüeh-i-an (Resolution on the Purge Work in the Soviet Area)*, dated January 29, 1932. *SSCM*, Reel 14.

[12] Hung Yi, "Chia-chin kai-tsao su-wei-ai ch'ü-yü nei wo-men tang ti tsu-chih" ("Stepping up the Reorganization of Our Party in the Soviet Areas") in *Tang-ti Chien-she (Reconstruction of the Party)*, No. 4 (March 8, 1931). *SSCM*, Reel 17.

provide an opportunity for the leadership cadres of the Party's higher echelon to observe directly the local Party in operation. By emphasizing the Party committee's collective decision-making, they greatly reduced the responsibilities and power of subordinate Party secretaries. At each level the decision-making body was "the Party Committee," which consisted of the chairmen of the functional committees — organization, propaganda, land reform, culture and education, and inspection. The secretary of the Party committee at each level was no longer the decision-maker, but served as the coordinator and recorder of the collective decision-making processes. The strengthening of the Party's committee system was of great concern to Mao Tse-tung in both the Kiangsi and Yenan periods. As he stressed during the latter, "The Party committee system is an important institution for ensuring collective leadership and preventing any individual from monopolizing the conduct of affairs." [13]

The inspection system had a dual function: it provided the opportunity for the Party committees, at the provincial and district levels, to ascertain whether each committee practiced collective decision-making, and it gave "intellectual" cadres practical experience. The cadres assigned to provincial or *hsien* Party committees after graduating from the Party schools were urged to take part in inspection work in order to learn how the local cadres performed their duties in establishing a close relationship between the Party and the masses. Both the provincial and *hsien* committees in the Kiangsi soviet base maintained a sizable body of inspection cadres to assure communication between the grass-roots organization and the upper echelons of the Party. According to instructional material published by the Party's Anfu *hsien* committee on February 16, 1932, inspection committees were established even at the district level during the Kiangsi soviet period. In response to the question, "How to develop worker-peasant cadres?" the instruction manual stressed:

> Each level of the Party, both district and branch, should not hesitate to recruit capable workers and peasants to the rank of cadres and assign them to leadership positions, including inspection. However, they must have demonstrated an exceptional ability to do their own work and they must be given special training.[14]

The same manual explains that the rationale for the expansion of the inspection-cadre system was to bring policy down to the grass

[13] Mao Tse-tung, "On Strengthening of the Party Committee System," *SW*, IV, 267.

[14] *Chih-pu shün-lien ts'ai-liao (Materials on the Training of the Branch Organizations)*, published by An-fu *hsien* committee of the CCP, dated February 16, 1932. *SSCM*, Reel 15.

roots, because formerly directives had tended to become stalled at the district level and subordinate branches could not act on them.[15]

The principal task of the inspection and coordination system, therefore, was to maintain close communication both between the Party's upper- and lower-echelon committees and among the functional committees formed within a Party committee. The *Ch'en Ch'eng Collection* contains a great deal of information about the ways in which inspection committees were created and how they were to function, but unfortunately, few judgments are rendered about their actual functioning.

One of the most important functions of the inspection committee, however, was closely related to the policy of cadre recruitment and training during the Kiangsi soviet period. As Lo Fu explained in his thesis on the "New Method of Leadership," leadership cadres were to be promoted from among those who had worked on inspection committees, because such background indicated a capacity for independent work, discipline, and responsibility. Leadership cadres, Lo Fu emphasized, "should be selected from those who have accumulated the experience of inspection work." [16]

The new concept of leadership based on the organizational techniques of the mass line had also begun to take shape in the early days of the period. "The most important components of the new leadership method," Lo Fu asserted, "are the questions of whether or not the Party is actually performing the function of leading the masses, whether or not the Party is able to meet quickly the aspirations of the masses and arouse them to respond to the call of the Party's policy line." [17] The rationale, as explained by Lo Fu, was to recruit and train those cadres who had led peasants in uprisings and demonstrations and who also were able to discern the aspirations of the masses and influence policy formulation to take such aspirations sufficiently into account so as to evoke loyalty. The new method of leadership, according to Lo Fu, required that the cadres should understand fully what the masses were really interested in, what aspirations they had, and to what kinds of appeal they responded quickly. The policies of the CCP that did not reflect or represent the majority will of the masses, he stressed, could not be successfully implemented, inasmuch as they would neither arouse enthusiasm nor win active support. What then, he asked, was the instrument through which the Party should actually ascertain the interests, desires, and needs of the masses? The answer lay in a strengthened recruitment of cadres and a training system for them. Without trained cadres, the new leadership emphasized, the CCP would never

[15] *Ibid.*
[16] Lo Fu, *Shin-ti ling-tao fang-shih (New Methods of Leadership)*, p. 28.
[17] Lo Fu, "Study the Art of Leading Masses," *ibid.*, p. 42.

be able to comprehend the aspirations of the masses or elicit support for its policies among the lower classes. The strengthening of cadre recruitment and the cadre-training program, therefore, were to be accompanied by the establishment and expansion of the Party's branch organizations at the grass-roots level.

When he established the General Action Committee in 1930, Li Li-san abolished the Party's mass organization, according to the new leadership, and local organizations of the Party were completely absorbed into the military-oriented committee, which was said to have functioned as an instrument for the implementation of Li Li-san's military policy. Faced with rebuilding the Party's branches at the grass-roots level and formulating a new policy of cadre recruitment and training, the Russian-returned-student leadership needed expert advice from the leaders of the soviet areas who had themselves acquired wide experience during several years of organizing and leading the peasants. The abstract theory of revolution learned by the new leaders during their student days in Moscow could not be applied directly to the revolutionary situation they perceived in China, but had to be modified or creatively applied to the realities of the Chinese situation. They could not do this without the endorsement or support of the leaders of the soviet areas, who had long since abandoned the illusion of a proletarian revolution in China.

The overriding concern of Mao at that time was not only how to integrate theory and practice, which was one of the major themes of cadre training during the Kiangsi soviet period, but also how to maintain unity of theory and experience, which he later expounded in *On Practice* during the Yenan period. The unity of theory and experience was emphasized in every class and manual for the education of cadres in the Kiangsi soviets. It was pointed out that a leadership cadre could not be created simply by appointing a person to a position of leadership — Li Li-san had attempted that and had failed — but that he should be selected from among those who demonstrated the ability to unite theory with practice. The chosen person should also be active, loyal, and dedicated to his work. He should emerge from those engaged in organizing the masses at the grass-roots level, whose needs and desires he must understand and by whom he must have been accepted as a leader.

Mao's concept of organization based on the mass-line style, as discussed earlier, was shaped by his several years' experience as an organizer and leader of the peasant and soviet institutions. As an instrument of mass mobilization during the Kiangsi period, the soviet performed the important function of providing the institutional framework through which the peasant masses were drawn closer to governmental affairs and were able to participate in the policy-making process. The creation of the Chinese Soviet Republic in November 1931 (with Mao as chairman of the central executive committee) was perhaps as important to revolutionary strategy as was peasant nationalism.[18] A new sense of participation among the peasant masses was provided by the soviet as the symbol of a new political institution, and it served as a medium through which they were able to articulate their interests and aspirations. What Mao achieved as the symbolic leader of the soviet government has already been described; Mao's ingenuity in integrating the new concepts of leadership and organizational techniques was quickly recognized by the Russian-returned students, and he and Lo Fu were able to collaborate, as has been mentioned, in developing the organizational method of soviet government at the district and *hsiang* level in 1933.[19]

As Mao and his Russian returned colleagues perceived in the Kiangsi soviet, what the peasant masses keenly desired was to feel that they were participating in bringing about revolutionary change and economic well-being in the face of landlord exploitation and imperialist aggression. This evaluation later proved to be an accurate basis for eliciting the support of the masses when translated into the policies of land reform and social mobilization through the institutions of the soviet. To the peasant masses, the soviet was a welcome alternative to the system of government that they had known for many years as an oppressive instrument of the landlord class. No accurate data are available, however, to measure the extent of mass support during the Kiangsi soviet period. One can only draw tentative conclusions from the scanty information concerning the high rate of increase in Party membership, the great expansion of the Red Army, and the rapid enlargement of the soviet areas themselves. Using these measures, though, one can easily see that the policies of the soviet during the Kiangsi period appealed to the peasant masses and won a wide range of support.[20] Such support was forthcoming until the spring of 1933, during the period when the mass-line style of work was still being enforced and a new offensive line had not yet been implemented. But the extent of

[18] For Chalmers Johnson's valuable thesis that the concept of nationalism served during the Yenan period, at the time of Japanese invasion, as the function of mass line, see his *Peasant Nationalism and Communist Power* and *Chinese Communist Leadership and Mass Response: The Yenan Period and the Socialist Education Campaign* (University of California Center for Chinese Studies, Reprint Series No. C-6).

[19] For example, see Chang Wen-t'ien and Mao Tse-tung, *Ch'ü-su yü Hsiang-su tsen-yang kung-tso (How to Work for the District and Hsiang Soviet Government)*. *SSCM*, Reels 7 and 8.

[20] For an effort to collect statistical data on the extent of mass support during the revolutionary period, see Roy Hofheinz, Jr., "The Ecology of Chinese Communist Success: Rural Influence Patterns, 1923–1945," in A. Doak Barnett, ed., *Chinese Communist Politics in Action* (Seattle, University of Washington Press, 1969), pp. 3–77.

mass support seems to have diminished when the CCP leaders changed from a policy based on the mass-line style to one based on the concept of "class line" and instituted economic extraction and political coercion.

The organizational techniques of the mass line developed on the basis of Mao's experience, and reflected in the form of soviet institutions, seem to have reappeared in late 1933 when the Land Investigation Movement and the mobilization campaigns for the soviet election were carried out. They later served as the foundation upon which the organizational strategy of the Yenan period was further refined and improved. While director of the general political department of the Red Army in 1932, Mao began to urge in his "Directive Concerning the Mass Work" that "tactics and working methods should not be separated from the tasks of winning the masses and establishing the soviet area. . . . In order to win the masses, our work must be divided into several stages." [21] First of all, he stressed, "you must try, by all means, to understand fully and realistically the situation and environment, and the feelings of the masses toward the campaigns, and listen to what they have to suggest. You ought to formulate a realistic strategy based on this information. If you follow the instructions, you will certainly produce remarkable results." [22] One can thus trace the roots of Mao's concept of a revolutionary strategy based on the concept of mass line to his experiences during the Kiangsi soviet period.

Cadre Training and Education

In 1945, almost a decade after the fall of the Kiangsi soviet, Mao charged that the Russian-returned students had failed during the Kiangsi soviet period to develop and train cadres properly. As he put it:

> They [i.e., the Russian-returned student leaders] did not give proper education to new cadres, nor did they handle the promotion of such cadres seriously (especially cadres of working-class origin), but carelessly replaced veterans in the central and local

[21] See *Mao Tse-tung kei Yüan Kuo-p'ing ti hsin — Kuan-yü Ch'ün-chung kung-tso ti chih-shih (Mao Tse-tung's Letter to Yuan Kuo-p'ing Concerning the Directive of the Mass Work)*, found in SSCM, Reel 14. Mao's concept of the mass-line method in the Kiangsi soviet should be compared with his pronouncements in the Yenan period. For example, "Resolution on Certain Questions in the History of Our Party," adopted on April 20, 1945, stressed that "as Comrade Mao Tse-tung says, the correct political line should be 'from the masses, to the masses.'" "To ensure that the line really comes from the masses and in particular that it really goes back to the masses, outside the Party (between the class and the people), but above all between the Party's leading bodies and the masses within the Party (between the cadres and the rank and file); in other words, there must be a correct organizational line." See Mao, *SW*, III, 208.

[22] See *Mao's Letter to Yüan Kuo-p'ing Concerning Mass Work, ibid.*

organizations with new cadres or cadres coming from other places who either lacked experience in work or had no close contact with the masses, but who proved congenial to them and did nothing but follow them blindly and chime in with them. In this manner, they not only disheartened the old cadres but also spoiled the new ones.[23]

Contrary to Mao's accusations, the Russian-returned student leadership did, in fact, develop — perhaps in collaboration with Mao himself — a policy governing the recruitment, training, and promotion of cadres. This was probably the first time in the Chinese Communist movement that a systematic attempt was made to develop and educate skillful cadres.[24] A careful study of the Party's resolutions on the question of cadres, a number of policy statements concerning cadre recruitment and training, and a series of discussions about the procedures for promoting cadres show clearly that the Russian-returned-student leadership did make a thoroughgoing effort to create a new group of leadership cadres.

Only a few months after the conclusion of the Fourth Plenum (1931), the CCP's new leadership began to consider seriously the problems of cadre recruitment and training. In accordance with the resolution adopted by the Party's central bureau in the soviet areas, "Concerning the Problems of Cadres," the Party began to formulate these policies only after the Fourth Plenum.[25] The basic policy line established by the resolution was later incorporated into the handbooks and instructional materials for cadre training and education that were widely circulated among Party secretaries and heads of departments. The resolution asserted also that past CCP leadership, from Ch'en Tu-hsiu to Li Li-san, had paid little or no attention to the systematic training and recruitment of cadres.

It was charged, moreover, that veteran leaders simply failed to draw up any rules or procedures to recruit, train, and promote the young cadres, especially those with a working-class background. Once a young man was picked by a veteran leader and placed in a leadership position in a Party organization, he was given no training or promotion; consequently, his performance became increasingly authoritarian and bu-

[23] *Ibid.*, pp. 209–210.

[24] *Tang-ti kan-pu wen-t'i chüeh-i-an (Resolution on the Party's Cadre Problems)*, published August 27, 1931, was probably the first resolution adopted by the Party's Central Politburo concerning the question of cadres. Other resolutions of the CCP usually contained sections on cadre problems, in which they discussed the reorganization of the Party structure or the reconstruction of the Party branches.

[25] See *Resolution on the Party's Cadre Problems*, the Chinese text of which may be found in Tso-liang Hsiao, *Power Relations*, II, 378–382.

reaucratic. Relying heavily on the orders transmitted from above, he failed to take any personal initiative in carrying out Party work.

The aim of the new policy governing the recruitment and training of cadres, therefore, was to rectify past mistakes and routinize the organizational techniques of the mass line on the basis of the emerging new concepts of leadership. The *Handbook for the Training of Cadres* defined the new cadre as a person who "follows correctly the political line established by the Party, fulfills each and all decisions of the Party, expands the political influence of the Party among the people and establishes a close relationship between the Party and the masses." [26] In order to create and maintain close ties he should be able not only to understand and influence the masses, but also to lead them in the direction desired by the Party. Therefore, "a cadre should be selected not only from the progressive element of the proletarian class but also from among the masses of poor peasant people," the CCP resolution on the problems of cadres emphasized. The first qualification for becoming a cadre was to demonstrate the ability to organize and lead the masses in demonstrations or uprisings as well as to disseminate the Party's policy line to the masses.[27] To sum up, the most important determinants in selecting cadres, according to the *Handbook*, were "class origin, political stand, and skill in leadership."

The new meaning of "cadre" became functionally associated with the emerging concept of leadership and the organizational techniques of the mass-line style of work. The term "cadre" had been applied in the past to only a few veteran leaders in top positions, but now it meant anyone who possessed the ability to lead and organize the masses. Once a person demonstrated that quality, he should be selected by the Party, given the proper training and education, and promoted to a position appropriate to his competence.

In setting up criteria for the selection of a cadre, the *Handbook* stressed that he must be chosen from among those who were loyal, brave, and positive members of the Party, and that it was always easier to discover a person's leadership ability during "demonstrations and campaigns such as workers' strikes, guerrilla warfare, the antiimperialist movement, or mass uprisings." [28] Once selected, he was usually given an assignment in the local party organization in a geographic region other than his own to test his ability to direct mass demonstrations or to organize mass groups such as the youth corps or the women's league. His second task would be to conduct inspection work in a party organization. His leadership skills, imagination, and determination were

[26] See *Tang-ti chien-she chiang-shu t'i-kang* (*Lecture Outlines for Reconstruction of the Party*), in *SSCM*, Reel 2. Hereafter cited as *Handbook*.
[27] *Ibid.*
[28] *Ibid.*

tested against his success in performing all the duties assigned to him during his work of inspection. Such work usually involved hardship because of the necessity of traveling a great deal in rural and backward areas. It also involved persuasive skills in helping to solve the problems of a local party organization. Successful performance entitled a man to be considered a qualified cadre.

Service in the inspection unit was a kind of job training usually given to cadres who had been graduated from various Party schools but who had not had an opportunity to acquire practical experience. Graduates were assigned to province, *hsien*, or district inspection committees and then sent to Party organizations at the grass-roots level or to the mass organizations. The cadre's inspection duties required imagination and creativity as well as discipline and adaptability in coping with local problems. The aim of the system was both to discover shortcomings or mistakes in the work of local-level organizations and to train the so-called "intellectual" cadres to help local cadres resolve difficulties. Another of its functions was to provide channels of communication between upper echelons of the Party and local cadres.

Once a CCP member qualified, what type of training and education did he undergo? The answer is somewhat complicated because during the Kiangsi period the CCP maintained training programs that varied from province to province. Although there was a general policy, actual operation was decentralized and left to the initiative and discretion of the local Party leader. The first principle governing the entire program — and it received heavy emphasis — was integration of theory and experience. According to the analysis of the cadre problem by the new leadership after the Fourth Plenum, there were many active and loyal Party leaders in the Soviet areas who had acquired valuable experience in the revolutionary movement but lacked theoretical training. On the other hand, there was also a large number of young cadres who had been well trained in the theories of Marxism-Leninism but who lacked experience in translating theory into action. Consequently, the main theme of cadre education in the Kiangsi soviet was learning to integrate theory and experience, on the ground that "theory makes practical experience much more meaningful and practical experience enriches theory."[29] The resolution on the "Reconstruction of the Party in the Soviet Areas" stressed that "all the resolutions and policy documents of the CCP should be read carefully and explained plainly in order to integrate theory, as represented by the Party's resolutions and policy statements, with practice, as represented by the actual experience being acquired by Party members."[30]

[29] *Ibid.*
[30] *Ibid.*

One of the most urgent necessities facing the new leadership during the Kiangsi period was to reduce tensions between two types of cadres: those with practical experience and those who had only theoretical knowledge learned in the Party schools. To bring about harmony, two types of training programs were developed: in-service for those with no theoretical background, and participation in the system of inspection for the "intellectual" cadres.

One training manual pointed out that the in-service classes were mainly designed to "improve the cadres' political consciousness and their ability to perform well."[31] They were meant not only to reduce tension between the two types of cadres, but also to cope with a rapid growth in Party membership. The sudden increase in new cadres in 1932 as the result of that growth[32] and the expansion of the soviet base areas[33] forced the CCP to formulate a policy governing in-service training programs that emphasized (1) cultivation of Party spirit to make the newly recruited cadre a fervent disciple of Marxism-Leninism and, by enriching his thought and determination, to make him an enthusiastic Party worker; (2) cultivation of the ability to work independently so that he could fulfill his responsibility under any circumstances; (3) cultivation of class consciousness so that he would be able to continue the class struggle; and (4) cultivation of the ability to integrate theory and practice by being soundly based in the theories of Marxism and Leninism.

Cadre preparation during the Kiangsi period emphasized theoretical education, political education, administrative education, and cultural education. Theoretical education involved the study of abstract theory through courses in subjects such as historical materialism and dialectical materialism and in "thought science" (ssu-hsiang k'e-hsüeh). Emphasis, however, was placed chiefly on the ways in which abstract theory could be linked to practical experience. Political education focused on revolutionary history, political movements in China and the West, the policies of the CCP, and current events. Administrative education dealt with the relationship between the Party and government agencies and mass organizations, and the relationships among

---

[31] For information concerning the in-service training of cadres, see *Kung-ch'an-tang ti tsai-chih kan-pu chao-yü (Communist Party Cadre In-Service Education)*. SSCM, Reel. 5.

[32] Party membership reached about 300,000 in 1933, the highest level since the founding of the Party and a record not broken until after the outbreak of the Sino-Japanese War in 1937.

[33] I have reached the somewhat deflated estimate of approximately 100 *hsien* that were under soviet rule and of approximately twelve million people who lived within the soviet districts. For this estimate, see my unpublished Ph.D. dissertation, *Communist Politics in China: A Study of Organizational Concepts, Techniques, and Behavior During the Kiangsi Soviet Period* (Columbia University, 1968).

the functional departments of the Party. Cultural education centered on raising the level of the cadres' general knowledge, and two categories were offered: one for cadres who were illiterate, which provided basic instruction in Chinese characters and simple arithmetic; the other for those who had a primary education, which included courses in Chinese literature, mathematics, history, geography, natural science, and so on.

All the cadre programs offered study in political science, history, and economics. Political science, of course, stressed the theory of Marxism and Leninism, whereas economics emphasized the economic development of China over the past hundred years and analyzed these developments in the light of Marxian theories. History accentuated the evolution of Chinese thought during the preceding century and included the study of revolutions in China and other countries, giving pride of place to the Bolshevik revolution.

These are some of the broad outlines of the cadre-training programs that can be traced from instructional materials contained in the *Ch'en Ch'eng Collection*, although the curricula used for the training varied to some degree from province to province because of differences in their respective levels of education. The most widely used source seems to have been the resolutions adopted by the Party's Central Committee or the central bureau of the Soviet Areas, numerous editions of which were reprinted by local Party committees and made available to the instructors. *Tang-ti chien-she*, an official publication of the organization department of the Party's central bureau of the soviet areas, was the most widely used instructional manual. Besides writings by Chinese and Russian theorists, the journal included practical accounts by cadres actually engaged in the work of structural reform and the rebuilding of local Party organizations.[34]

The institutional framework within which the training programs were conducted during the Kiangsi period was as complex and varied as the educational materials themselves. The Party's central bureau of the soviet areas maintained its own schools in Juichin and trained the so-called elite cadres, and each provincial Party committee and *hsien* Party committee operated its own schools. However, the in-service training program of each Party unit or government agency was the most popular and widespread method of cadre education. The first stage included a word-learning project in various Party units and branch organizations, in government agencies, and in the mass organizations. Those cadres with no primary education were urged to master between five hundred and one thousand Chinese characters in their

[34] See note 26.

spare time. Literate cadres usually served as instructors. The Party stressed this project throughout the base area during the Kiangsi period because the sudden increase in Party membership brought in a large number of illiterates.

One of the many difficulties encountered by the CCP leadership in developing educational policy in the Kiangsi soviet base was in transforming an ignorant worker or illiterate peasant into a good Communist cadre. Because the Party recruited many such persons under the assumption that they were much more politically conscious and active in the cause of revolution than they actually were, it had to devise an educational program that promoted literacy at the same time that it enhanced dedication to the revolution.

Cadres who were literate, even if only at a low level, were assigned to a different type of program, which usually was conducted in the evenings and had a slightly more advanced curriculum. They read simple texts (many of which are in the *Ch'en Ch'eng Collection*) and listened to lectures on the Chinese revolution, the Party's resolutions, policies, and political stand. As a rule, this program lasted five to six weeks.

The schools of the provincial, *hsien*, and district committees usually conducted higher-level training programs for administrative cadres who were engaged in specialized work such as the secretarial, organizational, propaganda, agitation, and cultural activities of the Party. In their basic content, the instructional materials used by the central bureau's Party school and those used by district-level schools were very similar, although the practical-training program varied from place to place and from time to time. Differences in the standard and quality of the staffs were more common. The central Party school, established under the auspices of the Party's central bureau of the soviet area, had been in operation since early 1931. When the Party's Central Committee completed its physical move in early 1933, however, the instructional staff was considerably strengthened and coordination between the central Party school and the local-level Party schools was improved. In the central Party school, the cadres from various provincial committees attended lectures by such Party leaders as Po Ku (Ch'in Pang-hsien), Lo Fu (Chang Wen-t'ien), and Mao Tse-tung, whereas the majority of the staff at the district or *hsien* schools were simply graduates of the provincial Party schools.

Besides the regular schools operated by the Party committees, a short-term training program existed at the regional level. Representative of this was the program in Ningtu. It was, of course, financed and operated by the provincial Party committee of Kiangsi, but the cadres were selected from four *hsien* adjacent to Ningtu *hsien*. On July 5, 1932, the *hsien* Party committee of Ningtu issued a circular to announce that the first class would soon begin. Three *hsien* (Shihchen, Luan, and Ihuang) were instructed to select five cadres each, and Nankuang *hsien* was to select eight cadres. Ningtu *hsien* selected one cadre from each district and each branch organization, making a total of forty cadres in the first class. The criteria for selecting them, according to the circular, were whether the cadre was active, whether he was superior to other cadres in his ability to learn, and whether he had a promising future in taking up a responsible position in the Party or other mass organization. All were to be of worker, poor-peasant, or hired-farmhand class origins. Another qualification was a minimum of three months' experience in guerrilla units. All cadres had to have at least some reading knowledge of the language. The circular also stressed that one female cadre or more should be selected from each *hsien*.[35]

The cadres were to supply their own rice bowls, chopsticks, and blankets. Return to their units would be at the expense of the provincial Party committee, but their transportation to Ningtu was provided by the *hsien* or district committees. Board and lodging during the training period were provided by the Ningtu *hsien* committee.

The forty students assembled in Ningtu on July 20, and classes began the next day. The first four days were devoted to lectures by seven speakers on general theoretical problems such as "The Political Situation and the Party's Tasks" (July 21), "The Party's Constitution and Organization" (July 22), "The Guerrilla Movement and the Resolutions Adopted by the Communist Youth Conference" (July 23), and "Organizational Work of the Soviets and the Women's Movement" (July 24). Next, the class was taken to nearby towns to observe and participate in the in-service training programs. It also participated in the actual work of labor organizations and attended meetings of the Party committees and branch organizations in the cities and towns. The cadres were given opportunities to attend meetings of district-level soviet government and to engage directly in its work. They also attended Red Army meetings in the district.

After five days of observation and participation in the in-service training program, the cadres were brought back to the classrooms for discussion and evaluation sessions. Each cadre drew up a project on "how to build up the Party's branch organization" in his own district, using what he had learned in the lectures and in the field. One full

[35] *Tang-ti chien-she* (*Reconstruction of the Party*) in *SSCM*, Reel 17. I have used the six issues, from No. 1 to No. 6, of this publication for information on the selection, education, and promotion of cadres. Another source of information is *Kuan-yü chao-yü kung-tso* (*On Educational Work*), Executive Order No. 17 of the People's Commissariat of the Central Executive Committee, the Chinese Soviet Republic, *SSCM*, Reel 5.

day was devoted to a discussion of each of the following topics: (1) the tasks of the workers' association; (2) propaganda, methods, and organization of the mass movement; and (3) the method of mass meetings. The final day was examination time, when each cadre was tested on how much he had learned in the classroom and also on how well he could integrate theory and experience.[36]

Like the short-term training program in Ningtu *hsien*, most of the educational programs for cadres in the Kiangsi soviet combined theoretical learning, practical field experience, and critical evaluation. The objective of theoretical learning, of course, was to instill in the cadres the correct political views to serve as a guide to revolutionary action. Field experience was intended to give the cadres an opportunity to demonstrate their ability to translate learning into practice — the major theme of cadre training during the Kiangsi soviet. The cadres were thus taught to function as living models of the way in which theory and action could be united. If they performed well, they not only would serve as model Party members, the CCP leaders asserted, but would become the embodiment of the mass-line style of work.

The promotion of cadres to higher leadership positions during the Kiangsi period was based upon what the new leadership perceived as their "good qualities," and these criteria stemmed from the new concept of leadership that emerged after the Fourth Plenum. The most important quality that a cadre was expected to possess in order to serve as a link between the Party and the masses was the ability to understand fully the ideas, emotions, and opinions of the masses. A cadre could not qualify for leadership unless he was considered by the masses to be a leader and was followed by them. The first criterion for promotion to a leadership position in the Party or government was the extent to which the individual cadre under consideration commanded the respect of the masses. This yardstick was also applied in electing Party cadres to leadership positions in the government and mass organizations. It may be that the Wang Ming and Po Ku leadership used the same criterion in electing Mao Tse-tung to the Chairmanship of the Chinese Soviet Republic. Fundamental to the new concept of leadership was the belief that if a cadre did not command the respect or support of the masses, as many of the veteran cadres under Li Li-san had failed to do, he was likely, if promoted, to become an authoritarian and bureaucratic type of leader.

The second criterion for promotion was demonstrated ability to make decisions based on broad Party policy lines and to resolve organizational problems quickly and independently. In a crisis situation, many of the middle-level cadres had to make decisions without consult-

---

[36] *Chung-kung Ning-tu chung-hsin hsien-wei t'ung-chih ti-san-hao* (Circular No. 3 of the Ning-tu *hsien* Committee of the CCP). SSCM, Reel 3.

ing with upper-echelon cadres. It was essential, therefore, that they should be able to grasp local situations quickly and to work within general policy established by the Party.

In the rules and regulations for the promotion of cadres, the CCP leaders during the Kiangsi period seemed to have emphasized actual performance on the basis of the new leadership criteria more than class origins or social background. Class origins had already been taken into account in the selection of cadres, so it was assumed that all cadres had the right background. Under the new promotion procedure, a review committee of cadres was set up by Party committees at every level from the central bureau to the branch organization, and a systematic and constant review of performance was carried out before a cadre was considered for promotion.

It is difficult to discover how rigorously the criteria of promotion were applied in actual practice. Political life being what it was in China, personal relationships or family ties almost certainly continued to play an important part. It is quite clear, however, from all the available documents and policy statements that, faced with the chaos caused by Li Li-san's method of organization, the new leadership of the Russian-returned students made a systematic and unremitting effort to establish effective rules and procedures to govern selection and promotion as a part of the larger program of the Party's structural reform.

Nevertheless, judging from what Lo Fu (Chang Wen-t'ien) stressed in his four articles on the "New Method of Leadership," the problems of "personalism," "commandism," and "sectarianism" seem to have persisted throughout the Kiangsi period as problems of organization and had to be combatted again during the Yenan period.

The new concept of leadership based on the organizational techniques of the "mass line" that began to emerge during the Kiangsi soviet period, especially in the soviet base areas, later served as the foundation on which the organizational strategy of the Yenan period was formulated. The structural reforms instituted by the new leadership after the Fourth Plenum in 1931 had the immediate goal of establishing a new style of leadership and new techniques of organization by replacing the followers of Li Li-san with new men. They also had the long-range objective of institutionalizing the new method of leadership — which was based on the concept of regularizing collective leadership — and the system of inspection, which was intended to strengthen the committee system and the mass-line style of work.

The development of the new concept of leadership style as well as the emergence of new organizational techniques based on the mass-line approach were by no means, therefore, merely by-products of the changes in leadership in the Party's central organs. They were, rather, the direct result of purposeful efforts on the part of the new leadership to create new structures and functions for the Party and to reorder the priorities of revolutionary strategy.

In the process of integrating the new concept of leadership developed by the Russian-returned students as a result of their training in Moscow into a mass-line organizational technique, which was mainly developed by the leaders of the Kiangsi soviet base, including Mao Tsetung himself, as the direct result of their long experience in organizing the peasant masses, the new leadership of Wang Ming and Po Ku seems to have collaborated with the guerrilla leaders of the soviet base. To integrate theory and practice in this way required a certain model by means of which new policies could be projected. The new type of leadership cadre emerged as this model and was expected to function as the unifying factor in bringing together the new concept of leadership and the new organizational techniques of the mass line. The process had already begun in the Kiangsi soviet base and later became a continuing one throughout the Yenan period.

Faced with constant attacks by KMT forces, the new leaders of the CCP and of the Chinese soviet government were not able really to resolve their organizational problems by unifying theory and experience and developing a revolutionary strategy that would carry them to victory. Nevertheless, the process was applied with considerable success in the training programs for leadership cadres and in the policies of mass mobilization. The evacuation of the soviet base in the fall of 1934 was more a result of relentless Nationalist military pressure than of the inability of the Communist leaders to mobilize the masses. Indeed, the Kiangsi soviet base possessed remarkably well-trained cadres and a relatively high degree of mass mobilization because the concept of "soviet" and the land-reform program (both based on the mass-line method) had strong appeal for the masses. It is not surprising, therefore, that the central soviet government was able to rally mass support behind its social and economic programs when it based its policies on Mao's concept of "mass line." The experience of the Kiangsi soviet leaders continued throughout the Yenan period to function as a basis for their unflagging efforts to resolve organizational problems through the concept of collective leadership, the system of strengthening the Party's committees, and the institutionalization of the mass-line style of work.

The attempts of the CCP leaders, in both the Kiangsi and Yenan periods, to create a governmental structure based on the new concept of leadership as well as on the new techniques of the mass line were so strikingly similar that one is compelled to conclude that it was the experience of institution-building acquired in the Kiangsi soviet, further refined and improved, that served as the organizational strategy during the Yenan period for the attainment of the final goal, the victory of the Chinese revolution.

CONCLUSION

It is the conclusion of this study that, by and large, the Communist leaders of the Kiangsi soviet period were successful in creating and operating an effective political system and in mobilizing the peasant masses under the soviets' rule, despite numerous problems, including internal factionalism and external military pressures from the Chinese Nationalist forces. The evacuation of the Kiangsi soviet base in 1934 probably was primarily the consequence of military failure, not of a lack of mass support or even of differences on issues among the top policy-makers.

During the Kiangsi period, the leadership of the central soviet government headed by Mao Tse-tung and Chang Kuo-t'ao, in collaboration with a group of the returned-student leaders, such as Chang Wen-t'ien and Wang Chia-hsiang, formulated distinctive mass mobilization policies, developed new organizational techniques that linked their peasant policy and the soviet movement, and worked out many of the administrative procedures and practices of local government that later were to serve as the foundation for the Chinese Communist political system, both in northwestern China after the Long March and on the Chinese mainland as a whole after the establishment of the People's Republic. Until the failure of their Kiangsi military strategy, which ultimately led to the evacuation of the Kiangsi soviet base in October 1934, the central soviet leadership achieved considerable success in mobilizing the peasant masses in the soviet base, and this can be attributed to their concept of "mass line."

During the Kiangsi period, the theoretical concepts and organizational techniques of "mass-line" politics were implemented by Mao Tse-tung, who headed the government's policy-making machinery, with the collaboration or acquiescence of some of the Russian-returned-student leadership elite who took over the Party's policy-making machinery and operated the Party apparatus. The experience of governing the base areas of the Kiangsi soviet was fundamentally one of building new political institutions to meet the needs and aspirations of the peasant masses as well as the requirements of revolutionary war. Such institutions as the soviet (delegate council), executive and functional committees, and the auxiliary organizations — the farm-labor unions, the

poor-peasant corps, and the cooperatives — had as one of their chief
aims to involve as many people as possible in the processes of local
politics. In short, the underlying concept of the political system in the
Kiangsi soviet base was that of "popular participation."

It was relatively easy to formulate theory, draft constitutions, devise
rules and regulations, and make policies for the functioning of various
organizations in Kiangsi, but to implement such rules, regulations, and
policies in the backward rural hinterland was much more difficult. The
border areas of southern Kiangsi where the soviet system emerged were
far less highly developed than the urban centers or the coastal cities
of China. The population in the region consisted predominantly of
peasants, and in large majority they were impoverished, illiterate, passive, and unwilling to respond to the appeals of revolutionary change.
Thus Mao's administrative concept of popular participation and his
organizational techniques of mass mobilization were gradually evolved
so as to cause fundamental changes in the attitudes and behavior of the
peasant population.

After the breakdown of CCP-KMT collaboration in August 1927,
Mao began to build the soviet system of government by restructuring
and reforming the existing peasant associations. The soviet government
in a newly conquered region was installed on the foundation already
laid by the revolutionary committee during the partisan warfare. The
newly created organization usually uprooted the existing power structure and ruling elites in order to replace them, which sometimes involved violent incidents. The ruling elites in the rural areas of China
were traditionally the land-owning class: the landlords, the local gentry, and the rich peasants. In order to establish new political institutions, Mao had to eliminate this group and replace them with newly
recruited people having proletarian or poor-peasant backgrounds.

To recruit the backward and illiterate peasants into the newly established institutions, Mao had to devise techniques by which the new
leadership could appeal to them and evoke their political consciousness and enthusiasm. Once the enthusiasm of the peasantry had been
aroused by new techniques, Mao thought, they would inevitably become a dynamic force, like a tornado, to carry the revolution to final
victory. The peasant masses, however, did not respond to Mao's appeals
as quickly as he expected them to, for they were neither willing to
join the revolutionary effort nor enthusiastic about participating in
the political processes of local organizations.

What Mao had to do, therefore, was to develop new techniques
based on his concept of "mass line," by which the rural peasants might
be won over, and then persuade them to join the newly created political institutions. Mao's obsession with his theory of institution-building,

as we have seen in this study, was grounded in his analysis of class structure in rural China. It was coupled with his intuitive notion that organization was a necessary means to attain his revolutionary goals. Such a notion was largely derived from his experience in directing the peasant movement in the late 1920s and also was influenced by his own perception and analysis of the revolutionary role of the peasant masses. Therefore, Mao's inconsistent policy toward the rich peasants and his active role in such campaigns as the economic-construction movement, the land-investigation drive, and the cooperative movement must be understood and analyzed against the background of his experience in ruling the base areas of the Kiangsi soviet.

In the course of creating and restructuring the soviet system of government in the base area, Mao was confronted with the challenge of the returned-student group. Fresh from their ideological training in Moscow and well versed in the theories of Marxism-Leninism, the returned students, after taking over the Party's policy-making machinery, challenged Mao's authority even in the base areas of Kiangsi. This action was carried out chiefly from the Party's Shanghai headquarters and only by means of sending directive letters. For the returned-student leaders the issue of "antiimperialism," which was also the Comintern's policy line, took precedence over the imperatives of social revolution on which Mao continued to place his emphasis.

After the formal transfer of the Party's Central Committee from Shanghai to Juichin in early 1933, however, the supporters of Mao's policy and a group of the returned students compromised in order to establish a division of labor based on the concept of collective leadership. By winning the support of some of the returned students, including Chang Wen-t'ien and Wang Chia-hsiang, Mao was able to maintain his authority and control the policy-making machinery of the central soviet government, whereas another group of the returned students, led by Ch'in Pang-hsien, presided over the Party's policy-making machinery and developed their own justification of the government's policies. The conflicting policy lines coexisted in the soviet base throughout the Kiangsi period, and apparently continued to do so, as Mark Selden has observed, in the Shen-Kan-Ning soviet during 1935–1936, even after Mao had assumed the unchallenged leadership of the Party.

Problems of bridging the gap between theory and practice frequently recurred in both the Kiangsi and the Yenan soviet periods, when the Chinese Communist leaders created new institutions such as the soviets and used them to govern the revolutionary societies of the Kiangsi and Shen-Kan-Ning base areas. Mao's real contribution to the theory of organization and administration, therefore, was the development of techniques based on his concept of mass line and the implementation of the political phenomena known as *yün-tung* (campaign or movement) in the form of the land-investigation movement, the cooperative movement, and the economic-construction movement. What Mao attempted to develop in the Kiangsi soviet was exactly what contemporary political theorists are concerned with: government and administration that would move mass organizations quickly, act decisively, and respond readily to the people's needs and demands.

Mao's development and implementation of such techniques as mass mobilization had taken shape in the Kiangsi period and had been gradually codified in the Yenan phase of development; they were finally institutionalized as a political style in the early years of the People's Republic. Today, Mao's concept of "mass line" politics continues to be a powerful force in mainland China and to guide the process of political development.

GLOSSARY OF CHINESE
TERMS AND NAMES

Ch'ang-chiang chü	長江局	Yangtse River Bureau
Ch'ang-kang *hsiang*	長岡鄉	
Chang Kuo-t'ao	張國燾	
Chang Wen-t'ien	張聞天	
Ch'a-t'ien yün-tung	查田運動	
Ch'en Chang-hao	陳昌浩	
Ch'en Shao-yü	陳紹禹 (陳韶玉)	
Ch'en T'u-hsiu	陳獨秀	
Ch'en Yüan-tao	陳原道	
(Chung-yang) Cheng-chih-chü	中央政治局	(Central Politburo)
Cheng-kang	政綱	Political Program
Ch'in Pang-hsien	秦邦憲	
Chingkangshan	井岡山	
Chou En-lai	周恩來	
Ch'ü	區	An administrative unit between the *hsien* and the *hsiang*

Ch'ü Ch'iu-pai	瞿秋白	
Ch'ü, Ch'ü-wei	區,區委	District, district committee
Chu Te	朱德	
Ch'üan-kuo su-wei-ai ch'ü-yü tai-piao hui-i	全國蘇維埃區域代表會議	National Conference of Delegates from the Soviet Areas
Ch'üan-kuo su-wei-ai ta-hui chung-yang chün-pei wei-yüan-hui	全國蘇維埃大會中央準備委員會	Central Preparatory Commission for the National Soviet Congress
Chung-kung chung-yang chu kuo-chi tai-piao-t'uan	中共中央駐國際代表團	Delegation of the CCP Central Committee to the Comintern
Ch'ün-chung kung-tso	群眾工作	Mass work
Ch'ün-chung lu-hsien	群眾路線	Mass line
Chung-kuo kung-ch'an-tang, Chung-kung	中國共產党中共	Chinese Communist Party (CCP)
Chung-kuo su-wei-ai kung-ho-kuo	中國蘇維埃共和國	Chinese Soviet Republic
Chung-kuo su-wei-ai yün-tung	中國蘇維埃運動	Chinese soviet movement
Chung-shan ta-hsüeh (Chung-ta)	中山大學(中大)	Sun Yat-sen University
Chung-yang fen-chü	中央分局	Central subBureau

Chung-yang su-wei-ai	中央蘇維埃	Central soviet
Fan fu-nung cheng-ts'e	反富農政策	Anti-rich-peasant policy
Fang Chih-min	方志敏	
Fu-nung, Fu-nung lu-hsien	富農，富農路線	Rich peasants, rich-peasant line
Ho Meng-hsiug	何孟雄	
Hsiang	鄉	A township, a rural administrative unit of three to five villages
Hsiang Chung-fa	向忠發	
Hsiang-o-hsi chung-yang fen-chü	湘鄂西中央分局	Hunan-West Hu-peh central sub-Bureau
Hsiang-o-kan su-ch'ü	湘鄂贛蘇區	Hunan-Hupeh Kiangsi soviet area
Hsiang Ying	項英	
Hsien-su	縣蘇	County soviet government
Hsin kan-pu	新幹部	New cadres
Hsing-kuo hsien	興國縣	
Juichin	瑞金	
Kan-chiang	贛江	Kan River
Kan-min-wan pien-ch'ü	贛閩皖邊區	Kiangsi-Fukien-Anhwei border area

Kuang-ta ch'ün-chung	廣大群衆	Broad masses
Kuang-ta ch'ün-chung cheng-chih shang-ti tung-yüan	廣大群衆政治上的動員	Political mobilization of the broad masses
Kung-ch'an kuo-chi yüan-tung-chü, tung-fang-pu	共産國際遠東局東方部	Comintern Far Eastern Bureau, Eastern Department
Ku-nung kung-hui	雇農工會	Hired farm hand (or labor) associations
Kung-nung min-chu chüan-cheng	工農民主専政	Democratic dictatorship of workers and peasants
Kuo-chia cheng-ch'ih pao-wei-ch'u	國家政治保衞處	State Political Security Bureau
K-uo-ta ti ts'u-chung ch'üan-hui	擴大第四次中全會	Enlarged Fourth Plenum
Lin Po-ch'ü (Lin Tsu-han)	林伯渠 (林祖涵)	
Liu-o p'ai	留俄派	Russian-returned-student group
Lo Chang-lung	羅章龍	
Lo Fu (Chang Wen-t'ien)	洛甫	
Lo Ming lu-hsien	羅明路線	Lo Ming line
Min-che-kan su-ch'ü	閩浙贛蘇區	Fukien-Chekiang-Kiangsi soviet area

Min-yüeh-kan su-ch'ü	閩粵贛蘇區	Fukien-Kwang-tung Kiangsi so-viet area
O-yü-wan su-ch'ü	鄂豫皖蘇區	Hupeh-Honan-Anhwei soviet area
Pa-ch'i hui-i, pa-ch'i chin-chi hui-i	八七會議 八七緊急會議	August 7 (1927) Conference, August 7 Emergency Conference
P'in-nung, P'in-nung t'uan	貧農，貧農團	Poor peasants, poor-peasant corps
Po Ku (alias of Ch'in Pang-hsien)	博古 (秦邦憲)	
Shang-hang *hsien*	上杭縣	
Shen Tse-min	沈澤民	
Su-ch'ü chung-yang chü	蘇區中央局	Central bureau of the soviet areas (CBSA)
Su-ch'ü chung-yang chü ti-i-tz'u k'uo-ta hui-i	蘇區中央局第一次擴大會議	First enlarged session of the central bureau, soviet areas
Su-wei-ai ch'ü-yü, su-ch'ü	蘇維埃區域蘇區	Soviet areas
Shun-chih (Chihli, Hopei)	順直	
Teng Tzu-hui	鄧子恢	
Ting-chow	汀洲	
Ts'ai Ho-shen	蔡和森	

Tsai-chi *hsiang*	才溪鄉	
Tsu-chih wen-t'i chüeh-i-an	組織問題決議案	Resolution on the organizational problems
Tsung cheng-chih-pu	總政治部	General political department
T'u-ti p'ing-chün fen-p'ei, p'ing-fen t'u-ti	土地平均分配 平分土地	Equal distribution of land
Tzu-ch'an chieh-chi min-chu ko-ming	資產階級民主革命	Bourgeois-democratic revolution
Wang Chia-ch'iang (Wang Chia-hsiang)	王稼薔 (祥)	
Wu-chung ch'üan hui	五中全會	Fifth Plenum

BIBLIOGRAPHY

It is necessary to provide here an explanatory note regarding the selected bibliography of Chinese, Japanese, Russian, and English source materials that follows. Almost all the references in this study are to items in the Ch'en Ch'eng archival materials, which are now available on microfilm at the Hoover Institution on War, Revolution, and Peace at Stanford University; the three-volume *Chung-kuo Kung-ch'an-tang shih-kao* (*Historical Materials of the Chinese Communist Party*), compiled by Wang Chien-min; and the seven-volume *Chūgoku Kyōsantō-shi* (*Documentary History of the Chinese Communist Party*), compiled by Hatano Ken'ichi.

The Ch'en Ch'eng archival materials were reproduced on microfilm by the Hoover Institution, and consist of twenty-one reels. This collection of documents contains Communist sources from the CCP and the Chinese soviet government that were collected on the spot by KMT troops under the command of General Ch'en Ch'eng in the early 1930s. The microfilm also contains *A Collection of Red Bandit Reactionary Documents*, compiled by the KMT for private circulation in 1935. This collection is cited below as *SSCM* (Shih Sou Collection in Microfilm).

The second volume of the *Chung-kuo Kung-ch'an-tang shih-kao* (hereafter cited as *Chung-kung shih-kao*) contains important documents and source materials of the Chinese Communist Party for the Kiangsi soviet period (1927–1937). These documents were obtained from the Collection of the Bureau of Investigation, Ministry of Justice in Ch'ing-tan, Taiwan. A series of seven important volumes on the Chinese Communist movement prepared by Hatano Ken'ichi for the Japanese Ministry of Foreign Affairs, *Chūgoku Kyōsantō-shi* (*A History of the Chinese Communist Party*), contains descriptions and evaluations of major events and trends during each year from 1921 through 1937. Translated texts of Party documents, Chinese reports, and analyses of Communist activities from Communist and non-Communist sources are included in this series, which is cited below as *Chūkyō-shi*.

The bibliography is divided into four parts: I, Chinese sources; II, Japanese sources; III, Russian sources; and IV, English sources.

I. CHINESE SOURCES

The CCP. *Kwangtung Nung-min Yün-tung Pao-kao (Report on the Peasant Movement in Kwangtung)*. Hoover Institution microfilm.

The CCP Central Committee. "Chung-kuo kung-ch'an-tang chung-yang wei-yuan-hui k'uo-ta-hui ti-szu-tz'u ch'üan-t'i hui-i i-chüeh-an" ("Resolution of the Enlarged Fourth Plenum of the CCP Central Committee"). Shanghai, January, 1931. In *Hung-se Wen-hsien (Red Documents)*, pp. 235–244. *SSCM*, Reel No. 15.

———. *Cheng Shih Nung-ts'un chih-nan (Directive for the Party Work in the Cities and Rural Areas)*. Shanghai, July 26, 1928. *SSCM*, Reel No. 14.

———. *Chung-yang cheng-chih kung-tso pao-kao chüeh-i-an (Resolution on the Report of the Work of the Central Politburo)*. Shanghai, 1930.

———. "Chung-yang tui su-ch'ü chih-shih hsin" (Directive Letter of the CCP Central Committee to the Soviet Areas"). September 1, 1931. *SSCM*, Reel No. 14.

———. *Hung-se Wen-hsien (Red Documents)*. *SSCM*, Reel No. 15.

———. "Kuan-yü k'ai ch'u Wang K'e-ch'üan tung-chih chüeh-i-an" ("Resolution Concerning the Dismissal of Wang K'en-ch'uan from the Party"), adopted by the Party's Central Politburo on January 30, 1930. *Tang-ti chien-she*, No. 3 (February 15, 1931), pp. 38–39.

———. *Tang-ti tsu-chih i-chüeh-an (Resolution on the Party's Organization)*. Shanghai, August 7, 1927.

The CCP Sixth Congress. "Ssu-wei-ai Cheng-ch'üan tsu-chih wen-t'i chüeh-i-an" ("Resolution on the Organizational Problems of the Soviet Government"), *CKSK*.

The Central Executive Committee of the Chinese Soviet Republic. "Chung-hua Su-wei-ai Kung-huo-kuo ti fang su-wei-ai chan-hsing tsu-chih-fa" ("Provisional Organization Law of the Local Soviet Government of the Chinese Soviet Republic"), December 12, 1933. *SSCM*, Reel No. 16.

———. *Wei Hang-Wu kung-tso kei Min-hsi ti i-feng-hsin (A Letter to the West Fukien Soviet Area for the Work in Shanghang and Wu-p'ing Areas)*. *SSCM*, Reel No. 16.

The Central Soviet Government. *Kuan-yü ch'a-t'ien yün-tung ti hsün-ling (Directive on the Land Classification Campaign)*. *Hung-se Chung-hua*, No. 87 (June 20, 1933).

Chang, Shao-tan. "Hsien Su-wei-ai kung-tso" ("The Work of the *Hsien* Soviet Government"), *Chūkyō-shi*, V, 215–241.

Chang, Wen-t'ien, and Mao Tse-tung. *Ch'u Hsiang Su-wei-ai Tsen-yang Kung-tso (How to Conduct the Work of the Ch'u and Hsiang Soviet Government)*. The People's Commissariat of the Chinese Soviet Republic. Jui-chin, Kiangsi, April, 1934. *SSCM*, Reel 10.

Ch'en, Tu-hsiu. *Kao ch'üan-tang t'ung-chih shu (An Open Letter to All Comrades of the Party)*. Shanghai, 1929.

Chiang, Yung-ching. *Pao-lo-t'ing yü Wu-han cheng-ch'üan (Borodin and the Wuhan Government)*. Taipei, Chung-kuo Hsüeh-shu chu-tso chiang-tsu wei-yüan-hui, 1963.

Ch'i, Ch'i-sheng. "Chih-ch'ü ti nung-yüeh cheng-chih" ("Agrarian Policy of the Red Areas"), *Kuo-wen Chou-pao, Chūkyō-shi*, V, 169–195.

Ch'ih-fei chi-mi wen-chien hui-pien (A Collection of Red Bandit Secret Documents). Compiled by the First Bandit-Suppression Propaganda Department, Headquarters of the Commander-in-Chief of the Land, Sea, and Air Forces. June–October, 1931. 6 vols. *SSCM*, Reel No. 20.

"Chih-se ch'ü ti tsu-chih yü chien-she" ("The Organization and Construction of the Red Areas"), *Ta Wan Pao*, Shanghai, May 15, 1932. *Mantetsu Chōsa Geppō*, September, 1932, pp. 140–149.

Tu, Chin-nung. "Kan tung-pei su-wei-ai ch'ü ti kung-tso pao-kao" (Report on the Soviet Work in Northeast Kiangsi), Hatano, *Chūkyō-shi*, III, 311–385.

Chou En-lai. *Mu-ch'ien Chung-kuo tang-ti tsu-chih wen-ti (Current Problems of the CCP Organizations)*. The CCP Central Committee, 1929. Hoover Institution microfilm.

———. "Ti-kuo chu-i ta-chüan ti wei-chi yü tang-ti mu-ch'ien chin-chih jen-wu" ("Crisis of the Imperialist War and the Present Urgent Task of the Party"), *Shih-hua (True Words)*, No. 1. (February 14, 1932).

Chün, "Lao-nung chih-tu yen-chiu" ("A Study of the Soviet System"), *Kung-ch'an-tang*, No. 5 (June 7, 1921), pp. 35–40.

"Chung-hua su-wei-ai kung-ho-kuo chung-yang cheng-fu chung-kuo kung-ch'an-tang chung-yang wei-yüan-hui wei fa-chan ch'ün-ch'ung ti yü-chi chan-cheng kao ch'üan-su-ch'ü min-chung" ("An Appeal of the Central Government of the Chinese Soviet Republic and the Central Committee of the CCP to All the People of the Soviet Areas for the Development of Mass Guerrilla Warfare"), *Hung-se Chung-hua*, No. 240 (October 3, 1934), p. 1.

"Chung-hua Su-wei-ai Kung-ho-Kuo Hua-fen shing-cheng ch'ü yü chan-hsing t'iao-li" ("Provisional Act to Reapportion the Administrative Districts of the Chinese Soviet Republic"), Bureau of Investigation, Ministry of Justice in Taiwan, Document No. 575.297/802.

Chung-hua su-wei-ai kung-ho-kuo ti-erh-tz'u ch'üan-kuo tai-piao ta-hui wen-hsien (Documents of the Second Soviet Congress of the Chinese Soviet Republic). Published by the People's Commissariat of the Chinese Soviet Republic, March 1934, p. 216. *SSCM*, Reel No. 16.

"Chung-hua Su-wei-ai Kung-ho-kuo ti-fang Su-wei-ai chan-hsing tsu-chih-fa" ("Provisional Organizational Law of the Local Soviet Government of the Chinese Soviet Republic"). *SSCM*, Reel No. 16.

"Chung-hua Su-wei-ai tai-piao ta-hui kei Chung-kung chung-yang tien" (Telegram from the Chinese Soviet Congress to the CCP Central Committee). *Chūkyō-shi*, I, 595–596.

Chung-kuo Ch'ing-nien (Chinese Youth), an official organ of the Chinese Communist Youth League, available in Hoover Institution microfilm.

Chung-kuo Kuomintang, Chung-yang Tsu-chih pu Tiao-ch'a k'e. *Chung-kuo kung-ch'an Tang chih t'ou-shih (Perspectives on the Chinese Communist Party)*. Taipei, Wen-Hsing shu-t'ien, 1962.

Chung-kuo Nung-min (The Chinese Peasants), an official organ of the Kuomintang Peasant Department.

"Chung-kuo Su-wei-ai cheng-kang" ("Political Program of the Chinese Soviets"), *SSCM*, Reel No. 20.

"Chung-kuo ti-i-tz'u Su-wei-ai ch'ü tai-piao ta-hui hsuan-ch'üan kang-yao" ("A Summary of the Declaration of the All-China Conference of Delegates from the Soviet Areas"), *Hung-ch'i (Red Flag)*, No. 112 (June 21, 1930). *Chūkyō-shi*, I, 388–394.

Hsiao, Tso-liang. *Power Relations in the Chinese Communist Movement, 1930–1934: A Study of Documents*. Seattle, University of Washington Press, 1967.

Hsüeh, Chün-tu, ed. *The Chinese Communist Movement, 1921–37*. Stanford, Hoover Institution, 1960.

Hu, Hua. *Chung-kuo hsin min-chu chu-i ko-ming shih (A History of New Democratic Revolution in China)*. Peking, Hsin-hua shu-tien, 1950.

Huang, T'ao. *Chung-kuo jen-min chieh-fang chun ti san-shih min (Thirty Years of the Chinese People's Liberation Army)*. Peking, Jen-min ch'u-pan she, 1958.

Huang, Ho. *Chung-kuo Kung-ch'an-tang san-shih wu nien chien shih (An Outline History of the Thiry-Five Years of the Chinese Communist Party)*. Peking, Hsin-hua ch'u-pan she, 1957.

Hui-i Chingkang-shan ch'ü ti tou-cheng (Reminiscence of the Struggle in the Chingkang Mountain Area). Peking, Kung-jen ch'u-pan she, 1955.

Hung-se Chung-hua (Red China), an official organ of the Chinese Soviet Republic. No. 1 (December 11, 1931)–No. 243 (October 20, 1934). *SSCM*, Reels No. 16 and 17.

"Hupeh-Hunan nan-hsi pu su-wei-ai kung-tso" ("The Soviet Work in the Hupeh and Southwest Hunan Areas"), *Mantetsu Chōsa Geppō* (September 1932), pp. 111–123.

Jao, Yung-chun. "Kuan-yu Oyüwan san-sheng ti chao-fei chün-shih yü cheng-chih" ("Extermination Campaign and Politics in Three Provinces of Hupeh-Honan-Anhwei"), *Chūkyō-shi*, II, 227–237.

Kung, Ch'u. *Wo yü Hung chün (I and the Red Army)*. Hong Kong, Nan-feng ch'u-pan she, 1954.

Kung-ch'an-tang (The Communists). Shanghai, The CCP, 1920–1921.

Kung-fei huo-kuo shih-liao hui-pien (Selected Documents on the Chinese Communist Plot in China). 3 vols. Taipei, 1964.

Kung-nung hung-chün hsüeh-hsiao. *Su-wei-ai Cheng-ch'üan (Soviet Political Power)*. Juichin, Kiangsi, January 1932.

Kuomintang, Bureau of Investigation. *Tzu 1931 nien chih 1933 nien liang-nien-lai chih Chung-kuo kung-ch'an-tang (Two Years of the Chinese Communist Party from 1931 to 1933)*. Bureau of Investigation Archives, Ministry of Justice, Taiwan. Document No. 291.2/811/9748.

Li Ang. *Hung-se Wu-t'ai (The Red Stage)*. Peking, 1946.

Li Chün-lung. "Chung-kuo Kung-ch'an tang ti t'u-ti cheng chih kai-kuan" ("Survey of the Land Policy of the Chinese Communist Party"), *Chungkuo chingchi (Chinese Economy)*, vol. I, Nos. 4 and 5. Shanghai, 1933.

Li Li-san. "Chün-fei chien li k'o-ming cheng-ch'üan" ("Prepare to Establish the Revolutionary Government"), *Hung-ch'i (Red Flag)*, March 26, 1930.

————. "Wu-ch'an chieh-chi ti ling-tao ch'uan wen-t'i" ("Problems of the Leadership of the Proletarian Class"), *Hung-ch'i (Red Flag)*, May 24, 1930.

Li Jui. "Ti-i-tz'u kuo-nei ko-ming chan-cheng shih-chi ti Hunan nung-min yün-tung" ("The Peasant Movement in Hunan During the Period of the First Civil War"), *Ti-i-tz'u kuo-nei ko-ming chan-cheng shih-chi ti nung-min yün-tung*. Peking, Jen-min ch'u-pan she, 1953.

Li Mu. "Kung-ch'an tang tung t'a-ti tsu-chih" ("The Communist Party and Its Organizations"), *Kung-ch'an-tang*, No. 1 (November 7, 1920), pp. 16–21.

Liao Yung-chün. "Kuan-yü Oyuwan san-sheng ti chiao fei yü cheng-chih" ("Extermination Campaign and Politics in Three Provinces of Oyuwan"), *Chūkyō-shi*, II, 227–239.

Lo Fu (Chang Wen-t'ien). *Shin-ti ling-tao fang-shih (New Methods of Leadership)*. Kiangsi, April 1934. *SSCM*, Reel No. 14.

Lu Wei. "Hsingkuo shan-huo kung-tso hu fei-ch'ü chuang-k'uang" ("Hsingkuo Rehabilitation and the State of Affairs in the Bandit Area"). November 4, 1934. *Chūkyō-shi*, IV, 719–738.

Ma Lo. "Report to the CCP Central Committee on the Situation of the Northeast Kiangsi Soviet Area," *Mantetsu Chōsa Geppō*, September 1932, pp. 57–66.

Mao Tse-tung. "Ch'a-t'ien yün-tung ch'u-pao tsung-chieh" ("Preliminary Summary of the Land Classification Campaign"), *Tou-cheng*, No. 24 (August 29, 1933).

————. *Chih-yu Su-wei-ai neng-kou chiu Chung-kuo (Only the Soviets Can Save China)*. Moscow, Foreign Workers' Press, 1934. 112 pp. Hoover Institution microfilm.

————. *Nung-ts'un tiao-ch'a (Rural Survey)*. Yenan, chieh-fang-she, 1941.

————. "Chung-hua Su-wei-ai Kung-ho-kuo Chung-yang chih-hsing wei-yüan-hui yü jen-min wei-yüan-hui tui ti erh-tz'u ch'üan-kuo su-wei-ai tai-piao ta-hui ti pao-kao" ("Report of the Central Executive Council and the People's Commissariat of the Chinese Soviet Republic to the Second National Soviet Congress"), *Hung-se Chung-hua*, No. 148 (February 12, 1934). Also a special issue of *Hung-se Chung-hua*, No. 7.

————. "Hsingkuo Changkang hsiang ti su-wei-ai kung-tso" ("The Soviet Work of the Changkang *Hsiang* in Hsingkuo *Hsien*"), *Tou-cheng*, No. 42 (January 12, 1934). *SSCM*, Reel 18.

————. *Mao Tse-tung chi (Collected Works of Mao Tse-tung)*. 10 vols. Tokyo, Hokobu Sha, 1970–1973.

————. *Mao Tse-tung hsuan-chi (Selected Works of Mao Tse-tung)*. 4 vols. Peking, Jen-min ch'u-pan-she, 1951–1961.

Mif, Pavel. "Chung-kuo ko-ming wei-chi ti hsin chieh-tuan" ("A New Stage of the Revolutionary Crisis in China"), *Tou-cheng*, Nos. 22 and 23 (August 1933). *SSCM*, Reel No. 18.

Po Ku. "Chung-kuo kung-ch'an-tang chung-yang wei-yuan-hui ti-wu-tz'u ch'üan-hui tsung-chieh" ("Conclusion of the Fifth Plenum of the CCP

Central Committee"), *Tou-cheng*, No. 48 (February 23, 1934), pp. 1–6. *SSCM*, Reel No. 18.

The Political Department of the Central Revolutionary Military Committee, *Ku-nung kung-hui ti kang-yao (A Summary of the Farm Laborers Union)*. Kiangsi, 1931. *SSCM*, Reel No. 17.

Sheng-wei T'ung-hsin (Provincial Committee Correspondence), issued by the Kiangsi Provincial Committee of the CCP, Nos. 11–20, 50, 81–83, 86–88 (July 6, 1933–May 15, 1934). *SSCM*, Reel No. 17.

Shih-hua (The True Story), an official organ of the Central Bureau of the Soviet Areas. No. 1 (February 14, 1932)–No. 10 (November 30, 1932).

"Su-ch'ü tang ti-i-tz'u tai-piao ta-hui tung-kuo cheng-chih chüeh-i-an" ("Political Resolution Passed by the First Party Congress of the Central Soviet Area"), November 1931. *SSCM*, Reel No. 15.

Su-wei-ai cheng-ch'üan (Soviet Political Power), Juichin, Kiangsi, 1932.

T'ien Chih. "Ch'ih-fei ti sheng-yin, tsu-chih, shan-hou" ("The Origin, Organizations, and Reconstruction of the Red Bandits"), *Tientsin Ta Kung Pao*, reproduced in *Chūkyō-shi*, I, 313–348.

T'ien Chih. "Fei-ch'ü shih-ch'a chi" ("Report on the Observation of the Soviet Area"), *Tientsin Ta Kung Pao*, reproduced in *Chūkyō-shi*, II, 277–312.

Ti-i-tz'u kuo-nei ko-ming chang-cheng shih-chi ti nung-min-yün-tung (The Peasant Movement During the Period of the First Revolutionary Civil War). Peking, Jen-min ch'u-pan she, 1953.

Tang-ti chien-she (Party Reconstruction), official organ of the CCP CBSA, 1931–1932.

Tou-cheng (Struggle), an official organ of the CCP Central Bureau of the Soviet Areas. No. 1 (February 4, 1933)–No. 73 (September 30, 1934). *SSCM*, Reel No. 18.

Ts'ai Ho-shen. *Chi-hui chu-i shih (History of Opportunism)*. *CKSK*.

Wang Chien-min. *Chung-kuo Kung-ch'an tang Shih-kao (Historical Materials of the Chinese Communist Party)*. Taipei, 1965. *CKSK*.

Wang Hsiao-wen. *Chung-kuo t'u-t'i wen-t'i (Land Problems in China)*. Shanghai, Commercial Press, 1937.

Wang Ming (Ch'en Shao-yü). "Chung-kuo kung-ch'an-tang shih Chung-kuo fan-ti yü t'u-ti ko-ming chung ti ling-hsiu" ("The Chinese Communist Party is the Only Leader in the Antiimperialist and Agrarian Revolution in China"), *Tou-cheng*, No. 66 (June 30, 1934), pp. 1–12. *SSCM*, Reel No. 18.

————. "Kuan-yü szu-chung ch'üan-hui chien fan-tui li-san lu-hsien tou-cheng ti ching-kuo" ("On the Story of the Struggle Against the Li Li-san Line Before the Fourth Plenum"), in *CKSK*, II, 96–97.

————. *Liang t'iao lu-hsien (The Two Lines)*. First ed., Shanghai, Wu-ch'an chieh-chi shu-tien, 1931. Second ed., Moscow, 1932. Third ed., retitled *Wei chung-kung keng-chia pu-erh shih-wei-k'e-hua erh tou-cheng (Struggle for the More Complete Bolshevization of the Chinese Communist Party)*, Yenan, July 1940.

————. "On the Revolutionary Movement in Colonial and Semicolonial Countries and the Tactics of the Communist Party," a speech delivered to the Seventh Comintern Congress (July 25–August 20, 1935) in *Chūkyō-shi*, V, 53–93.

―――. "The Revolutionary Movement in China," *Communist International*, Vol. XII, No. 17–18 (September 20, 1935).

―――. *Su-wei-ai Chung-kuo* (*Soviets in China*). Moscow, Foreign Workers' Publishing House, 1933.

――― and Kan Sing (K'ang Sheng). *Revolutionary China Today*. Moscow, Foreign Language Press, 1934.

Wang T'ieh-chang. "Fan-tui li-san lu-hsien tou-cheng ti ching-kuo" ("Story of the Struggle Against the Li Li-san Line"), *Tang-ti Chien-she* (*Reconstruction of the Party*), No. 3 (February 15, 1931), pp. 16–30.

'Wei chi-nien Hsiang Chung-fa tung-chih" ("In Commemoration of Comrade Hsiang Chung-fa"), *SSCM*, Reel No. 15.

Wei ling-tao min-chung ko-ming chien-li min-chung ti su-wei-ai cheng-ch'üan erh tou-cheng (*A Struggle for Leading the Masses in the Revolution and Establishing Their Soviet Regime*), a collection of documents published by the Central Bureau of the CCP in the Soviet Area, April 1932. *SSCM*, Reel No. 16.

"Wu-chung ch'üan-hui kei erh-tz'u ch'uan-su ta-hui tang-t'uan ti chih-ling" ("Directive of the Fifth Plenum to the Party Fraction of the Second Soviet Congress"), *Tou-cheng*, No. 47 (February 16, 1934). *SSCM*, Reel No. 18.

Yun Hai-sheng. "Ningtu Hsien ti shih-ching" ("The Situation in Ningtu Hsien"), November 10, 1934, *Chūkyō-shi*, IV, 738–753.

II. JAPANESE SOURCES

The CCP Central Committee. *Chūgoku Kyōsan-tō Chō Shikko Iinkai Dainiji zentai kaigi ketsugian* (*Resolutions of the Second Plenum of the CCP Central Executive Committee*). Tairen, Mantetsu cho-sa ka, 1930.

Chūgoku Kyōsantō bunken ishū (*Collection of Documents issued by the Chinese Communist Party*). Shanghai, Mantetsu Chōsa shiryō, 1933.

Hara, Masarū. "Chūgoku sovietō ni okeru hinnō oyobi kōnō no soshiki to sono tōsō koŕyo" ("Organizations and their Programs for the Poor Peasants and Farm Laborers in the Chinese Soviet Areas"), *Mantetsu Chōsa Geppo*. 15, No. 5 (May 1935), 137–148.

Hatano, Ken'ichi. *Chūgoku Kyōsan-tō shi* (*A History of the Chinese Communist Party*). 7 vols. Tokyo, Ji Ji Press, 1962.

―――. *Shina no seiji to jinbutsu*. Tokyo, Kaizō sha, 1937.

―――. "The Chinese Communist Party and the Red Army," *Shina Nenkan* (*The China Yearbook*). Tokyo, Toa Tōbun Kai, 1930.

―――. "Chūgoku kyōsan-tō, kyōsan-gun, sovietō" ("The Chinese Communist Party, the Communist Army, and the Soviets"), *Chūo-kōron* (*The Central Forum*), May 1934, pp. 42–47.

Hatano, Ken-ichi. "Shina kyōsan-gun no rekishi to gensei" ("History and Present Situation of the Chinese Communist Army"), *Shina* (*China*), March 1935.

————. "Shū On-rai ten" ("Biography of Chou En-lai"), *Kaizō*, 19, No. 7 (July 1937), 86–91.

Himori, Torao, *Chukyō 20 nen shi, 1920–1940* (*History of the Chinese Communist Party, 1920–1940*). Shanghai, Himori kenkyujo, 1942.

————. "Shina sekigun oyobi sovietō kuiki no hatsuten chōkyo" ("The Chinese Red Army and the Development of the Soviet Area"), *Mantetsu Chōsa Geppō* (*Monthly Research Report of the South Manchurian Railway Co.*). Tairen, 1932, pp. 94–119.

Ishikawa, Tatao. *Chūgoku Kyōsantō shi ghenkyū* (*A Study of the History of the Chinese Communist Party*). Tokyo, Keio University Press, 1961.

Mantetsu Chōsa Geppō (*Monthly Research Report of the South Manchurian Railway Company*). Dairen, 1931–1935.

Minami Manshu tetsudō kabushiki kaishā, comp. *Chūgoku Kyōsantō no kinjō* (*The Present Situation of the Chinese Communist Party*). Dairen, 1934.

Minami Manshu tetsudō kabushiki kaishā *Iwayuru "Kōgun Mondai"* (*The So-called Problems of the Red Army*). Dairen, Sōmbu chōsa-ka, 1930.

Nakanishi, Kō. *Chūgoku Kyōsantō shi* (*History of the Chinese Communist Party*). Tokyo, Hakuto sha, 1949.

Nihon Gaiji Kyōkai. *Shina ni okeru kyōsan undō* (*The Communist Movement in China*). Tokyo, Nihon Gaiji Kyōkai, p. 1933.

Okubō, Yasushi, *Chūkyo sanjūnen* (*Thirty Years of Chinese Communism*). Tokyo, Nyūsusha, 1949.

Ōtsuka, Reizō, *Chūgoku Kyōsantō-shi* (*A History of the Chinese Communist Party*). 2 vols. Tokyo, Seikatsu sha, 1940.

————. *Chūgoku Kyōsan-tō Soshiki Mondai* (*Source Materials on the Organizational Problems of the CCP*). Tairen, South Manchurian Railway Company, 1930.

————. "Shina kyōsan-tō no gensei" ("Present Situation of the Chinese Communist Party"), *Kaizō*, 13, No. 7 (July 1931), 44–53.

Ōzaki, Hotsumi. "Shū On-rai no chii" ("The Position of Chou-En-lai"), *Chūo Kōron*, 52, No. 12 (November 1937), 97–105.

Sambō Honbū (the Chief of Staff). *Shina Kyōsan-tō Undō-shi* (*A History of the Chinese Communist Movement*). Tokyo, 1931.

Sangyō Rōdō Chōsajo, ed. *Shina ni okeru saikin no nōmin mondai*. Tokyo, 1930.

Tanaka, Tatao. "Shina sovietō no gensei to sono shisetsu" ("Present Situation of the Chinese Soviets and their Establishment"), *Tō-a* (*East Asia*), November 1930.

Tōa Keizai Chōsa-kyoku. *Shina Sovietō Undō no Genkyū* (*A Study of the Chinese Soviet Movement*). Tokyo, Toa Keizai Chōsa-kyoku, 1934.

Yoshikawa, Shigezō, comp. *Chūkyo sōran* (*Handbook on Communist China*). Tokyo, JJijitsushin sha, 1950.

III. RUSSIAN SOURCES

Erenburg, G. B. *Sovetskii Kitaii* (*Soviet China*). Moscow, 1934.

Manuil'skii, D. Z. *Otchetnyi doklad XVII s'ezdu VKP (b) o rabote delegatsii*

VKP (b) *v IKKI* (*Report to the XVIIth Congress of the CPSU Concerning the Work of the CPSU Delegation to the Executive Committee of the Communist International*). Moscow, 1934.

Mif, Pavel. "Novoe v razvittii revoliutsionn ogo krizisa v Kitae" ("New Development in the Progress of the Revolutionary Crisis in China"), *Kommunisticheskii internatsional*, No. 10 (April 1, 1933), p. 38.

————, ed. *Strategiia i taktika Kominterna v natsional' no-kolonial'noi revoliutsii na primere Kitaia* (*Strategy and Tactics of the Comintern in the National-Colonial Revolution, Primarily in China*). Moscow, 1934. This book is a collection of Comintern documents on Chinese policy.

Revoliutsionnyi Vostok (*The Revolutionary East*), the Organ of the Research Institute for the Study of the National and Colonial Problems of the Soviet Academy of Science, 1927–1937. This was the only Soviet quarterly journal specializing in Far Eastern problems during the Kiangsi period.

Sovety v Kitae, sbornik materialov im dokumentov (*The Soviets in China: A Collection of Materials and Documents*). Moscow, China Research Institute, 1934.

Vladimirova, T. *Bor'bz za sovety v Kitae* (*The Struggle for Soviets in China*). Moscow, 1931.

IV. ENGLISH SOURCES

Barnett, A. Doak. *China on the Eve of Communist Takeover*. New York, Praeger, 1963.

————. *Communist China: The Early Years*. New York, Praeger, 1964.

————. *Cadres, Bureaucracy and Political Power in Communist China*. New York, Columbia University Press, 1967.

Brandt, Conrad. *Stalin's Failure in China 1924–1927*. Cambridge, Harvard University Press, 1958.

————, Benjamin Schwartz, and John K. Fairbank. *A Documentary History of Chinese Communism*. Cambridge, Harvard University Press, 1952.

Buck, John Lossing. *Land Utilization in China*. Chicago, University of Chicago Press, 1937.

Chao, Kuo-chun. *Agrarian Policy of the Chinese Communist Party*. New Delhi, Asia Publishing House, 1960.

Ch'en, Kung-po. *The Communist Movement in China*. New York, East Asian Institute of Columbia University, 1960.

Chen Po-ta. *Notes on Ten Years of Civil War (1927–1936)*. Peking, Foreign Language Press, 1958.

Chen Po-ta. *A Study of Land Rent in Pre-Liberation China*. Peking, Foreign Language Press, 1958.

Ch'en, Jerome. *Mao and the Chinese Revolution*. London, Oxford University Press, 1965.

Ch'u, T'ung-tsu. *Local Government in China Under the Ch'ing*. Cambridge, Harvard University Press, 1962.

Clubb, O. Edmund. *Twentieth Century China*. New York, Columbia University Press, 1964.

The Columbia Lippincott Gazetteer of the World. New York, Columbia University Press, 1961.

Cressey, George. *China's Geographic Foundation.* New York, 1934.

Degras, Jane. *The Communist International 1919–1943 Documents.* London, Oxford University Press, 1965.

Elegant, Robert S. *China's Red Masters: Political Biographies of the Chinese Communist Leaders.* New York, Twayne Publishers, 1951.

Eto, Shinkichi. "Hai-lu-feng — The First Chinese Soviet Government," *The China Quarterly,* No. 8 (October–December 1961), pp. 161–183; No. 9 (January–March 1962), pp. 149–181.

Florinsky, Michael T. *Russia: A History and an Interpretation.* New York, Macmillan, 1955.

Harrison, James P. "The Li Li-san line and the CCP in 1930," *The China Quarterly,* No. 14 (April-June 1963), 178–194.

Ho, Kan-chih. *A History of the Modern Chinese Revolution.* Peking, Foreign Language Press, 1958.

Hsiao, Tso-liang. *Power Relations within the Chinese Communist Movement 1930–1934: A Study of Documents.* Seattle, University of Washington Press, 1961.

———. *Land Revolution in China, 1930–1934: A Study of Documents.* Seattle, University of Washington Press, 1969.

Hu, Chiao-mu. *Thirty Years of the Communist Party of China.* Peking, Foreign Language Press, 1959.

Isaacs, Harold R. *The Tragedy of the Chinese Revolution.* Stanford, Stanford University Press, 1961.

James, M. and R. Doomping. *Soviet China.* New York, International Publishers, 1932.

Johnson, Chalmers A. *Peasant Nationalism and Communist Power: The Emergence of Revolutionary China 1937–1945.* Stanford, Stanford University Press, 1962.

Klein, Donald and Anne Clark. *Biographical Dictionary of the Chinese Communist Movement, 1921–1965.* Cambridge, Harvard University Press, 1971.

Lenin, V. *Two Tactics of Social Democracy.* New York, International Publishers.

Lewis, John Wilson. *Leadership in Communist China.* Ithaca, Cornell University Press, 1963.

Li, Wei-han. *The Struggle for Proletarian Leadership in the Period of the New-Democratic Revolution in China.* Peking, Foreign Language Press, 1962.

Liu, Shao-chi. *The Victory of Marxism-Leninism in China.* Peking, Foreign Language Press, 1959.

McKenzie, Kermit E. *Comintern and World Revolution, 1928–1943.* New York, Columbia University Press, 1964.

McLane, Charles B. *Soviet Policy and the Chinese Communists 1931–1946.* New York, Columbia University Press, 1958.

MacNair, H. F. *China in Revolution.* Berkeley, University of California Press, 1946.

Mao Tse-tung. *Selected Works of Mao Tse-tung.* Peking, Foreign Language Press, 1961–1965. 4 vols.

————. "Report of an Investigation into the Peasant Movement in Hunan," *Selected Works of Mao Tse-tung.* Peking, Foreign Language Press, 1964.

Mif, Pavel. *Heroic China: Fifteen Years of the Communist Party of China.* New York, Workers Library Publishers, 1937.

Nollau, Gunther. *International Communism and World Revolution.* New York, Praeger, 1961.

North, Robert C. *Kuomintang and Chinese Communist Elites.* Stanford, Stanford University Press, 1952.

————. *Moscow and the Chinese Communists.* Stanford, Stanford University Press, 1963.

————. and Xenia J. Eudin. *M.N. Roy's Mission to China.* Berkeley, University of California Press, 1963.

————. *Soviet Russia and the East 1920–1927: A Documentary Survey.* Stanford, Stanford University Press, 1957.

"Resolution of November Plenum of the CC of the CCP," *International Press Correspondence,* VIII, No. 5 (January 26, 1928), 122–123.

Rue, John E. *Mao Tse-tung in Opposition, 1927–1935.* Stanford, Stanford University Press, 1966.

Schram, Stuart R. *Mao Tse-tung.* New York, Simon and Shuster, 1967.

————. "On the Nature of Mao Tse-tung's 'Deviation' in 1927," *The China Quarterly,* No. 18 (April–June 1964), pp. 55–66.

————. *The Political Thought of Mao Tse-tung.* New York, Praeger, 1963.

Schwartz, Benjamin. *Chinese Communism and the Rise of Mao.* Cambridge, Harvard University Press, 1958.

Selden, Mark. *The Yenan Way in Revolutionary China.* Cambridge, Harvard University Press, 1971.

Snow, Edgar. *Red Star over China.* New York, Random House, 1938.

Snow, Helen Foster (Nym Wales). *Red Dust.* Stanford, Stanford University Press, 1952.

Stalin, Joseph. "China on the Eve of the Bourgeois-Democratic Revolution," *Soviet Russia and the East 1920–1937: A Documentary Survey.* Stanford, Stanford University Press, 1957.

————. "The Political Tasks of the University of the Peoples of the East," *Works.* Moscow, Foreign Language Publishing House, 1954. VII, 146–154.

————. "The Prospects of the Chinese Revolution," *International Press Correspondence,* No. 90 (December 23, 1926), pp. 1581–1584.

————. *Sochineniia (Selected Works).* Moscow, Foreign Language Publishing House, 1951.

————. "Stalin's Interview with the Chinese Students at Sun-Yat-sen University," *Works.* Moscow, Foreign Language Publishing House, 1954. IX, 243–273.

Swarup, Shanti. *A Study of the Chinese Communist Movement 1927–1934.* Oxford, Clarendon Press, 1966.

Thornton, Richard. *The Comintern and the Chinese Communists, 1928–1931.* Seattle, University of Washington Press, 1969.

Townsend, James R. *Political Participation in Communist China.* Berkeley, University of California Press, 1967.

Trotsky, Leon. *Problems of the Chinese Revolution.* New York, Pioneer Publishers, 1932.

Wilbur, C. Martin. "The Ashes of Defeat," *The China Quarterly*, No. 2 (April–June 1964), pp. 3–54.

———— and Julie Lienying How. *Documents on Communism, Nationalism, and Soviet Advisers in China 1918–1927.* New York, Columbia University Press, 1956.

Wittfogel, K. A. "The Legend of 'Maoism'," *The China Quarterly*, No. 2 (April–June 1960), pp. 16–34.

Who's Who in Communist China. Hong Kong, The Union Research Institute, 1966.

Woodhead, H. G. W. *The China Yearbook 1933.* Shanghai, The North-China Daily News and Herald, Ltd., 1933.

Yang, Shang-kuei. *The Red Kiangsi-Kwangtung Border Region.* Peking, Foreign Language Press, 1961.

Yakhontoff, V. A. *The Chinese Soviets.* New York, Coward-McCann, 1934.

INDEX

Agrarian policy, 104; administrative processes to implement, 122–126; dual characteristics of, 113–114
Agrarian revolution, 2; Mao's viewpoint on three stages of, 115; role of different peasant classes in, 105–111. *See also* Land distribution; Land Investigation Movement
Agricultural productivity, and cooperative movement, 147
All-China Federation of Trade Unions, 72
Anhwei province, 27, 154, 155
Antiimperialism: as basis for mobilization tactics, 103–104; issue of supported by Ch'in Pang-hsien, 100; use of as war tactic debated by policy-makers, 101–104
Anti-rich-peasant policy, and poor-peasant corps, 129, 136
Anti-rich-peasant struggle, 115, 122
anti-Wang Ming group, 56, 57
Appeals bureau: at *hsien* level, 164; of worker-peasant inspection department, 78
"Armed struggles," 2

Barnett, A. Doak, 19, 118
Bolshevik Revolution, 155, 195
Bolsheviks, the twenty-eight, 56. *See also* returned-student group
Bourgeois-democratic revolution, 20, 110
Braun, Otto, military strategy of, 97, 98, 99
Bureaucratic corruption: and appeals bureau, 78; at *hsien* level, 164
Bureaucratic formalism, 44–45, 48

CBSA. *See* Central Bureau of the Soviet Area
CCP. *See* Chinese Communist Party
CCP-KMT collaboration, breakdown of, 2, 6, 15, 29, 42, 202
CSR. *See* Chinese Soviet Republic
Cadres: administrative, 118; to ascertain for CCP needs of peasants, 187–188; criteria for promotion of, 198–199; cri-

teria for selection of, 192; defined, 180, 192; educated to integrate theory and experience, 193–194; education and training of, 190–200; essential functions of, 180; of inspection department, 78, 80–81; as link of Party to masses, 198; shortage of, 46, 51–52, 53; in southwest Kiangsi soviet, 40; training of in Yenan period and Kiangsi soviet period compared, 181–182; trained for cooperatives, 151; trained to manage land distribution, 123
Caplow, Theodore, 21
Cash crops, 27
Central Bureau of the Soviet Area (CBSA): amalgamated with Central Committee, 62; balance of power in, 67; Circular Letter No. 1, 66; collective leadership policy and, 184; influence of Mao on resolution for land-investigation movement, 88; interactions with Party's Central Committee in Shanghai, 66–67; official journals of, 62–63; organization and function of, 63–68; programs of to counter KMT forces, 144; relation to central soviet government, 63; role of in cadre education, 195; standing committee of in (1931), 90, 91
Central Committee of CCP: move from Shanghai to Juichin (1932), 9, 61–62, 87, 116; poor communications with CBSA, 66–67. *See also* Fourth Plenum
Central Executive Council (CEC), 44; creation of, 68; development of mutual-aid program and, 145 n.49; elected members of in (1931 and 1934), 82–85; establishes presidium, 73; legislative functions of, 69
Central Revolutionary Military Commission (CRMC): controls military policy-making after (1933), 116; creation of, 68; function of, 95–96; as major center for military strategy, 89; strengthening of to combat KMT forces, 94
Chang Kuo-t'ao: as Chinese student in Moscow, 56, 57; elected vice-chairman

223